Faulkner and Mystery
FAULKNER AND YOKNAPATAWPHA

2009

Faulkner and Mystery

FAULKNER AND YOKNAPATAWPHA, 2009

EDITED BY
ANNETTE TREFZER
AND
ANN J. ABADIE

UNIVERSITY PRESS OF MISSISSIPPI
JACKSON

www.upress.state.ms.us

The University Press of Mississippi is a member of the Association of
American University Presses.

First printing 2014

∞

Library of Congress Cataloging-in-Publication Data

Faulkner and Yoknapatawpha Conference (36th : 2009 : University of
Mississippi)
Faulkner and mystery : Faulkner and Yoknapatawpha, 2009 / edited
by Annette Trefzer, Ann J. Abadie.
pages cm. — (Faulkner and Yoknapatawpha series)
Includes bibliographical references and index.
ISBN 978-1-62846-029-2 (hardback) — ISBN 978-1-62846-030-8
(ebook) 1. Faulkner, William, 1897–1962—Criticism and interpreta-
tion—Congresses. 2. Mystery in literature—Congresses. I. Trefzer,
Annette, 1960– II. Abadie, Ann J. III. Title.
PS3511.A86Z7832113 2009
813'.52—DC23   2013042773

British Library Cataloging-in-Publication Data available

In Memoriam,

André Bleikasten
1933–15 February 2009

Ella Vasser Bishop
15 August 1917–25 October 2010

Dean Faulkner Wells
March 22, 1936–July 27, 2011

Thomas Henry "Hal" Freeland
24 March 1930–10 May 2012

John Pilkington Jr.
1 July 1918–4 June 2012

Mary Lillian "Sue" Hart
2 May 1928–21 July 2012

Noel Polk
23 February 1943–21 August 2012

Marion Beckett Howorth Jr.
5 December 1922–31 October 2012

Josephine Ayres Haxton (Ellen Douglas)
12 July 1921–7 November 2012

Joseph Blotner
21 June 1923–16 November 2012

David Aston Holley
10 January 1923–5 December 2012

Contents

Introduction

Few readers might dispute the claim that Faulkner's fiction is filled with mystery. Even after turning the last page of his novels, there is something that stubbornly remains unexplained. This puzzling "something" needs clarification, demands explanation, and calls for interpretation. Some mysteries in Faulkner's texts refer most obviously to anything that is cleverly kept secret from the reader. Such a mystery might arise as a result of Faulkner's calculated attempt at hiding a secret. In "A Rose for Emily," for instance, Faulkner conceals Homer Barron's corpse and the iron-gray hair on the pillow next to him until the shocking moment of planned and staged discovery in the last section of the story. The presence of a secret that will be discovered is hinted at throughout the story in its gothic setting, fragmented narrative structure, mysterious events, and the prying eyes of the townspeople. On all narrative levels, the story is laced with elements of obscurity that invite curiosity and speculation not only on behalf of Emily's neighbors but Faulkner's readers as well.

There is another deeper sense of mystery, however, that hints at what remains unexplained even after we have pried open the door to the ghastly bedroom scene. This sense of mystery taps into questions of what is ultimately knowable, or what sort of truth can or cannot be known. When we come to the end of Faulkner's famous short story, we may have discovered the mysterious source of the smell and the hair on the pillow, but the mysteries of Emily's eccentric behavior and her motivations for killing Homer Barron remain. Did she in fact do it? And if so, why? Was Homer's social class unacceptable to her aristocratic family's expectations? Was it because Homer was a self-confessed "nonmarrying man," or simply a Yankee in the wrong place at the wrong time? Was it because Emily sought revenge on her father, or because she wanted to fool the town with her indomitable ways? Did she in fact sleep with Homer's corpse? And if she did, was it because of mental illness in her family, or because of her sexual perversions? Did she desire to vanquish death itself? Such unanswered questions point to the deeper mysteries of human motivation and the limits of knowledge. Although some of the answers might garner more substantial textual support than others, the "truth" eludes us and the mystery remains.

Ultimately, what is at stake in Faulkner is not simply the uncovering of a secret, the revelation of some insight, or the conveyance of a grand idea, but the crafting of a plot and the telling of a compelling story. Faulkner famously claimed that he was not much interested in sociological or historical truths but in the process of telling about them. Asked in 1962 what his objective is in writing and whether he is "trying to portray the South . . . as essentially an area of depravity and poverty," he answered: "I am a story-teller. I am telling a story, introducing comic and tragic elements as I like. I'm telling a story to be repeated and retold. I don't claim to be truthful."[1] Faulkner insists that what his work reveals about the South (and what knowledge or truth is conveyed) is never mimetic—never simply reflective of an environment—but always narratively crafted and reordered in the telling. In this gap between what is conveyed and *how* it is conveyed, there is room for revelation and insight but also for the presence of obscurity and mystery. In one sense then, mystery in Faulkner's fiction emerges in the act of storytelling; it arises from narrative contingencies and reversals. Pointing to the often radical disjunction between the telling and the tale, Michael Gorra argues in this volume that Faulkner's deepest mystery touches on "his sense of the world in which truth is always uncertain and knowledge is forever incomplete."

Faulkner and Mystery presents a wide spectrum of definitions and arguments about the role and function of mystery in his fiction. Most fundamentally, scholars in this volume urge us to distinguish between the mystery of the detective form and the mystery of novels that in their plot development complicate questions rather than solve them. The wide range of work in Faulkner's canon includes texts that resemble the genre of mystery and detective fiction and play with or allude to those conventions. The detective story was widely popular in the 1920s and '30s when Faulkner came into his own as a writer. After the author of Sherlock Holmes, Sir Arthur Conan Doyle, died in 1930, the heroines of Agatha Christy's formulaic detective fiction, including most famously Hercule Poirot and Miss Maples, kept suffusing the popular imagination on both sides of the Atlantic with stories of crime detection for many decades.[2] Among Faulkner's texts most interested in the format of crime and detection is his novel *Intruder in the Dust* (1948), which assumes a central role in this volume. Three essays are dedicated to exploring the narrative strategies and ideological functions of Faulkner's take on the detective story. Even though *Intruder* resembles the genre of detective fiction with its central interest in unraveling a murder case that is to be solved, some contributors to the volume propose that mystery is least present in such a narrative: "If there's one place where we *do not* find that mystery-producing disjunction [between telling and tale], it is in those works that he actually called mysteries," Gorra argues.

Many of Faulkner's texts do not attempt to solve mysteries; in fact, in some of his best work each plot element adds to the thickening of the mystery and the elusiveness of truth in a movement quite contrary to that of the detective story. In *Unknowing: The Work of Modernist Fiction*, Philip Weinstein argues that, as a modernist writer interested in the mysteries of identity, Faulkner figures prominently among those writers who question the confidence in Enlightenment notions of truth, knowledge, and subjectivity. Faulkner's modernist strategies of "unknowing," he argues, function as "an attack on the confidence in Western norms for securing identity" and open deep mysteries in the logic of subjectivity.[3] Faulkner's greatest work, Weinstein believes, addresses the (im)possibility of transparency in self-knowledge and the knowledge of others in novels that least resemble the detective form.

The discussion of Faulkner and mystery begins with a group of essays interested in examining such a sense of thickening mystery that gathers particularly around issues of identity and subjectivity in novels that attempt to eschew, in Sean McCann's words, the "moral, epistemological, and formal clarity that characterizes the mystery novel." McCann, Weinstein, Donald M. Kartiganer, and Richard Godden locate one of the most impenetrable mysteries at the heart of Faulkner's fiction in questions of racial identity. Particularly central to such an agenda are Faulkner's novels of the 1930s, especially *Light in August* and *Absalom, Absalom!*, which accrue mystery around social and racial prohibitions in the South. Moving from the mysteries of identity to the mysteries of detective fiction, the next cluster of essays focuses on *Intruder in the Dust*, a novel that both invokes and subverts genre expectations of the crime novel. Rachel Watson, Hosam Aboul-Ela, and Esther Sánchez-Pardo focus on the role of crime solving in Cold War America and Faulkner's representation of the justice system in the South in his 1948 novel. Crime and punishment are also central topics for Susan V. Donaldson and Lisa Hinrichsen, who address the mysteries surrounding Faulkner's inscrutable women in *Sanctuary* and *Requiem for a Nun*. What can be known and what should remain a mystery are the questions at the center of Sarah Mahurin's essay on *The Unvanquished*, and the two concluding essays by Michael Gorra and Noel Polk focus on the crafting of plot and return the discussion to the mysteries in Faulkner's storytelling.

In the opening essay of the collection, *"And you are ——? Faulkner's Mysteries of Race and Identity,"* Philip Weinstein traces the etymological origins of the word *mystery* from Greek. Mystery was understood not only quite literally as a "secret rite or doctrine" but as the idea that we cannot be "self-knowing": "In its most religious forms, mystery engages the reality that, ultimately, we cannot remain ourselves—self-owned, self-defined, self-knowing. Put otherwise, mystery at its heart intimates the undoing of identity." Weinstein cites Sophocles's *Oedipus Rex* as the archetypal text that offers mystery in relation both to detection *and* to the undoing of identity. Here mystery is understood as a "terrifying, quasi-religious mode" of recognition where identity glimpses its own limits. He suggests that "quasi-religious mystery and reason-fueled detection—even though they are regularly coupled—may point in opposed directions." After presenting these opposing trajectories in the Greek tragedy, Weinstein turns to Faulkner's changing representations of racial identity as mystery in four of his novels. He argues that Faulkner first moves toward race as mystery in *Light in August*, then "plunges into the heart of such mystery" in *Absalom, Absalom!*, and finally turns away from an understanding of racial identity as mystery in *Go Down, Moses* and towards "pure detection" in *Intruder in the Dust*. Weinstein concludes that, whereas Faulkner delves into the mysteries of racial identity and the question of self-knowing in his fiction of the 1930s, by 1948 he "had come to respect, enshrine, and reify black difference."

Faulkner's treatment of racial difference is also at stake in "The Blackness of *Absalom, Absalom!*" Donald M. Kartiganer argues that "the great mystery of *Absalom, Absalom!* is not why Thomas Supten rejected Charles Bon as a husband for his daughter Judith, but why it takes four internal narrators of the story . . . so incredibly long to answer the question." In order to conceal Bon's racial heritage, the narrators put up various screening mechanisms that shield what they have trouble acknowledging. Kartiganer claims that "the great originality of *Absalom* is that, despite the defenses of its narrators, Faulkner offers a 'new vision' while continuing to explore the old racial dilemma." Kartiganer begins his argument by putting Faulkner's novel into conversation with the influential manifesto *I'll Take My Stand*, which denied, in his words, "not just the significance but virtually the presence of African Americans" in the South of the 1930s. In contrast to the imagined racial and sectional homogeneity sketched by the Twelve Southerners, Faulkner noticed the blindness to the African American presence in discourses about the South and exposed it in his novel. What brought him to see? Kartiganer provocatively suggests that it may have been Faulkner's own family history. In *Absalom, Absalom!* Faulkner "exposes the 1930s 'invisibility' of Southern blackness as a social and psychic pathology of devastating consequence." At the center of this drama is Thomas Supten, the character most threatened by "blackness" because he believes that racial identity is more than a fantasy. This awareness differs from the fantasized blackness that Rosa attributes to Supten, whom she characterizes as "behaviorally black," and also from Mr. Compson's fantasies centering around Bon's octoroon mistress. These fantasies form screening mechanisms around race that are present in Quentin's and Shreve's narrations as well. Here homosexual desires and incest are covering up the most profound mystery at the heart of the novel: racial identity. For Kartiganer, the racial mystery in *Absalom Absalom!* is hiding in plain sight, present in the layers of concealment and the various screening mechanisms carefully embedded in the narrative strategies of the novel.

Mystery also surrounds Faulkner's representations of race relations in his Indian stories from the 1930s. In "Reading 'Red Leaves': Mouths, Labor Power, and Revolutions," Richard Godden contemplates the relationship of the African American slave to his Indian master. Faulkner's short story revolves in part around the death of Issetibbeha, the Choctaw chief whose black body servant must be killed at the death of his master. Although the slave runs away, he is running in a circle, eventually returning to face his doom, but not before he engages with the meaning of his own dying. Godden's essay draws on the Hegelian master-slave dialectic, with specific regard to the slave's former function as a "taster" for his master. He argues that "the food, carried first to the slave's mouth and only then to the mouth of the master, constitutes a congealed form of the slave's labor power." The taster's function is to prevent the master's death by poisoning; however, in the slave's awakening consciousness of his own power, he invites death by poison when he lets himself be repeatedly struck by a poisonous cottonmouth snake. Godden examines the significance of this bite, which causes the slave's arm to shrivel up, resulting in his uselessness to his master and in an ironic reversal of their relationship: Issetibbeha would now have to assist such a disabled servant until the end of his days. According to Godden, Faulkner's story grants "a layered and positively Hegelian irony to the slave, by means of which, even as he provokes the deformation of his arm (the instrument of his labor), he recognizes that in order 'not . . . to die' (as an 'independent consciousness') he must die first (as a 'dependent consciousness'), doing so, moreover, by poisoning himself in a manner that will poison the limb of the very tree that he (and his class) have sustained." The feeding and poisoning of the master, as well as the circulation of foods and fluids in the world of "Red Leaves" more generally, draw attention to the binding of labor power in the nineteenth century and the imminent economic restructuring of Faulkner's contemporary South. In Godden's close reading of various processes of ingestion, what remains in the text "semantically indigestible" is the mystery at the heart of Faulkner's "Red Leaves."

Published in 1930, "Red Leaves" indicates Faulkner's concern with the colonial racial history of Mississippi, and while the time period of the setting changes in *Light in August*, published only two years later, Faulkner's interest in the meaning of race remains constant. In "'Nice Believing': Mystery and Mysteries in *Light in August*," Sean McCann argues that *Light in August* both resembles and subverts the popular crime narrative. This is the case on the level of character where a murderer (Christmas), a victim (Burden), and a vigilante (Grimm) come together to act out a familiar drama. But unlike in the detective genre, there is no easy resolution to the murder, resulting in an ending that would leave us with a sense of resolution and a world at peace. Instead, Faulkner's *Light in August* "directly reverses the logic at the core of most murder mysteries" by ending with an act of ritualistic violence that moves us away from social solutions towards spiritual questions and mysteries. Whereas *Knight's Gambit* and *Intruder in the Dust* are narratives more genuinely true to the detective genre, *Light in August* is interested in complicating the questions. The intellectual figures in each text—Gavin Stevens in *Knight's Gambit* and Gail Hightower in *Light in August*—illuminate the "key problems of the text," which turn out to be very different: according to McCann, *Knight's Gambit* concerns an agrarian society in conflict with modernity. The question here is a secular one—how to "accommodate the energies of an increasingly commercialized society"—whereas the question in *Light in August* is a spiritual one. McCann reads *Light in August* within a national climate marked by anxieties over religious liberalism that "allegedly transferred devotion from sacred authority to secular visions of social progress." These anxieties are apparent in the "self-sufficient zealotry of McEachern, the eccentric fervor of Hines, the solitary devotion of Byron Bunch, and the personal torment of Joe Christmas and Joanna Burden." The novel addresses the religious battles of the 1920s in Faulkner's portrayal of these characters and in Hightower's "culminating religious vision."[4]

McCann's distinction between spiritual and secular mystery is helpful in grouping the essays in this volume. The next three essays address the secular mysteries of Faulkner's *Intruder in the Dust*: Rachel Watson examines the role of scientific forensic evidence, Esther Sánchez-Pardo investigates the merging of crime fiction with a coming of age story, and Hosam Aboul-Ela probes the function of civil disobedience and the role of the state. Watson's essay, "'To Survive What Looked Out': The Forensic Trail and William Faulkner's *Intruder in the Dust*," analyzes the novel's positioning as informed by two competing narratives: the sociological "motive narrative" and the "forensic narrative." She suggests that these narratives constitute meditations not only on types of evidence but how such evidence is linked to national and racial ideologies of the 1940s. The plot of *Intruder*, Watson argues, "is actually made possible by a fantasy of dispassionate crime solving" through scientific evidence, but this narrative is "crossed" by specific racial and regional signifiers. Watson writes that *Intruder* is a story about "hard evidence: how it is recognized, how it works on us, how we feel about it, and how we use it as a category with which to mark and revise our competing desires for 'pure' signs of a scientific discourse on the one hand and the messier, contingent signs of the cultural and social world on the other." She argues that Faulkner's "most serious attempt at detective fiction emerges as an engagement with Americans' evolving interest in forensic certainty." Faulkner wrote in the context of the FBI's new technologies of scientific crime solving, saw movies such as *You Can't Get Away with It* (1936), which deals with finger printing, and observed the work of his own brother Murray Falkner, who was a "G-man" in the Hoover administration. These cultural contexts may have prompted Faulkner's meditation on the reading of evidence in the South, an environment where no white man could properly read the evidence and solve a crime when a black man was implicated.

Faulkner's ideological positioning in the postwar South also plays a role in "The Mysterious Case of the Cold War Imaginary: Faulkner's *Intruder in the Dust* and Paul Bowles's *The Sheltering Sky*." Hosam Aboul-Ela argues that Faulkner makes several moves that align his detective story with novels of the postcolonial world. "Faulkner's position as a Southerner infused his work with insights into the processes of imperialism—particularly economic imperialism." *Intruder* not only challenges the normative form of detective fiction, it also explicitly seeks to address challenges to authority. In the novel the "threat against authority of the state emanates from a specific piece of land, Beat Four, to which the power of law enforcement does not extend." Contested land, as Aboul-Ela reminds us, is at the center of much literature of occupation. Further, in Faulkner's novel Gavin Stevens is circumvented by detective figures who come from the margins of society and include "an elderly black man, a young dependent white boy, a young dependent black boy, and an elderly single woman." These marginal detectives can be read as subverting the "entire structure of colonialism with its centralized hierarchy of power." Gavin Stevens, by contrast, represents such power; he is connected with Cold War anxieties that originate beyond the borders of the state. Aboul-Ela compares how Faulkner and Bowles critique mainstream society: Faulkner by valorizing marginal characters, crossing racial lines, and rewriting the detective story; and Bowles by focusing on American outsiders and expatriates, crossing sexual lines,

and twisting the genre of the captivity narrative. This bending of conventions, he argues, can be read as a form of "disobedience" that challenges
the order and conformity of society and criticizes the ideologies of Cold
War America.

Faulkner's alteration of the genre of detective fiction is also at stake
in Esther Sánchez-Pardo's essay, "Critical Intruders: Unraveling Race
and Mystery in *Intruder in the Dust*." This essay positions *Intruder in
the Dust* as a text that conforms neither entirely to the conventions of
crime fiction, nor the coming of age story, nor the black liberation story.
The mystery in *Intruder*, Sánchez-Pardo writes, "is not necessarily who
killed Vinson Gowrie . . . but rather what precisely is going on in the
mind of this black man whose individual subjectivity resists being categorized, contained, and understood by whites." Faulkner, she argues,
prefers racial opacity and refuses simple dichotomies, including those of
race and morality. The essay traces Faulkner's own shifting conceptions
of the story he was composing and adds to the critical debate about
Lucas's political positioning in the pre–civil rights South. Sánchez-Pardo
observes that Faulkner places Lucas within the context of liberal individualism, on the one hand, and "collective black political struggle" of the
1940s on the other. But in the end, Lucas, isolated from his community
and characterized as a "supremely singular hero," symbolizes neither.
Sánchez-Pardo focuses on the centrality of the jail cell and the ways
in which Lucas "directs" his own release from behind bars. He is the
titular intruder, she argues, who in Glissant's words "disturbs the order
of things." But for such disruption to succeed, he needs help, and it is
only by the joint efforts of the "transgressive interracial couple"—Chick,
the white boy, and Lucas, the black man—that justice can be attained.

Public spaces like the jail cell and the courtroom are also central loca-
tions for mysteries surrounding Faulkner's female characters. Mystery
as a problem of knowledge connected to gender and sexuality is pervasive in Faulkner's fiction. The essays by Susan V. Donaldson and Lisa
Hinrichsen address the different ways by which women become figures
for the ultimately unknowable, Freud's Dark Continent. As Donaldson argues, Faulkner's female characters form the nexus for racial and
sexual fantasies expressive not only of the time and culture, but of his
own mixed feelings about women. In "Reimagining the Femme Fatale:
Requiem for a Nun and the Lessons of Film Noir," Donaldson focuses
on Faulkner's notoriously mysterious and illegible female characters,
especially Nancy Manigoe and Temple Drake. These characters come
into sharper focus, she argues, when read as femmes fatales and put
into the context of the film noir tradition of the 1940s and '50s. During
and after World War II, when women entered the work force in greater

numbers, the boundaries between black and white women and "ladies" and "fallen" women became more blurred. This created a social anxiety to which film noir responded by introducing the femme fatale who, according to Mary Ann Doane, represents "a potential epistemological trauma" because "she never really is what she seems to be." Most of all, writes Donaldson, she is not legible or manageable. Faulkner's work, too, is marked by this anxiety as he was searching "with increasing desperation—for a vocabulary to address black restiveness, women's new ambitions, and his mounting sense of the wrongs wrought not just by segregation but by the cultural narratives of black and white womanhood that had long served as the legitimizing underpinnings of American apartheid." Donaldson traces Faulkner's concern with female illegibility and ambiguity back to Caddy in the *Sound and the Fury* who, she argues, "anticipates the disruptive and ambiguous presence of femmes fatales in those hard-boiled detective movies charged with anxiety over violated boundaries between femininity and masculinity and between blackness and whiteness." When Faulkner was working on *Requiem*, he was looking back to assess his earlier work, including *Sanctuary* and "That Evening Sun," and he may have been inspired by some of the conventions of Hollywood film noir and crime fiction. Nancy and Temple are Faulkner's femmes fatales in a society marked by "literal and figurative violence that has gone into the making of narratives about black sexuality and white purity." In *Requiem for a Nun*, Nancy ends up in the jail that looks out over the community and oversees the "entrenchment of segregation," but, Donaldson suggests, this space also bears the important unrecorded histories of women who break social codes.

In "Open Spaces, Open Secrets: *Sanctuary's* Mysterious 'Something,'" Lisa Hinrichsen also focuses on Temple Drake as a mysterious female figure. In dramatizing the story of the crime—Popeye's rape of Temple—Faulkner, she argues, "locates *Sanctuary's* central formal and thematic inquiry in the tension between acting and knowing." Faulkner emphasizes the telling of this story in three ways: first, by "eliding direct narrative representation of Temple's rape"; second, "by undermining Horace Benbow's reliability as 'detective'"; and third, by dramatizing Temple's inability to testify in court. A severely traumatized Temple, Hinrichsen argues, cannot properly testify, and her gaze, fixated on the back of the courtroom, functions as an ellipses that represents "at once the silence of her trauma . . . as well as the gap in the symbolic order of Southern culture itself, which the trial exposes." The place where Temple's rape occurs, Frenchman's Bend, is significant for its plantation setting and a "planter culture in which white ownership doubles as legal authority." This setting effectively silences Temple and shows us that the patriarchal planter culture is complicit with violence against women and that this aspect of Southern society is "an open secret." During her testimony in court, Temple's gaze, fixated on the back wall of the courtroom, points to this open secret. Hinrichsen argues that her fixed gaze and her passivity in court form "her means of telling us 'something' the community doesn't want to know." Using the work of Slavoj Žižek, Hinrichsen identifies this spot on the back wall as Žižek's "meaningless stain," which, when looked at from a different vantage point, acquires shape and yields new social meaning. This "something" that Temple sees at the back wall "significantly undercuts the symbolic order" and the masculine law of the courtroom. Temple's gaze, Hinrichsen concludes, makes us see "through the trial" and its façade for achieving social justice.

Mystery in Faulkner's novels then is concerned with the central problem of seeing, knowing, and understanding and with questions of what we can and choose to know and what must or should remain hidden and unknowable. Faulkner's fiction repeatedly returns to this problem of a mystery, whether in the seemingly irrational behavior of women, or in the social and racial mores of society even in seemingly straightforward texts. In "*Unvanquished* Uncertainty" Sarah Mahurin examines one of Faulkner's apparently clear and "easily decipherable texts." On closer examination, however, the novel is actually "suffused with moments of mystery" and "studded with nuggets of uncertainty," as Mahurin argues. The novel, she posits, is concerned with the central problem of knowledge—that is, with what we can and choose to know and what must or should remain unknowable. The light-hearted episodes that make up the lives and adventures of Bayard and Ringo easily mask the epistemological mystery at the heart of the novel. Picking up on the opening story when Bayard and Ringo hide under Granny's skirt after having shot a Yankee horse, Mahurin describes their vantage point as an epistemological "underskirtedness," a condition that functions more broadly in her argument as a description for sheltered uncertainty. Mahurin asks us to note the importance and "the predominance of not knowing" that Faulkner introduces as a central feature of his text. For instance, Bayard "incessantly notes the things he didn't—or doesn't—realize." These uncertainties are explicitly addressed in many scenes, especially in the opening Vicksburg episode, as well as in the discussion of the railroad and the "cokynut" cake. The pervasive "ethos of uncertainty" suggests not simply indecision but a desire for and a pleasure in not knowing certain things for strategic purposes. To remain ignorant of whether or not he has ever eaten coconut cake is preferable for Ringo over knowing for sure that he lacks an experience that his white friend Bayard has had and therefore admitting his inferior social and racial position. This ethos also fits with the Civil War context in which uncertainty of events and ignorance of casualties were often preferable to knowing the devastating truth. Taking into consideration historical testimony by women of the Civil War, Mahurin concludes that "the hermeneutics of the Civil War are not so different from the hermeneutics of Ringo's coconut cake."

The concluding essays by Michael Gorra and Noel Polk consider the relation, in Faulkner's work, between narrative structure and mystery. Gorra argues that Faulkner, unlike some of his well-known modernist contemporaries, was fond of crafting novels with a story line, and he was "not in the least shy about drawing on popular forms." "Faulkner's Plots" begins with a review of the relationship between plot and story (or the telling and the tale) within the theoretical framework of Russian formalist critics. Gorra believes that "Faulkner's work finds its greatest power when that tension [between plot and story] reaches its highest pitch." In the often radical disjunction between the telling and the tale, Faulkner was able to "represent his deepest sense of mystery, his sense of the world in which truth is always uncertain and knowledge forever incomplete." Like Weinstein, Gorra distinguishes between the mystery of the detective form (in *Intruder in the Dust* and *Knight's Gambit*, for instance) and the greater sense of mystery in *The Sound and the Fury* and *Absalom, Absalom!* In these novels some truth remains veiled. Gorra believes that, even though *Absalom, Absalom!* has a less technically diffi-cult plot than some of Faulkner's other works, it presents a much greater mystery because each plot element adds to the opacity of situation and human motivation. Gorra's essay ends with a brief consideration of *As I Lay Dying*, a novel that proves that its seemingly linear narration and rationality based on cause and effect contain mysteries that transcend the apparent chronology. Gorra concludes that Faulkner's characters "live in a world of imperfect knowledge," and, as Polk goes on to show, Faulkner's readers do, too. For Gorra, mystery is a kind of friction cre-ated by the imperfect matching up of plot and story material; for Polk, it is the utterly unplotable present in some of Faulkner's lesser-known stories.

Noel Polk finds mystery in some of the more obscure if not down-right unreadable stories in the "Beyond" section of Faulkner's *Collected Stories*. In "'It Just Doesn't Explain': 'The Leg,' "'Mistral,' Evelyn Nes-bit, and the Unreadable World," Polk argues that these stories present "the unsolved and unsolvable enigmas" resistant to even the most care-ful critical scrutiny. Polk brings Faulkner into productive conversation with Edgar Allan Poe and his fascination with crimes and experiences beyond the "normal." In Poe's fiction the "possibility of disorder that attaches itself to the inexplicable" is straightened out and illuminated by a detective figure who unlocks the mystery and reads the apparently unreadable. The case for these Faulkner stories, however, is different. "The Leg" and "Mistral" present mysterious deaths and unanswered questions, but both stories "spiral away from their own clues," leaving mysteries that remain unknowable even for the best detective critic. Polk argues that the characters in Faulkner's stories "move into the twilight between what we know and what we can never understand, and perhaps, as we shall see, do not want to know. What's *beyond* in these stories is precisely what's on the other side of that by no means liminal divide." He proceeds to show how these stories confront "the limits of rationality" with an in-depth look at the mysterious triangles in both stories: in "The Leg" the triangle is between Davy, George, and Everbe Corinthia; in "Mistral" it is between the narrator, his friend Don, and a girl raised by a priest in the Italian town they visit. Polk attempts to unravel the tricky knots of plotting by drawing connections between the stories that help illuminate character motivation. He notices that "trouble occurs when the narrator's male companion abandons him for a heterosexual liaison." The mysteries of these unreadable stories, he suggests, have to do with homosexual desire.

As the essays in this volume demonstrate, mystery is layered into every stratum of Faulkner's texts: it is present in the plot structure, and as an effect of plot, mystery primarily points to a hermeneutic problem. It is present in Faulkner's concern with questions of truth and knowledge, and as such it points towards epistemological questions. It is present in questions of self and other that lead us into the ontological sphere for answers about the mysteries of reality and the nature of existence. It is also present in Faulkner's language, which serves not only as a tool for discovery and communication, but as a conveyor of the illegible and the linguistically inscrutable. Faulkner's concern with the inexplicable in his fiction challenges our interpretive and explanatory capacities in an effort to unlock these mysteries. Reflecting on the desire for critical demystification, Rita Felski writes that mystery and enchantment are terms "with precious little currency in literary theory."[5] "Contemporary critics," she adds, "pride themselves on their power to disenchant, to mercilessly direct laser-sharp beams of critique at every imaginable object." Felski urges us to "face up to the limits of demystification as a critical method and a theoretical ideal" and promises that, "once we relinquish the modern dogma that our lives should become thoroughly disenchanted, we can truly begin to engage the affective and absorptive, sensuous and somatic qualities of aesthetic experience."[6] Reading Faulkner is such a multifaceted experience marked by pleasure, confusion, and an encounter with mystery; however, it is the job of the critic

nevertheless to attempt to explain the "mysterious something" that emanates from his work. And, it is the job of Faulkner, and any writer worth
his salt, to sprinkle it liberally into his fiction.

Annette Trefzer
University of Mississippi

NOTES

1. *Lion in the Garden: Interviews with William Faulkner, 1926–1962*, ed. James B.
Meriwether and Michael Millgate (Random House, 1968), 277.

2. References to detective fiction can be found in Faulkner's work as well; for instance,
in *The Wild Palms* (1938) one of the characters (the tall convict) reads the *Detectives'
Gazette*.

3. Philip Weinstein, *Unknowing: The Work of Modernist Fiction* (Ithaca: Cornell
University Press, 2005), 3.

4. It may be worth mentioning here that the word *mystery*, as Webster's reminds us,
derives from the Latin *mysterium*, a root word that carries religious and sacramental
connotations hinting at a truth that is unknowable except by divine revelation. In *Light
in August*, for instance, Faulkner strongly suggests such a sacramental sense of religious
mystery in Joe Christmas's crucifixion at the end of the novel.

5. Rita Felski, *Uses of Literature* (Hoboken, N.J.: Wiley-Blackwell Publishing, 2008), 54.

6. Ibid, 76.

Note on the Conference

The thirty-sixth Faulkner and Yoknapatawpha Conference sponsored by the University of Mississippi in Oxford took place 19–23 July 2009, with more than two hundred of the author's admirers in attendance. Twelve presentations on the theme "Faulkner and Mystery" are collected as essays in this volume. Brief mention is made here of other activities that took place during the five-day conference.

The program began on Sunday with lectures on "Faulkner's Plots" by Michael Gorra and "The Blackness of *Absalom, Absalom!*" by Donald Kartiganer. Following a buffet supper at the home of Dr. M. B. Howorth Jr. there was a screening of *The Story of Temple Drake*, the rarely seen 1933 film version of *Sanctuary*. Before the film, Richard Howorth, owner of Square Books in Oxford, and Ivo Kamps, chairman of the University English Department, welcomed participants and conference director Donald Kartiganer introduced winners of the 2009 William Faulkner Society Fellowships. These fellowships, awarded to young scholars selected to present conference papers, are funded by the Faulkner Society, the *Faulkner Journal*, and donations in memory of John W. Hunt, Faulkner scholar and emeritus professor of literature at Lehigh University. Ted Ownby, director of the Center for the Study of Southern Culture, presented the twenty-third annual Eudora Welty Awards in Creative Writing. Tiffany Croft won first prize, $500, for her poem "Off to Route 22," and Elizabeth Seratt won second prize, $250, for her short story "Jobe." Both winners are from Vicksburg and are students of Emma Richardson at the Mississippi School of Math and Science located in Columbus on the campus of the Mississippi College for Women. The late Frances Patterson of Tupelo, a longtime member of the Center Advisory Committee, established and endowed the awards, which are selected through a competition held in high schools throughout Mississippi.

Sean McCann and Philip Weinstein presented lectures on Monday, and James B. Carothers and Theresa M. Towner discussed "Some Mysteries of Faulkner's Short Stories" during the first of three "Teaching Faulkner" sessions. The day's program also included sessions during which Seth Berner, a book dealer from Portland, Maine, talked about

"Collecting Faulkner" and Kelley Hayden, Daniel Pecchenino, and Randall Wilhelm made presentations for the first of four panels featuring short papers selected through an annual call for papers. Authors Ace Atkins and Jere Hoar talked about their experiences writing "crime" fiction and commented on Faulkner's work in this genre. The day ended with Colby Kullman moderating the tenth annual Faulkner Fringe Festival, an open-mike evening at Southside Gallery on the Oxford Square. Among the highlights of the evening were Donald Kartiganer's playing his guitar and singing Faulkner-inspired songs and James Carothers's presentation to Kartiganer of a signed photograph of his lifelong baseball hero Joe DiMaggio as a retirement gift from conference friends.

Tuesday's program began with Charles A. Peek and Terrell L. Tebbetts conducting the second "Teaching Faulkner" session, which focused on the topic "As I Lay Missing: Vision and Detection in *Light in August.*" Noel Polk and Richard Godden presented lectures, and Margaret Rayburn Kramar, Esther Sánchez-Pardo, and Rachel Watson made panel presentations. Colby Kullman and his neighbors Harold and Dinah Clark hosted an afternoon party at Tyler place. A special event that evening was a conversation between Oxford attorneys Hal Freeland and his son, Tom, on Hal's experience as Phil Stone's law partner in the 1950s, when Faulkner was a regular visitor at the law office.

Susan V. Donaldson and Hosam Aboul-Ela were the lecturers for Wednesday's program, which also included a "Teaching Faulkner" session and panels with scholarly papers by John Padgett, Marta Puxan, and Rachel Walsh in the morning and Lisa Hinrichsen, Sarah Mahurin, and Conor Picken in the afternoon. Attendees gathered for the annual afternoon picnic at Faulkner's home, Rowan Oak. Guided tours of North Mississippi, the Delta, and Memphis took place on Thursday, and the conference ended with a party at Off Square Books.

Four exhibitions were available throughout the conference. The Department of Archives and Special Collections at the University's John Davis Williams Library mounted a display of materials on Faulkner and mysteries. The University Museum sponsored an exhibition of Boyd Saunders's original stone lithographs and etchings of Faulkner's "The Bear" and *The Sound and the Fury. Mississippi Delta Photographs and Other Recent Work* by Maude Clay was on exhibit at Barnard Observatory's Gammill Gallery. The University Press of Mississippi exhibited Faulkner books published by university presses throughout the United States.

The conference planners are grateful to all the individuals and organizations that support the Faulkner and Yoknapatawpha Conference annually. In addition to those mentioned above, we thank conference patron

Greg Perkins, Square Books, Southside Gallery, the City of Oxford, and the Oxford Convention and Visitors Bureau.

Faulkner and Mystery
FAULKNER AND YOKNAPATAWPHA

2009

"*And you are* ——?": Faulkner's Mysteries of Race and Identity

PHILIP WEINSTEIN

1

What is mystery? Long before detective fiction, long before fiction itself, the term was operative, deriving apparently from Latin *mysterium*, which comes from Greek *mysterion*, meaning "secret rite or doctrine." Someone participating in such a "Mystery" was a *mystes*, "one who has been initiated."[1] The earliest and most important ceremonies seem to have been the Greek Eleusinian Mysteries, centered on the cult of Demeter and Persephone.[2] These secret ceremonies endured for some two millennia, and subsequent mystery "cults" have flourished throughout Western history: often in opposition to hegemonic Christianity, but also—ever since the rise of science in the sixteenth century—in opposition to Enlightenment reason. Freemasonry, for example, recurrently seems to operate like a Mystery; as does the rise of antirational theosophy—associated with Madame Blavatsky—at the end of the nineteenth century.

With respect to Enlightenment assumptions, "Mystery" seems to involve a set of secret procedures for addressing a scandal at the core of life itself: a blind spot or radical limitation that Enlightenment reason alone is incapable of overcoming. Reliance on initiation, on privileged access to secret doctrine and ritual, points to a project for engaging that scandal. The ultimate blind spot and radical limitation that unaided reason cannot accommodate is death itself: the fact—so offensive to reason—that we are born to die, that our self itself is destined to conclude in a space of unknowable darkness, where we cease to be. Mystery seeks to engage the limits hemming in ego and operative beyond its sway—the ways in which, intolerably, we remain creatures in the dark rather than creators in the light. It is no accident that the Eleusinian Mysteries centered on Demeter and Persephone—the story of the goddess of agriculture and fertility who lost her daughter to Hades, the god of death and the underworld. Determined to retrieve Persephone, Demeter could extract from Zeus no more than a promise of her daughter's return for

3

six months out of the year. Darkness and death insist on their claim for the other six months, the myth thus signaling the binding of summer to winter, of light to dark, of life to death. In its most powerful religious forms, mystery engages the reality that, ultimately, we cannot remain ourselves—self-owned, self-defined, self-knowing. Put otherwise, mystery, at its heart, intimates the undoing of identity.

Freud's notion of "uncanny" addresses something of the same dispossession of self. It engages those moments when our habitual self-world relation slips its coherence and we find ourselves in an unmappable other space—a space where we are no longer canny, no longer familiar with the procedures, no longer ourselves.[3] This dynamic induces vertigo as the normal traffic between self and world comes to a halt. As long as our world had continued to remain recognizable, we managed to move through it with our conventions intact. This is what "canny" means: the capacity to make our ambient world "work" for us, to believe with justification that "I can." The "uncanny," like Mystery, arises when those conventions rupture. The outbreak of the "uncanny" involves the unfurnishing of a previously furnished ego.

Freud takes such moments of unfurnishing as signs of the original frailty of ego itself. Arguing that life takes initial shape as the infant's unindividuated extension into world—no distinctions yet established between here and there, inner and outer—Freud envisages the painful path we pursue toward individuation as beset on all sides by pitfalls of relapse. At such moments of relapse the exterior world sheds its reliable objectivity—its vouchsafed otherness obedient to scientific mapping—and becomes once more a scene shaped by unconscious projection. It all becomes strange: estranged. What we took to be "out there" turns bizarre, is recognized as coming from "in here." Horrifyingly, we seem to be doing it ourselves.

The supreme mystery text of Western culture is Sophocles's *Oedipus the King*: where individual identity reveals itself as not only saturated in scandal but *conceived* in it. Oedipus's entire personal history is founded on the breaking of familial and social taboo. What had appeared to be outer catastrophe—the plague of Thebes—is shown to be inner scandal—the crimes of Oedipus. Unbeknownst to himself, he is in intolerable relation to his father, his mother, and his city. Inner and outer are joined at the hip. The canniest of men—greatest of warriors and leaders—emerges as uncanny disaster. To cure the plague of Thebes requires destroying Oedipus. Sophocles's play intimates that we as individuals may be in relation to others and to the culture we inhabit in ways we did not know and cannot bear to learn, all this through no correctable fault of our own, yet our fault nevertheless. We were not forced.

Confronted with what he has done and therefore who he unknowingly has been all along and still is, Oedipus undoes himself, tears out his eyes, relinquishes identity. The mystery of identity—identity *as* mystery—can go no further.

In contrast to this terrifying, quasi-religious mode of mystery—where identity glimpses its own limits, its own shattering—the West has produced for centuries (creating in the late nineteenth century an entire subgenre) a literature of "detective fiction." This mode, fueled by an Enlightenment faith in reason, seeks less to acknowledge mystery than to eradicate it—"to create a mystery for the sole purpose of effecting its effortless dissipation."[4] In detective fiction, the procedures are reason guided rather than ritualistic, and the corpse in question rarely registers as a death's head presaging our own coming extinction.

For a classic example of mystery thus sanitized, protected from the menace of death and the collapse of ego—of mystery engaged as pure adventure and made safe for consumption—think of Dan Brown's *The Da Vinci Code*. This novel pursues an external mystery centered on the game of detection itself, not on engaging the threat of mortality that uncannily attaches to the career of ego. There are no memorable figures in *The Da Vinci Code*—no doomed Oedipus or Jocasta—only flat characters acting as counters in the service of the game: the great impersonal game of finding out. Not that that game of detecting is trivial: Western culture has insisted immemorially that someone or something must know what is going on. Someone or something must be accountable for the fall of a sparrow and the suffering of Job—must, however silent, know why these things occur, be responsible for their occurring. Our traditional name for this knowing function is God or the gods—or, in Faulkner's vocabulary, "fate." God serves, precisely, to name and contain mystery. "[G]od represents . . . man's most strenuous attempt to overcome mystery."[5] In detective fiction, the detached detective himself—Holmes and all his counterparts—stands in for God. He overcomes mystery—by explaining it. Mystery cedes to the reasoning mind, the scandal is contained, our own coming death can once again be put out of mind. The detective refurnishes our menaced egos by curing the plague of Thebes—or London or Los Angeles or Jefferson—at least for a time, at least until it breaks out again.

What has this to do with Faulkner and race? A great deal. In the conference description this year, the two terms—mystery and detective fiction—are treated as interchangeable. The rubric is "Faulkner and Mystery," and the opening sentence of the "Call for Papers" speaks of Faulkner's "deep interest if not in what is normally regarded as detective fiction, then in its thematic and formal staple: the process of detection."

But quasi-religious mystery and reason-fueled detection—even though they are regularly coupled—may point in opposed directions. With respect to Faulkner's mysteries of race and identity, I argue that they do point in opposed directions, and that his work enacts a parabolic arc of changing values. His fiction begins by ignoring race, then—charged with new energy—moves toward race as mystery (*Light in August*), then plunges into the heart of such mystery (*Absalom, Absalom!*), then turns away from race as mystery (*Go Down, Moses*), and ends in pure detection (*Intruder in the Dust*).

2

Light in August is Faulkner's breakthrough novel about racial identity as mystery. In his career, blacks emerge as significant only in *Flags in the Dust* and *The Sound and the Fury*, where no mystery attaches to them.[6] There they bask in their author's keen observation, kept by their blackness from inner development, protected as well from the turmoil besetting Horace Benbow, Bayard Sartoris, and the Compson brothers. White turmoil takes center stage, begetting the stylistic innovations of *The Sound and the Fury* and then of *As I Lay Dying*. Blacks are minor in *Sanctuary* as well, but everything changes in *Light in August*.

It is as though Faulkner sat up in bed after a nightmare sometime in 1931 and asked himself: what would I feel like if I suddenly found myself to be one of them? What would *I* feel like: there was no question of *them*. The novel didn't ask who (as a community living in segregated "freedman's" districts of every town in the South) they might be. No empathic entry into Southern blackness, virtually no blacks in the novel at all. No: what was required was that the one suffering from race relations be taken as white—yet be trapped in a weave of racial rumor about his identity at its core genetic level. The man had to be unable to know what blood ran in his veins. That would be the mystery he embodied, a mystery of identity scrupulously guarded not only from others in the novel, but from the man himself, as well as from the novel's readers. This narrow optic brought to focus an extraordinary insight. Beneath the surface confidence of Southern whites ran a racial insecurity bordering on hysteria.[7] If a drop of black blood was thought to make a white man black, who might not unknowingly carry this toxic drop? No one could see the internal wreckage that drop would have wrought. Invisibly infected carriers might be anywhere. Such anxiety might be enough to make many a white man in the segregated South have trouble going back to sleep, once he had sat bolt upright at 3:00 a.m. and wondered: what if I were black and didn't know it?

How can racial identity be a serious mystery in a novel that has virtually no black characters? Yet racial hysteria—like a bomb threat—can flare up, uncontrollably, with neither blacks nor bombs anywhere to be found. In an essay entitled "Stranger in the Village" James Baldwin explains the logic of this hysteria: "At the root of the American Negro problem," he writes, "is the necessity of the American white man to find a way of living with the Negro in order to live with himself. . . . 'the Negro-in-America is a form of insanity which overtakes white men.'"[8] It is as though the American white man has been surreptitiously infected with Negroness. The insanity such infection releases is white alone. My figure of speech invokes the blood, which is *Light in August's* obsessive concern. Joe Christmas is incapable of finding a way of living with the Negro in order to live with himself, and this because he senses his dark twin living inejectably, blood-coiled, beneath his skin. How does Christmas come to believe this? How does Faulkner let us find it out?

The first scene where we realize that Christmas may be black occurs some seventy pages into the book. Far enough along for readers to feel tricked: which is to say, to resent the author's not giving us in advance the racial information we require. (We have spent fifty pages already in Christmas's company: we deserve better.) Such resentment boomerangs on us once we ask what is at stake in our demanding to know, first off, a character's racial pedigree. Here is the scene. Joe Brown, Christmas's erstwhile partner, is being grilled as he tries to explain to an angry public what he has been doing with Christmas. The latter is suspected of having slit Joanna Burden's throat, set fire to her house, and fled. A thousand-dollar reward has been offered to anyone who can identify the killer, and Brown wants to collect it. The riled town, however, wants to know what Brown was doing at the scene of the fire. Byron Bunch narrates what comes next:

> "I reckon he was desperate by then. I reckon he could not only see that thousand dollars getting further away from him, but that he could begin to see somebody else getting it. . . . Because they said it was just like he had been saving what he told them next for just such a time as this. Like he had knowed that if it come to a pinch, this would save him. . . . 'That's right,' he says. 'Go on. Accuse me. Accuse the white man that's trying to help you with what he knows. Accuse the white man and let the nigger go free. Accuse the white and let the nigger run.'
>
> "'Nigger?' the sheriff said. 'Nigger?'
>
> "It's like he knew he had them then. Like nothing they could believe he had done would be as bad as what he could tell that somebody else had done. 'You're so smart,' he says. 'The folks in this town is so smart. Fooled for three years. Calling him a foreigner for three years, when soon as I watched him

three days I knew he wasn't no more a foreigner than I am. I knew before he even told me himself.' And them watching him now, and looking now and then at one another.

"'You better be careful what you are saying, if it is a white man you are talking about,' the marshall says. 'I don't care if he is a murderer or not.' . . .

"'A nigger,' the marshall said. 'I always thought there was something funny about that fellow.'"[9]

Five times hurled into that space of contestation, the word "nigger" magically reconfigures the stakes involved. Brown exits from the space of suspicion, as Christmas comes to fill (overfill) that space by himself. All eyes—with previously blurred vision now corrected to 20/20—are turned on this absent figure. "Nigger" is bad enough, but it could be dealt with. What is intolerable is that none of them spotted him in advance. The marshall warningly trots out to Brown the South's hierarchy of crimes. To murder someone is less culpable than to call a white man a "nigger."

Subsequent recognitions click into place: "I always thought there was something funny about that fellow," the marshall says. His access to this recognition is revealing. The lack of clarity he and his countrymen felt during their actual experience of Christmas has been satisfyingly dispelled. *Now* they know what that was all about. Retrospective judgment silently reconfigures earlier experience so that it fits ongoing prejudice. Uncertainty gets "corrected" into fixed (and fatal) conviction. It doesn't stop there. Joanna Burden—while alive, a strange Yankee woman living alone in their vicinity—becomes, once dead, a martyr to Southern honor, the victim of black bestiality: "Among them [were those] who believed aloud that it was an anonymous negro crime committed not by a negro but by Negro and who knew, believed, and hoped that she had been ravished too: at least once before her throat was cut and at least once afterward" (611). "Nigger" carries with it an inalterably subhuman narrative. As for Brown, wielder of the term, we can infer that he is lying about his own process of recognition. He too was blind to Christmas's racial identity, until Christmas informed him otherwise. But he has forgotten that he *is* lying about it, so soothing is it to rewrite earlier blindness into later enlightenment. Except that it is not enlightenment. No one knows if Christmas is black, but none of this not knowing will prevent the citizens of Jefferson from killing and castrating him. We alone are sure that his racial identity remains a mystery: there is nothing satisfying about knowing this.

Although Christmas outwits the pursuers who are convinced that he is a nigger-murderer-rapist, he chooses, finally, to turn himself in: "*I am tired of running of having to carry my life like it was a basket of eggs*"

(648, emphasis in the original). He makes sure that the day he starts trying to do so is a Friday. On Saturday he succeeds in getting recognized and caught. Of all of *Light in August*'s narratives moves, this is perhaps the most brilliant. Faulkner turns over the telling of Christmas's capture to an anonymous townsman, who speaks to other anonymous townsmen as follows:

> "He don't look any more like a nigger than I do. But it must have been the nigger blood in him. It looked like he had set out to get himself caught like a man might set out to get married. He had got clean away for a whole week. . . . Then yesterday morning he come into Mottstown in broad daylight, on a Saturday with the town full of folks. He went into a white barbershop like a white man, and because he looked like a white man they never suspected him. . . . They shaved him and cut his hair and he payed them and walked out and right into a store and bought a new shirt and a tie and a straw hat. . . . And then he walked the streets in broad daylight, like he owned the town, walking back and forth with people passing him a dozen times and not knowing it, until Halliday saw him and ran up and grabbed him and said, 'Aint your name Christmas?' and the nigger said that it was. He never denied it. He never did anything. He never acted like either a nigger or a white man. That was it. That was what made the folks so mad. For him to be a murderer and all dressed up and walking the town like he dared them to touch him, when he ought to have been skulking and hiding in the woods, muddy and dirty and running. It was like he never even knew he was a murderer, let along a nigger too." (657–58)

A culture's racist vernacular speaks here. In this vernacular, all "niggers" are capable—it is their default position—of being rapist-murderers who skulk and hide in the woods. They are typically dirty as well—and recognizable as such. Joe Christmas's final gestures eloquently transcend this racial stereotype. With exquisite irony, he bestrides the town as though he owned it. A white barbershop, a new shirt and tie and hat, an unhurried parading through Mottstown while waiting to be recognized: his moves counter white expectations, point for point. He does not say a word. His performance says it for him: "I look like you, perhaps better than you. I am clean, tall, and self-possessed. I enter and exit your segregated spaces—your barbershop and stores—and you do not see my difference. You do not see it because it does not exist. It takes you forever to catch up to me." I have invented this silent speech, yet something like it roils inside this mob of enraged whites. Inchoately, they register his insult and grasp that he is mocking the racial conventions that underwrite their sanity. "The Negro-in-America is a form of insanity which overtakes white men," Baldwin wrote. *Light in August* is the first of Faulkner's masterpieces to express the fallout of that insanity.

Light in August treats Joe Christmas's racial identity as a mystery at once radioactive and unsolvable. Given white anxiety toward miscegenation, as well as whites' urgent need to decode racial identity accurately so as to tether their responses accordingly, Christmas's racial mystery provokes in them outrage. The social contract that had remained relatively benign in Faulkner's previous novels now reveals its darker elements. A long-festering wound opens up at the heart of the body politic, launching a race-fueled violence that would solicit Faulkner's diagnostic scrutiny for years to come. Submitted to this new racial optic, Southern history shows him not the sleepiness of antebellum ways, but a disease that had ravaged the country (not just the South) since its founding centuries earlier, and whose virulence in 1932 was unabated. Faulkner now had rawer and more damaging social materials on his hands than ever before, and the imaginative labor of how best to deploy those materials—to make them tell most resonantly—would beget his most inventive forms.

Mystery has now become central to those narrative forms (there is distress everywhere in the earlier work, but little mystery). It takes the concealed mystery of Christmas's blood to make certain intimate encounters between him and whites possible at all. My distinction is crucial: *concealed* mystery lets Faulkner narrate as normal black-white relations that would otherwise be taboo. Put in different terms, Faulkner is beginning to dramatize what he will later call the "might have been." For all its focus on the meanness of Southern race relations, *Light in August* lets us glimpse—through Bobbie, Joanna, Mrs. Hines, and Joe himself—the pathos, the waste, of feelings that will be mangled by the racial status quo. This Utopian glimpse is short-lived: once Joe's racial mystery becomes visible, it must cease—for all white characters in the novel—to *be* a mystery. Racial identity cannot be tolerated in Faulkner's South *as* mystery. Selfhood is accessible in his culture only through the fixed lens of a racial binary. Exposing the mystery of Christmas's racial identity launches—ritualistically, inevitably—outbursts of violence. The cunning of the book lodges in Faulkner's keeping that mystery known only to us and to Joe, but *unknown* to others. Faulkner thus makes it a working mystery, begetting outrage or perversity whenever it is outed for white comprehension.

What are the results of this narrative experiment? It lets us see that no love in *Light in August* can acknowledge racial difference (revealed or assumed) and remain intact. Such love as crosses the barrier of race gets scarred and deformed in its passage, manifesting as abjection, perversity, hysteria. The implicit racial stance operative in *Light in August* emerges: sustainable love can develop between two people only if they share the same race. You have to know your love partner as racially akin, in order to experience appropriate feelings. The love comedy of Byron and Lena is luridly silhouetted by the love fiasco of Christmas and every white woman he becomes involved with. Everything *known* in *Light in August* proceeds on the premise that a crossing of races—in the same character or between characters—cannot be borne. But if *unknown*? To launch those racial crossings nevertheless—and to take the diagnostic measure of the violence unleashed, the tenderness despoiled—Faulkner needed Christmas's racial identity *as* mystery.

3

I turn now to *Absalom, Absalom!* There, the love-race-mystery equation deepens; we are granted much more than *Light in August*'s Utopian glimpses. Once again, a central character's racial identity is kept a mystery. However, no reader is permitted to know—until virtually the end of the narrative—that there *is* a racial mystery centered on Charles Bon. Everyone, we included, remained unaware that the mysterious *what*—his unexplained murder—kept from view a mysterious *who*: his racial identity.

Rather than descending into the morass of recrimination and violence that that mystery—whenever revealed—launched in *Light in August*, *Absalom* reaches towards love. It does so by staging a series of imaginative projections. This is the most openly projective of Faulkner's novels. It cannot "work" at all without Judith and Henry's projections onto Bon, Quentin and Shreve's projections onto the Sutpen and Coldfield families, the reader's projections—through the mediating discourses of several narrators—onto the entire cast of characters. *Absalom* is rife with vicarious projections into others' lives, and such projections can go anywhere.[10]

Inasmuch as vicarious projection fuels the dynamic of love itself, *Absalom* aspires—more than any other work of Faulkner—toward an "overpass to love." By keeping the reader uninformed, like the characters themselves, of the racial identity of its most enigmatic character, *Absalom* establishes Bon as the fantasy center of the book: a blank slate on whom a range of lovers and narrators may project their fondest desires. Ellen sees in him the refinement missing in her husband and children, Henry sees in him the sophistication and beauty he himself lacks, Judith sees in him a marital destiny she yearns for. As for the narrators, Rosa sees in Bon the ideal husband she is never to have, Mr. Compson sees in him an unillusioned intelligence that yet avoids nihilism, and Quentin and Shreve see in him a New Orleans–funded finesse and freedom from northern Mississippi rigidities of thought, feeling, and behavior.

Faulkner writes Bon in such a way that the other characters—with the fatal exception of Sutpen—see in Bon a greater fund of possibility than they themselves possess. They love in him the larger life they cannot conceptualize or access without him. This novel is difficult to read primarily because the chronology of its narration is so different from the chronology of its events. And it is precisely that difference—which keeps Bon's identity a mystery—that produces everyone's sense of him as a blank slate rather than part black. No one knows until the end that they've been wrong about him. Thanks to Faulkner's sustaining of racial mystery, Bon has become the touchstone for extraordinary identifications. Faulkner thus yokes the mystery of his identity to the capacity for love itself—the human propensity to project into the other and see one's own possibilities at stake there.

Their love for him—which in Henry's case will not survive the "revelation" of black blood—takes *Absalom* into racial territory Faulkner had never entered before and would never do so again. Whites loving blacks, always on condition of not knowing that they are black: this arrangement bristles with implication. Half French in his sophistication, half American in his vulnerability; half female in his charm, half male in his strength; half white by his father, part black by his mother: Bon blends elegance and power, sophisticated shrewdness, and generosity of spirit. These come together to produce a suppleness of being that no pure line of descent could make available. He is the text's Utopian image of what miscegenation might *really* enable, though no one in the story is prepared to consider this possibility once he is outed as black. Identified thus—his history exposed—Bon cannot be loved, nor admired, nor admitted into the precincts of his white family. Once racially fixed, he must either submit to be "nigger" or die the death. Given Bon's courage, his choice is not surprising.

Henry pleads with Bon—"You are my brother"—to forego his quest, not force the issue. Bon replies: "No I'm not. I'm the nigger that's going to sleep with your sister."[11] Bon is unpacifiably both. No other fiction writer approaches Faulkner when it comes to loving what you hate, hating what you love. This unmanageable heart truth underwrites *Absalom* and makes it live and breathe. "The human heart in conflict with itself": so Faulkner characterized his core concern when receiving the Nobel Prize in 1950. What is this but to center his great work on the plight of human beings who find themselves intolerably self-entrapped? Doomed by what their culture has taught them they must be—yet can no longer bear to be? Faulkner's most compelling protagonists seethe with convictions at odds with their feelings. The territory Faulkner opens to anguished reilluming is the reality—at once his own and his region's—of interracial intimacy cohabiting with repudiation. They are us and not us, cherished and abandoned—dark twins bonded by blood, beyond joining because of that shared blood.

By the end *Absalom* has revealed in Charles Bon all that he is and cannot be. Bon a nigger? Given what we have seen, the inappropriateness of "nigger" virtually explodes on the page. In mid-nineteenth-century Mississippi, if Bon "were" black, he would have been a slave, and none of *Absalom*'s love investments would have been possible. Since he "is" black—as we learn at the end—we recognize with renewed power the absurd brutality of racial stereotype. Absurd because Bon so transcends the stereotype, brutal because its daily imposition prevented Mississippi blacks from remotely becoming Bon. Faulkner has created, in the guise of this socially impossible figure, so much that the South had experienced but could not allow itself to conceptualize.

The murder of Bon finally takes on its meaning. The morganatic marriage only goes so far, not very far at all. The incest motive goes further, tormenting Henry for the four years of the war. Finally, there is miscegenation, and this barrier is nonnegotiable—Henry "thinking not what he would do but what he would have to do. Because he knew what he would do" (292). Perhaps the book's brilliance is most on display here. *Absalom* must *think through* something that its actors—once they know that the obstacle to marriage is miscegenation—are incapable of thinking about at all.

This revelation must come last because we, Bon, and the others in the novel must experience him otherwise until the end. We internalize (as Henry does) the developing emotional value of his becoming a brother before he can be unmasked as black. We live inside his subjectivity as a man who does not know he is black. He figures it out, finally, because the refusal of acknowledgment he receives at the hands of his father tells him eventually, by process of elimination, who he has to be. He must be suffering from the one condition no white Southern patriarch *can* acknowledge: black blood. Finally it clicks into coherence.

The resemblance between *Absalom* and *Oedipus the King* is not fortuitous. Both works center on the mystery of identity, on identity *as* mystery. Both Oedipus and Bon turn out to be what no one—including themselves—can bear them to be. Their inner coherence is revealed as social transgression—enabled by the rupture of taboo. *Absalom* stages this in such a way as to maximize the horror of X and non-X being one and the same. *"And you are——?"*—Quentin's hushed question to a dying Henry Sutpen—here takes on its deeper resonance: the mystery of identity as at once inner and outer, self-sustaining yet socially constructed. "And you are——?" becomes unanswerable, a question that is itself in question. The resonance of the question is not far to find if we ask how blacks in the South can be both anathema to whites and at the same time their siblings, parents, and offspring—kept tenaciously out of homes that they are always already inside of, how Charles Bon can be at once paragon and scapegoat.

Sophocles treats that question more benignly than Faulkner does. Finally self-identified, Oedipus exacts punishment on himself, and the plague of Thebes is lifted. Not so for Faulkner: If Charles Bon can be the love object for every questing character in *Absalom*, if he can house their fondest desires and aspiration, then the racial structure of the South that eventually claims and destroys him—once his racial identity is outed—loses its cogency and conceptually shatters, like a house of cards. Not the lifting of the plague of race but the recognition, finally, of all that that plague portends. "I don't hate the South," Quentin keeps repeating at the end of *Absalom*. Given what Faulkner has shown, no reader has trouble understanding why Quentin cannot convince himself.

The indispensable condition required for these mysteries to work is that neither Christmas nor Bon looks black. It follows that Faulkner could produce his most penetrating racial diagnoses only if the "black" men in question seemed white. Let us take this a step further: Faulkner could enter them vividly only if, within his own imaginary, they *were* white—yet tragically ensnared by being read (by others, perhaps by themselves as well) as black. This line of argument seems to me persuasive, and it points in two directions.

Most compellingly, it suggests that, in *Light in August* and *Absalom, Absalom!*, Faulkner is envisaging a transcendence of racial difference itself. The mystery of racial difference he narrates reveals at its core—no difference. Rumor, dread, violence—all of these fueled by a hysterical social mandate: but no difference. Put otherwise, Faulkner's choice to enter the turmoil of race in America by way of white anxiety permitted him to expose the entire deforming edifice of racial constructedness. Blacks and whites do not otherwise differ. And more, these two novels keep Utopianly whispering, deep down, that whites—at an unconscious level—do not want them to differ.[12] Deep down, whites long for reunion—however forbidden by social norms—reunion with their repudiated siblings and parents and offspring, with their disowned lovers.

The other direction this insight points to is more obvious: when Faulkner undertakes to narrate the plight of visibly and vocally identifiable blacks, the imaginative terms at his disposal shift. His fiction embarks on a different pathway, one that shows more markedly the influence of his culture's thinking and feeling about blacks. I want to close this argument by suggesting that *Go Down, Moses* and *Intruder in the Dust* pursue this later pathway, and that the mystery of racial identity explored in *Light in August* and *Absalom* transforms into a drama of detection.

4

Go Down, Moses informs us, racially, at the outset. We learn in "Was" that the slave the two McCaslin brothers are hunting, Tomey's Turl, is a "half-white McCaslin." Buck and Buddy do not register that mixed race identity as scandal, neither does the narrator, the nine-year-old Cass. Tomey's Turl's cultural identity and language—his behavior in all its facets—are comfortably represented as black. No one within the novel projects into Tomey's Turl's being as also white—the damage imposed by his abusive begetting has done its cultural work—and the reader, likewise, is not invited to imagine Turl as white either. Instead, we are urged to recognize the unspoken inhumanity in two brothers' casually racist treatment of their half-brother, and thus to envisage what it meant, in 1859, to own a white-spawned "nigger-slave." The racial wrong wrought into that begetting is of course *Go Down, Moses*'s central moral concern. But the focus of that concern is Old Carothers's white guilt—and its descent first to Buck and Buddy, and then to Ike. The focus is not Tomey Turl's identity *as* mystery. For his part, Turl accepts and exploits his status as McCaslin slave. We are worlds away from the vertigo of Joe Christmas, the anguish of Charles Bon.

Turl's son, Lucas, is significantly white descended as well, and Lucas's speech and projects and behavior are—like his father's—wily Negro normative. Lucas, however, makes much larger claims than Turl on both the whites within the novel and the reader outside it. But these claims invoke his resourcefulness and dignity more than they invite a rethinking of his racial makeup. Lucas's racially crossed history registers as white abuse, not as a mystery of identity. More, Lucas's various shenanigans throughout "The Fire and the Hearth" reveal, precisely, his canniness— his capacity to operate effectively within his given racial conditions.

In keeping with the premise of a narrative centered on shrewd "dealing" with obstacles, even the race-focused sleuthing that occupies Ike in part 4 of "The Bear" (via the ledgers) seems to be presented in order to be resolved. Detection triumphs, and the concealed mystery of Old Carothers's miscegenated begettings—first on Eunice and then on Tomasina—is outed and dispelled. These recognitions, however moving (and they *are* moving), resonate quite differently from the outrage of *Light in August*'s race mystery, the tragedy of *Absalom*'s race mystery. They have little to do with intimate projections unknowingly launched across the racial binary—with the pathos of such projections once they are revealed as scandalous, once they collapse or turn to violence. There is (white) ceremonial grief and mourning aplenty in *Go Down, Moses*, but no mystery that would allow love to cross racial lines—for a time. Put otherwise, there is in this novel no visionary grasp of the need for a postracial South.

To care for Lucas Beauchamp as some whites did care for blacks in Faulkner's 1940s culture, Faulkner had to posit him as knowably black. How he got to be black is a story Faulkner invests with enormous significance, but that is a white story. Moreover, now that he is black, Lucas is a good black, inextricably composed of what Faulkner's culture took to be the range of behaviors that signified: good black. Lucas emerges thus as one of ours, but this according to white racial norms for understanding him. He is to be protected—and the novel insists on protecting him—but only as such. We know throughout *Go Down, Moses* how we're supposed to think about him. His begetting is born of outrage, but his being is not a mystery.

The pattern of racial identity I am pursuing completes itself in *Intruder in the Dust*. Every reader realizes swiftly, even as almost no one in Jefferson does, that Lucas is not guilty. No real mystery here: Lucas is being framed—as innocent blacks are framed. The mystery in *Intruder in the Dust* centers elsewhere: on the dead man in that coffin. And this is a death we do not care about—a death mandated by the story of detection Faulkner has chosen to narrate, virtually a Macguffin (in cinematic terms). His death does not threaten the security of *our* identity, does not remind us, uncannily, that we too are destined for that coffin, that our social arrangements (including our racial ones) extend past our own control and comprehension and could—should fate wish it—turn and annihilate us. Such mystery as attaches to that coffin submits wholly to detection. More, Lucas Beauchamp is not genuinely menaced either. All readers gather (this is the implicit narrative contract embedded in the genre) that his innocence will be revealed. Rather than menaced, Lucas remains encased in his dignity, a throwback to earlier mores. His plight, external only, is designed to engage white Jeffersonians and the white reader as an unmistakable call to come to his aid. Put otherwise, by 1948 Faulkner had come to respect, enshrine, and reify black difference. He envisaged it as a sturdy composite of Southern-white-liberal-approved traits: minority traits in no need of alteration. Let them stay who they essentially are—Sambos with grounded, imperturbable dignity—and let us whites begin the long-delayed business of emancipating them. No meddling Yankees needed for this: an old Southern lady, a couple of enterprising boys, and an avuncular white liberal are sufficient for the deed.

Light in August and *Absalom, Absalom!* are Faulkner's supreme mysteries of race. Each novel raised the question of racial difference itself. Without mystery, Faulkner came to recognize, without the veils of misrecognition it imposed, interracial intimacy could not take place. He provided the mystery so that it would happen. Once that veil is shorn, and racial difference revealed, none of his whites could sustain interracial love. The best they could do—and by the 1940s it was all he asked of them—was to care for blacks in a less projective way, a way that upheld racial difference even as it humanized it: paternally, guiltily, tardily.[13] To care for blacks not as versions of themselves but as the others the whites had for so long abused. In the end, Faulkner sought less to transcend racial difference than to acknowledge white and black as separate but equal. For this he no longer needed a mystery centered on race at all. It was enough for detection to figure out who was in that coffin. Thus his work took on lesser mysteries while abandoning a greater one: the mystery of a racial difference that is, however devastating for centuries to Southern and American society, no difference at all.

NOTES

1. This definition is taken from Douglas Harper's commentary on "Mystery" in the *Online Etymology Dictionary* (2001), Lancaster, Pa. etymology.com.

2. For more on ancient ceremonial mysteries, see Georg Luck, *Ancient Pathways and Hidden Priests: Religion, Morals, and Magic in the Ancient World* (Ann Arbor: University of Michigan Press, 2000).

3. The locus classicus of Freud's thinking on these matters is his essay entitled "The Uncanny," in *The Standard Edition of the Complete Psychological Works of Sigmund Freud*, 23 vols. (London: Hogarth Press, 1954–1974), 17: 219–53. For the resonance of "uncanny" in modernist literature, see my *Unknowing: The Work of Modernist Fiction* (Ithaca: Cornell University Press, 2005), 79–120.

4. David I. Grossvogel, *Mystery and Its Fictions* (Baltimore: Johns Hopkins University Press, 1979), 15.

5. Ibid., 4.

6. Much of this argument is indebted to the chapter on race in my *Becoming Faulkner* (New York: Oxford University Press, 2010).

7. Racial anxiety in the South is of course widely recognized in Faulkner studies. For an incisive recent treatment of this concern, see John T. Matthews, "This Race Which Is Not One: The 'More Inextricable Compositeness' of William Faulkner's South," in *Look Away! The U.S. South in New World Studies*, ed. Jon Smith and Deborah Cohn (Durham: Duke University Press, 2004), 201–26.

8. James Baldwin, "Stranger in the Village," in *The Price of the Ticket: Collected Nonfiction, 1948–1985* (New York: St. Martin's, 1985), 88.

9. William Faulkner, *Light in August* (1932), in Joseph Blotner and Noel Polk, eds., *Faulkner: Novels 1930–1935* (New York: Library of America: 1985), 470–71. All citations will refer to this edition.

10. For more on the centrality of projection in modernist fiction, see my *Unknowing*, 202–5.

11. William Faulkner, *Absalom, Absalom!* (1936), in Joseph Blotner and Noel Polk, eds., *Faulkner: Novels 1936–1940* (New York: Library of America: 1990), 294.

12. Eric Sundquist offers (in *Faulkner: The House Divided* [Baltimore: Johns Hopkins University Press, 1983]) what is still the best meditation on Southern whites' unacknowledgeable desire to love the blacks whom they must at the same time disown. See especially his commentary on *Absalom, Absalom!*

13. For fuller discussion of Faulkner's vexed stance—at once penetrating and blindsighted—toward racial turmoil throughout the 1950s, see Charles Peavy's *Go Slow Now: Faulkner and the Race Question* (Eugene: University of Oregon Press, 1971), as well as the chapter "Dark Twins: Faulkner and Race" in *Becoming Faulkner*.

The Blackness of *Absalom, Absalom!*

DONALD M. KARTIGANER

The great mystery of *Absalom, Absalom!* is not why Thomas Sutpen rejected Charles Bon as a husband for his daughter Judith, but why it takes the four internal narrators of the story—these extraordinarily gifted prose artists and analysts of character—so incredibly long to answer that question. The motive for murder turns out to be what they have always known but dare not consciously acknowledge: the power of the African life that emerges as the inescapable core of the Southern history Thomas Sutpen enacts and represents. Racial and cultural blackness is the repressed reality the narrators dwell in and deny, exploit and dismiss, like a dark pleasure to be obsessively indulged even as it arouses a horror and a guilt that are not to be borne.

Rosa Coldfield, Mr. Compson, Quentin Compson, and Shreve immerse themselves in the imagery, literal and figurative, of the African: Haitian, Creole, American. Quentin, in his account of Sutpen and his slaves chasing the New Orleans architect in flight from the project of designing and building the Sutpen mansion, exemplifies the sensibility that permeates the entire text: "'the niggers (the niggers mostly still naked except for a pair of pants here and there) with the pine torches smoking and flaring above them and the red light on their round heads and arms and the mud they wore in the swamp to keep the mosquitoes off dried hard and shiny, glinting like glass or china and the shadows they cast taller than they were at one moment then gone the next and even the trees and brakes and thickets there one moment and gone the next'"—the blacks, their shadows, like the woods and underbrush through which they move, "'they were still there because you could feel them with your breathing, as though, invisible, they pressed down and condensed the invisible air you breathed.'"[1]

However rich the imagery they employ, the narrators resist its fullest meaning, concealing the blackness of the history with various screens: the Satanic force of Sutpen's depravity, the fatalism of the cosmopolitan Charles Bon, the incestuous, homoerotic desires of Bon and Henry. Whatever the motive for the murder of Charles Bon, it must have nothing to do with race, nothing to do with the blackness that circumscribes all the events, "'there one moment and gone the next.'"

The most succinct statement of resistance comes from Sutpen, the man whose grand "design" rests on his conviction that blackness is not integral to, but an aberration from, his rise from poor white to plantation master. He tells Quentin's grandfather how, as a boy of ten arriving with his family in Virginia, he discovered the ubiquity of blacks and their frequent roles as objects of white anger and resentment, and yet quickly learned that they are not the true object of that anger: "'you knew that you could hit them, he told Grandfather, and they would not hit back or even resist. But you did not want to, because they (the niggers) were not it, not what you wanted to hit'" (186). What Sutpen learns is a truth that conceals a deeper deception which the narrators of *Absalom* invariably resort to as the mask, the "balloon face" (186) of their obsession. They "'were not it, not what you wanted to hit,'" and yet the constant presence in their lives and imaginations of that which is *not it* reflects a doubled-edged desire of attraction and repulsion, a desperate need to claim difference in the very act of experiencing a profound intimacy.

Absalom, Absalom! is the most complete representation in American literature—and the most complete analysis—of what Toni Morrison has described as the standard white American literary practice of "gathering identity . . . from the wholly available and serviceable lives of Africanist others." Blackness becomes "a playground for the imagination . . . a fabricated brew of darkness, otherness, alarm, and desire that is uniquely American." The anxiety accompanying the practice, however, requires simultaneous repression of the blackness evoked; that "fabricated brew" must not be brought to full fictional life. White writers create a "language that mystifies what it cannot bring itself to articulate but still attempts to register."[2]

To register but not articulate, exploit but not acknowledge. In the South, the culture of which is complicated and intensified by the continuous, close relationship that, despite constant tension, exists between white and black, there is indeed a need to register Southern history as a shared experience, lived, as *Absalom, Absalom!* makes clear, at every level of life—in love and hatred, labor and pleasure, honor and vengeance—but to write that experience through strategic screens that reverse intimacy into a hierarchical binary, reducing the African to secondary significance, as if determined to empty the imagery of the power that inspires it. The great originality of *Absalom* is that, despite the defenses of its narrators, it evokes the knowing and the not knowing as equal adversaries. Moreover, it ultimately shatters the impasse on a breakthrough that offers new vision, but without diminishing the devastating effects of the old. The triumph of the novel, that is, also foresees the continuation of the tragic dilemma.

❀ ❀ ❀

Absalom, Absalom! is the first of Faulkner's novels to take as its theme the African American as a central, not a marginal, figure in the South. In *The Sound and the Fury*, Faulkner's first novel that has a major black character, the emphasis is clearly on the condition of black instrumentality to the white community. Dilsey Gibson is the epitome of the servant sharply divided from the family she serves: variously appreciated, but quite unknown to the Compsons because it is inconceivable to them that, other than her service, there is anything more to *be* known. What we may judge to be her moral superiority to the Compsons is itself a function of that service, since it too rests largely on her single-minded, selfless devotion to them. The African American Easter service she attends performs a comparable functionality for the novel as a whole, a means of exposing the Compson's spiritual decay while remaining itself beyond our understanding. The Reverend Shegog's sermon and the congregation's response to it comes to us as a strange, contorted Christianity performed in order to reap a spiritual knowledge whose very inscrutability constitutes its power: "And the congregation seemed to watch with its own eyes while the [preacher's] voice consumed him, until he was nothing and they were nothing and there was not even a voice but instead their hearts were speaking to one another in chanting measures beyond the need for words."³

In *Light in August* the African American is not merely marginal, but nonexistent. What is most remarkable about a novel in which Faulkner seems to be moving toward a more complex rendering of the role of the African American in Southern life is the fact that there is scarcely a black character in it. Joe Christmas is the blank figure at the center who in childhood assumes a possible but never verified black identity, wholly derived from the white cultural stereotypes in which he lives. The initial source of that identity is his grandfather, Doc Hines, for whom blackness and "bitchery" are one, and who literally *gazes* Joe into the difference that he will adopt as his working definition: *"That is why I am different from the others: because he is watching me all the time."*⁴ The name of difference, for Joe and for the other children at the orphanage, is "nigger." In *Light in August* the African American is invisible, a freestanding, portable word that whites use in order to name the chaos that occasionally surfaces in their community: an orphan child's unwitting voyeurism or the depths of sexuality or the alleged murderer of a white woman. The novel is essentially about how blackness effectively disappears, leaving the white community complete freedom to exploit it.

The Unvanquished, written as a series of short stories largely before *Absalom*, but expanded and revised afterwards for publication as a novel,

returns African Americans to visibility. They remain, however, peripheral figures, despite the fact that the war that frees the slaves is the
book's most momentous action. While Barbara Ladd has made a strong
argument for the autonomy of the slave Loosh as he joins the other
slaves marching northward, in the concluding story, as she points out,
Loosh is back on the plantation, absent of any explanation for his return.[5]
More importantly, the slave Ringo, despite John Sartoris's claim that he
is "smarter" than the narrator, Bayard Sartoris, and who for much of the
novel plays a pivotal role in the action, has become by the end a secondary figure, his marginal status secured. Although they have been raised
virtually as brothers, Bayard is the one who shoots Grumby, the man
responsible for the death of "Granny" Rosa Millard, and Bayard alone
will plan and execute a unique vengeance against his father's killer.

In all these novels African American marginality is a given. Faulkner
deepens the stereotypical roles of blacks, yet he continues to depend on
them, only rarely pausing, as Ralph Ellison acknowledged, to "seek out
the human truth which [stereotype] hides."[6] He makes clear the white
exploitation of blackness, yet he seems to be decrying the brutality (and
at times the absurdity) of the exploitation without providing an alternative image to the assumption of black subserviency on which it is based.
There is no fictional vision of the white mind truly engaging, even if not
with full consciousness, its own desires and fears, the paradox of practic-
ing, simultaneously, intimacy and difference.

◦ ◦ ◦

The question that arises, to put it baldly, is how and why does *Absalom,
Absalom!* happen? Blackness in the novel remains within a language of
white appropriation, but now it threatens constantly to break through
what Morrison calls its "registration," its "mystification," into a fearful
"articulation." Ultimately it comes forth as the son, the brother, the lover
who *must* be recognized—if necessary by compelling the white man into
an act of murder. This is not the death, however, of the "black" man
of *Light in August*, which becomes the topic at "suppertables on that
Monday night" (443), the townspeople calmly speculating on the day's
violent doings, their lives returned to order with Christmas's necessary, if
horrifying, end. The death in *Absalom, Absalom!* brings down the entire
Sutpen edifice—the design, the dynasty, and the world they imply—and
leaves its primary teller in a state of shock, turned toward the suicide his
creator has already put in place.

How does Faulkner get from his novels of African American marginality to the novel of their centrality—and not only get there but to insist,
as I will be arguing in the following pages, that this centrality is the most

difficult and the most necessary knowledge that the South must acquire? What is going on in Faulkner's life, his reading, his writing, his north Mississippi world, or the South generally, that leads him to present what is for him and white Southern writing a strikingly new understanding of how the culture of race in the South works?

Definitive answers, of course, are out of the question, given not only the innumerable possible sources of influence and impact, but even more so the great complexity of how historical, social, economic, cultural, and biographical materials make their way into literary texts. In the course of representation does a text record, revise, or recreate its context? Or does it—can it?—imagine the acontextual: "a world elsewhere," as Richard Poirier, more than a half century ago, proposed as the driving force in American literature?[7] Nevertheless, if we look at Faulkner's scene as he writes what will prove to be the beginning of *Absalom, Absalom!*—the story "Evangeline," (1931)—and completes the typescript of the novel in January 1936, there are certain texts, conditions, biographical details I find suggestive, although hardly beyond dispute as significant factors in the shaping of *Absalom*.[8] One is the collection of essays published in 1930 by "Twelve Southerners," *I'll Take My Stand*, analyzing the current state of the South. Another is what the historian Joel Williamson, in *The Crucible of Race* (1984), designates as a significant shift in black-white social relations in the 1920s and 1930s. Finally, there is the still unproven biographical speculation concerning a half-black daughter of Faulkner's great-grandfather, William C. Falkner, proposed by Williamson in *Faulkner and Southern History* (1993).

Joining the two books of 1930 and 1984 is the fact that the first effectively illustrates the white attitude toward race diagnosed by the second. And the thrust of that attitude confirms the conditions of subserviency or absence that exist in *The Sound and the Fury*, *Light in August*, and *The Unvanquished*. In *The Crucible of Race* Joel Williamson describes a Southern white perspective in the 1920s and 1930s that relegated the black population of the South to an absolutely peripheral status. Added to the customary domination of white over black was a new element, a remarkable psychic leap in the white mind, by means of which the African American population, numbering in the millions, virtually ceased to exist.

During this period, Williamson argues, the South abandoned the attitudes of what he calls the Radical era of 1889–1915, which focused sharply and narrowly on the supposed primitiveness of blacks, emphasizing an inherent savagery epitomized in the image of the "black beast" rapist of white women. Instead of presenting the black as menace, allegedly the result of the relaxation of white control once imposed by

slavery, the conservatives of the '20s and '30s minimized the very presence of African Americans, reducing them to a necessary but shadowy
instrumentality.

They were a people unto themselves, serving the whites but distinctly
separate from them—not merely according to the system of strict segregation, but as if they constituted another species entirely. There was,
Williamson maintains, a "white withdrawal from blackness both in the
body and in the mind. A logical result of such thinking was the pro-
motion of the invisibility of black people, the further removal of white
people from the possibility of recognizing the equal humanity of blacks,
and, finally, the loss of the black problem in the white mind."[9]

While this kind of thinking might be regarded as an improvement
over earlier Radical attitudes, it generated a detachment from the reality
of black life that was equally dehumanizing. Blacks had, and would stay
in, their "place," becoming in the white mind the objects of a kind of
complacent if strategic indifference. Supplanting the black beast was an
older image renewed, what Williamson calls the "neo-Sambo" image. No
longer the "child" of the antebellum period nor the "savage" of the Radical period, neo-Sambo was a useful adjunct to the white community and,
like his earlier manifestation, "docile, subordinate, pliable, conforming,
and loyal" (463).

To be sure, the guarantee of docility continued to be the violence
that could be inflicted on those who refused that role. Lynching sharply
declined in the 1930s, in part because of the crushing domination that
prevailed, yet it still functioned as a very real threat. The fear of it, as
Richard Wright writes in *Black Boy*, "hung over every male black in the
South."[10] When it erupted again, it had the intended double effect of a
punishment for what whites had decided was the exceptional case, and
as what Neil R. McMillen refers to as "an instrument of social discipline,
an object lesson of general value to the entire black community."[11] Primarily, however, Williamson characterizes the racial situation at this time
as that of a white South bound solidly together, with an attitude toward
blacks similar to that of the last generation of slavery: "their Negroes
were good Negroes, and there was really no Negro problem at all as long
as Negroes remained in the place made for them, and misguided and
ill-intentioned whites left them alone" (464). The difference is that now
it is not only the "misguided and ill-intentioned" who should let African
Americans be, but the Southern white culture at large, for whom they
have become pure accessory, except on those rare occasions when they
must be reminded of the consequences of becoming anything more. As
Richard Gray puts it, the African American became "an unremarkable
part of life's furniture, something not to be noticed or noted, and then
subsequently turn[ed] . . . into an object of fear."[12]

Perfectly consistent with this strange combination of awareness and indifference is the landmark volume of 1930, *I'll Take My Stand: The South and the Agrarian Tradition*. Although conceived in resistance to the New South and its emergent industrialism, it symptomizes the white attitudes Williamson sees characterizing the entire society. What is so striking about the book as a whole is not its occasionally egregious pronouncements about blacks, such as John Crowe Ransom's infamous description of slavery as "monstrous enough in theory, but, more often than not, humane in practice," or Frank Lawrence Owsley's reference to the emancipated slaves of the Reconstruction, "some of whom could still remember the taste of human flesh."[13] Rather it is the glaring historical distortion of its treatment of slavery and blacks in general as topics of strictly secondary or tertiary importance.

Examples are legion: Owsley writes, "Without slavery the economic and social life of the South would not have been radically different. Perhaps the plantation life would not have been as pronounced without it, yet the South would long have remained agricultural" (76). The comment is echoed by Ransom: "it is impossible to believe that [slavery's] abolition alone could have effected any great revolution in society" (14). Donald Davidson doesn't even need to specify the white South when he claims that at the beginning of the 1930s the "promise of the South . . . offers the possibility of an integrated life, American in the older rather than the newer sense. Its population is homogeneous. Its people share a common past, which they are not likely to forget; for aside from having Civil War battlefields at their doorsteps, the Southern people have long cultivated a historical consciousness that permeates manners, localities, institutions, the very words and cadence of social intercourse" (53).

In "The Briar Patch," the only essay in the collection devoted entirely to the African American situation in the South, Robert Penn Warren presumes segregation to be virtually a natural order, any alteration of which requires documentation and justification. "Does [the African American] simply want to spend the night in a hotel as comfortable as the one from which he is turned away, or does he want to spend the night in that same hotel?" If the latter, then "a good deal depends," namely, whether the second option is legitimate (253–54). Perhaps most revealing is Warren's program for where the African American will live and what his labor will consist of: "the Southern negro has always been a creature of the small town and farm. That is where he still chiefly belongs, by temperament and capacity" (260). It is there, away from the industrializing cities, where he may be a provocation, a "scab," a possible competitor with white workers, where the "negro" belongs. On farms and in small towns. Not exactly out of sight, but pushed to the spatial and psychic margins.

The volume's "stand" on race relations is fundamentally to deny not just the significance but virtually the presence of African Americans. With millions still in their midst, the authors speak of a sectional homogeneity, a "common past," that simply excludes them. With the institution of slavery so recent a phenomenon that ex-slaves are still in abundance, the allegedly great historical consciousness of the Southerner recalls a South only minimally affected by slavery's presence or absence—less an economic base than a convenience, possibly adding to or subtracting somewhat from the "pronounced" impact of the great plantations.

With segregation in the period of its most crushing implementation, there is not a word to question either its utility or its justice. The claims of the antebellum defenders of slavery that the institution is justified by the Bible, by the inherent inferiority of blacks, by its humaneness beneath the skin, were no longer necessary. The black population, when properly treated and placed, is, to all intents and purposes, not really there. Titling this subsection of his book "The White South Loses the Black Problem," Williamson captures the spirit of the attitude of *I'll Take My Stand*: Whatever the problems of the South, the African American is the least of them, having contributed little to the past and less to the present.

Whether Faulkner observed in Oxford, Mississippi, the "invisibility" of its African American population, whether he recognized the vast contradiction, the doublethink Williamson describes, or whether he was aware of the agrarian manifesto of "Twelve Southerners," we do not know. If indeed he recognized a regional blindness, not only in others but in himself, there is still the question of what it was that might have brought him at this particular point in his career to the writing of *Absalom* and its profound analysis and ultimate exposure of that blindness.[14]

Here a recent biographical suggestion may come into play. This is the theory Joel Williamson puts forth in his biography, *Faulkner and Southern History*, that Faulkner's great-grandfather, William Clark Falkner, the Old Colonel, in 1864 fathered at least one daughter with a mulatto slave, Emmeline Lacy Falkner.[15] The daughter was named Fannie Forrest Falkner, possibly after Falkner's favorite sister, Frances, and Nathan Bedford Forrest, whom Falkner much admired. Falkner's subsequent care for the daughter, sending her to Rust College and visiting her regularly; the widespread conviction of members of the African American community of Ripley that Fannie Forrest was indeed the Old Colonel's daughter; and the continued belief of her descendants that they are related to the Faulkner family—these facts and the evidence of census and chancery court records that Williamson makes use of enable him to make a persuasive if circumstantial argument.

The answer to the most important question, however, still eludes us: did Faulkner know that he had a great aunt and several cousins living in Texas who would be considered unquestionably black? Williamson claims that he did, but offers no proof, circumstantial or otherwise. Was it while he was working on *Absalom, Absalom!* that the split between awareness and denial in his own life finally merged with that of the Southern mind, erupting into full writing awareness? In *Absalom, Absalom!* and again, several years later, in *Go Down, Moses*, the white denial of black kin comes forth as the critical event of history, two versions of the Fall: white denial as the great moral crime of the South. Was this Faulkner's way of acknowledging his history—even making atonement for it—in the form that would always matter most to him?[16]

⁕ ⁕ ⁕

Absalom, Absalom! exposes the 1930s "invisibility" of Southern blackness as a social and psychic pathology of devastating consequence. Blackness is now brilliantly, fearfully present: always marginalized—often frantically so—but in that uncanny way in which margin broadens and thickens into the center, until center becomes a white dot of desperate neurotic registering of and resistance to an always encroaching black reality.

The novel revolves around Thomas Sutpen because he is the one most steeped in and threatened by blackness. His arrival in the Virginia Tidewater at the age of ten is a second birth into a world that for him is essentially black. At least this is how he tells his story to Quentin's grandfather. Blackness is what he constantly confronts, from the "'huge bull of a nigger, the first black man, slave, they had even seen'" (182), who ejects Sutpen's father from one of the "doggeries" where he stops to drink, to the "monkey nigger" servant who orders Sutpen away from the front door of "the big house" (185), to his own Haitian slaves, whose subservience to himself he must periodically reassert through hand-to-hand combat. His peculiar "innocence" is that he cannot merely deny the significance of black people, but must prove it every day of his life. Unlike that white Southern world in terms of which he chooses to claim his own significance, Sutpen cannot regard black inferiority as an inherent condition, requiring no more demonstration than the inferiority of an animal. For him, the difference of blackness is a definition always in process, proven not by biblical or anthropological authority but according to the criteria of his original mountain code of merit: a difference to be demonstrated by such acts as "lifting anvils or gouging eyes or how much whiskey you could drink then get up and walk out of the room" (183). Sutpen can prove his own identity solely by establishing—not by decree but by action—the unlikeness of himself and blackness.

This is especially evident in the episode of the native uprising in Haiti. Grandfather tells the story, but the dynamic of black and white difference is Sutpen's: "[he] walked out into the darkness and subdued them, maybe by yelling louder, maybe by standing, bearing more than they believed any bones and flesh could or should (should, yes: that would be the terrible thing: to find flesh to stand more than flesh should be asked to stand); maybe at last they themselves turning in horror and fleeing from the white arms and legs shaped like theirs and from which blood could be made to spurt and flow as it could from theirs and containing an indomitable spirit which should have come from the same primary fire which theirs came from but which could not have, could not possibly have" (205).

Whiteness is of a different "primary fire"—or so Sutpen must believe. The great irony of his life is that in Haiti, having saved the plantation and won its owner's daughter in marriage, he could be prince and heir, but according to Quentin and Shreve's final reading of the Sutpen history, he would have had to revise his identity across racial boundaries, accept the blackness he has married and sired, and this he cannot do. Sutpen returns to the South because he defines himself by those boundaries, yet he never truly comprehends the paradoxical language that brings them into being, that thinks black and white as an interdependence that must not exist. Were Sutpen capable of simply assuming black difference, he could confront Charles Bon as the rest of the white planter class would, assigning him at the outset to the subhuman condition inherent to his race. But Sutpen will not make that assumption, given what Quentin and Shreve finally determine is the phenomenon of his own blood in Charles Bon: the black son in whom burns "the same primary fire" as his own.[17]

The only lasting proof of the difference, and the fulfillment of Sutpen's "design," will be the establishment of a white male heir who will have what the "nameless stranger" whom Sutpen imagines taking in will also come to possess, what Sutpen himself can never quite own: the capacity to "shut that door himself forever behind him on all that he had ever known" (210). Sutpen's dynasty will be his triumph because it will consist of white descendants who do not know they had to win their whiteness. It is only the white son, Henry or any white male Sutpen fathers, who may confront and kill the black son, as if the fraternal blood ties were looser than those of the paternal bond that holds Sutpen in check.

The emergence of Charles Bon requires that Sutpen play what, grandfather tells Quentin, is his "last trump card" (220). The trump in this novel is always the effort to distinguish the white superior self by naming someone "nigger": a word that assumes almost magical properties, capable of bending the reality of intimacy to the sound that negates it. In Sutpen's case, however, as he well knows, the trump is not only the dismissal of the black, but also the acknowledgment of the blood bond between the white Sutpen and the black one. It will "'destroy my design with my own hand'" (220), shattering what for him has always been an existential rather than a foundational hierarchical difference. In a sense, Sutpen himself is the "nigger" of the novel and the South. He is the gigantic presence of a conscious awareness that blackness is real, not, in the paradoxes of neurotic repression, to be fantasized away or rendered invisible.

With Miss Rosa and Mr. Compson we engage with two of the major narrators of the novel, exemplary performers of the doublethink Sutpen is incapable of. This is not because they are shrewder but because, unlike Sutpen, they come to the African presence already fully armed, already groomed in the codes of white superiority. A rude black butler will not undo them. And yet their power and insight as narrators, their susceptibility to the reality that intrudes on them, finally compels them to play the Sutpen trump card. They are each drawn to a black woman—Rosa to Clytie, Compson to Charles Bon's octoroon mistress—only to dismiss them to the margins of the Sutpen history. Then they turn to more dangerous representatives of the truth they are searching for, to a white man—Rosa to Sutpen, Compson to Charles Bon—in whom they infer black qualities. From their obsessions with literal blackness, that is, Rosa and Compson turn to screens for blackness: ostensibly white males whose source of fascination for Rosa and Compson is a blackness they can never consciously acknowledge.

For Rosa, Clytie is always Sutpen's black daughter, her *"Sutpen coffee-colored face"* the *"replica of his own,"* but Clytie also embodies a blackness that is the archaic source of Sutpen, *"antedating time and house and doom and all."* She belongs to *"an older and a purer race than mine"* (109–10), yet it is one whose power Sutpen has borrowed by crossing his blood with it. Rosa's courage and insight are such that she understands the need to embrace that blackness, as if it might be the breath that would bring her to life: *"something in the touch of flesh with flesh"* that would shatter *"all the eggshell shibboleth of caste and color too"* (111–12). But courage and insight fail, and although *"it was not to her I spoke,"* but to *"it,"* the house, it is to that coffee-colored Sutpen face that Rosa directs the words, plays her "trump" card of denial: *"'Take your hand off me, nigger!'"* (112).

The most compelling object of Rosa's racial attraction, however, is Thomas Sutpen. The imagery she surrounds him with is invariably black. For Rosa, Sutpen is indistinguishable from his slaves: *"his face exactly like the negro's save for the teeth"* (16); *"So he and the twenty negroes worked together, plastered over with mud against the mosquitoes and . . . distinguishable one from another by his beard and eyes alone"* (28). Unlike her infatuation with Charles Bon, whom she never sees alive or dead—*"that might-have-been which is the single rock we cling to above the maelstrom of unbearable reality"* (120)—Rosa Coldfield's Sutpen is colossally real, and her imagery for their growing intimacy is that of the man of darkness struggling toward the promise of light from *"black morass and snarled vine and creeper . . . a swamp with nothing to guide or drive him"*: a man beholden to *"the very dark forces of fate which he had evoked and dared"* (133–34). A man, she wants to imagine, who would come to her as *"the sun and light"* (135) he yearns for.

For Rosa, Sutpen has all the trappings of alleged black sexual power. Moreover, in his behavior generally, such as his prevention of the marriage of Bon and Judith "without rhyme or reason or shadow of excuse" (12), and specifically his outrageous proposal to her that they consummate their relationship prior to marriage, testing for her capacity to produce a male heir, he demonstrates those qualities that by the 1900s were regarded as those of someone Joel Williamson refers to as "behaviorally black." Williamson notes that by 1900, through immoral actions, "it was possible in the South for one who was biologically purely white to become behaviorally black. . . . Thus there was created in the white mind a new and curious kind of mulatto—a mulatto who was in fact genetically white but morally black. In sum 'Negro' became an idea."[18]

But for Miss Rosa, Sutpen is more than behaviorally black, dangerously more. At the very beginning of her narration, Rosa's references to Sutpen suggest an inference on her part that he may be literally black. Here, as in the above reference to behavioral blackness, the time of her telling, rather than the experience itself is crucial. Not in 1831, when he first appears in Jefferson, nor during Rosa's experience with him in the 1860s, but certainly in 1909 when she is telling the story to Quentin, Rosa's account of Sutpen's mysterious arrival in Jefferson emphasizes qualities that constitute a stereotype of the man whose unknown background would make him highly suspect to Southern whites, who, by the turn of the century were bent on discerning and maintaining the boundaries between blacks and whites. Sutpen is a man with "a name which nobody ever heard before" (9), who "either had no past at all or did not dare reveal it" (10), a man whose past "must have been some opposite of respectability too dark to talk about" (11).[19]

The form of intimacy this man offers Rosa Coldfield in 1866, in violation of every social code, is also a violation of racial difference, behavioral or biological. That she initially accepts his offer of marriage is an act of rebellion, her readiness to put aside *"all the shibboleth erupting of cannot, will not, never will in one red instant's fierce obliteration. This was my instant, who could have fled then and did not"* (132). Sutpen's subsequent condition that she must produce a male heir before he will marry her is an insurmountable shock for Rosa, virtually the violation by the "black beast" rapist of Southern mythology. *This* blackness is not to be borne. Unlike her moment on the stairs with Clytie, with another "shibboleth" being tested, this ultimate insult is the one she can neither accept nor respond to with the trump card of "nigger." To do so would be to admit the unpardonable passion of being ready, at least at one point in her life, to marry a "black" or black man.

Sutpen thus becomes for Rosa the devil: no longer merely *"an ogre of my childhood"* (135), but the being *"not articulated in this world. He was a walking shadow. He was the light-blinded bat-like image of his own torment cast by the fierce demoniac lantern up from beneath the earth's crust"* (139). Rosa is the woman wailing for her demon lover— but he is not the "nigger" she agreed to marry. Remarkably, a Satanic Sutpen is the screen Rosa chooses to conceal the black one.

Mr. Compson follows a similar pattern in his explanation of the Sutpen history. Regarding the bigamy threatened by Charles Bon as the reason Sutpen forbids the marriage, Compson focuses initially on the extraordinary attraction of Bon's octoroon mistress, imagining her through a white stereotypical view of black female sexuality. As Rosa Coldfield sees in Clytie "an older and purer race," so Compson, exploiting blackness in Morrison's words as "a playground for the imagination" (38), attributes to the octoroon "'a female principle which existed, queenly and complete, in the hot equatorial groin of the world long before that white one of ours came down from trees and lost its hair and bleached out'" (92). He creates on Bon's behalf an erotic fantasy of the woman groomed solely to practice "'strange and ancient curious pleasures of the flesh (which is all: there is nothing else),'" which then becomes part of Bon's strategy in trying to seduce Henry into accepting Bon as suitable husband to Judith. The imagined scene builds on the blackness of sexuality and vulnerability and, if anything, is intensified by Bon's absurd claims of the true chastity and fidelity attending this particular purchase of female flesh. When all this fails to persuade Henry, however, Compson has Bon resort to what should be the final argument, the insult Rosa has used against Clytie: "'and Bon—the trump now, the voice gentle now: 'Have you forgot that this woman, this child, are niggers?'" (94).

Blackness defined, exploited, and discarded—Compson executes the white strategy that dominates *Absalom* and the world in which it was written. But, again like Miss Rosa, he cannot go further into this representative Southern story without taking the African presence with him. He turns to Bon himself for further explanation, still harboring blackness, but now in a subtly screened form, as the core of his quest for historical meaning. Like Miss Rosa's Sutpen, Charles Bon will remain "publicly" white, but Compson depicts him as the consummate New Orleans Creole of French extraction, whose potentially dangerous identity for white Mississippi Southerners was that of the man who, beneath his apparently white skin, is behaviorally or biologically black.

As Barbara Ladd points out, once Louisiana became part of the United States, moving from an assimilationist to a segregationist society, Creoles of color were no more privileged than free blacks in the South. Moreover, owing to the more assimilationist practices in the Caribbean colonies that had been extended to the Louisiana Territory, white Southerners associated all Creoles, white or mulatto, with "colonialist race mixing" and, even without evidence of color, with miscegenation and general cultural degeneration.[20]

New Orleans for Compson is "'foreign and paradoxical, with its atmosphere at once fatal and languorous, at once feminine and steel-hard'" (86). From it Charles Bon suddenly appears, unaccountably, at the recently founded University of Mississippi, "'in a flowered, almost feminised gown . . . with some tangible effluvium of knowledge, surfeit: of actions done and situations plumbed and pleasures exhausted and even forgotten'" (76). Narrating in 1909, Compson finds in Bon the alleged sophistication and worldliness of the Creole as well as of the fin de siècle decadence with which the Bon he imagines would have felt easily at home. Particularly attracted to the exotic stranger, "'the curious one to me'" (74), Compson fills out the portrait with various forms of depravity: the homosexual attraction to Henry (86), the courting of Judith in the manner of the "metropolitan gallant" (102), the letters "flowery indolent frequent and insincere"—above all, the abiding fatalism of the man who follows, almost indifferently, the path that opens before him. Bon will not renounce his octoroon wife (although only a "nigger," he has said earlier) because, having given the chance of war the opportunity to settle the issue for him, he can only conclude that he and Judith are, in the letter to Judith that survives, *"doomed to live"* (105).

Compson's refusal even to consider the possibility that Bon's racial background might have been the reason for Sutpen's rejection of him—especially given his own admission that bigamy, even, or especially, with an octoroon, "just does not explain" (80)—suggests how powerful his resistance is.[21] Rather than screening Bon with the devil, Compson clings to a principle of fatalism to explain the mystery: a combination of history as a "horrible and bloody mischancing of human affairs" (80) and the motives of a man culturally groomed to accept the "doom" of life or death as a difference without significant distinction. If Compson were to follow up the full implications of his own recreation of Bon, the story might lead him to something more. If Bon were black, this would no longer be a story of jaded sophistication, the fatalist taking (what is for him) the less-traveled path to destruction, but the story of the long struggle of the black toward recognition, toward meeting, and the violent white response to that struggle. There is indeed, as Compson imagines the suspicious citizens of Jefferson thinking, "a nigger in the woodpile somewhere" (56), but on the brink of discovery, indeed virtually *within* discovery, he backs off. Like Miss Rosa, Compson cannot follow through to a genuinely revisionary statement. Their powerful intimations of a blackness central to Southern history yield to what has become the official, double-think narrative, the viciously dismissive epithet, the imagery that censors its most dangerous implications.

* * *

For Quentin and Shreve, there is no unambiguous black intermediary, no Clytie or octoroon mistress whose attraction they can exploit and then safely withdraw from, as do Miss Rosa and Mr. Compson. In fact, for the larger part of their narrative, chapters 7 and 8, they appear to ignore race entirely, executing a sharp swerve in the narrative from the obsessions, explicit and implicit, that have dominated the novel up to this point. But theirs is only a subtler form of screening, for throughout Quentin and Shreve's focus on incest, as well as the homoerotic desires they infer and manifest, the bottom line of blackness is driving them and the history toward its most profound meaning.

The two boys concern themselves chiefly with Henry and Charles Bon, whose relationship Quentin radically alters by introducing the idea—the source of which is never disclosed—that Bon is Sutpen's son from his first marriage. Quentin's purposes as a narrator are threefold. From the outset he identifies primarily with Henry and his desire to protect his sister Judith from a dishonorable marriage. Now, however, that desire is complicated by the fact that the male threat is Henry's own brother and the violation is not bigamy but incest. He also wants to gain greater autonomy, one that will take the form of proposing a new reading of the Southern history that seems to have surrounded his life: "*Yes. I have heard too much, I have been told too much; I have had to listen to too much*" (168). And thirdly, he needs to engage the blackness that, like the narrators before him, he has always known and not known is at the heart of that history.

Shreve's purposes are those of the Northerner, but they gradually evolve until they become integral with the story he and Quentin cooperatively devise. First, to understand the South, a desire first raised in

September 1909 when they meet at Harvard: *"Tell about the South. What's it like there. What do they do there. Why do they live there. Why do they live at all"* (142). Shreve's interest is by no means merely cynical or academic, although it is January 1910 before he makes that explicitly clear: "'Wait. Listen. I'm not trying to be funny, smart. I just want to understand it if I can and I don't know how to say it better. Because it's something my people haven't got, or if we have got it, it all happened long ago across the water'" (289). He focuses on Charles Bon because they are both outsiders seeking entrance into what is essentially a different world. And, like all the narrators, Shreve wants the blackness, not only in the sense of what Morrison calls the American inference of "darkness [and] otherness" (38), but in that Southern sense of a desire for intimacy however encircled by fear and contempt.

In bringing Bon into the story as the half-brother of Henry and Judith, Quentin has not only established a new motive for murder. He has also introduced (quite possibly without Shreve's awareness) one more version of the hidden blackness of the history. From the antebellum period well into the twentieth century, incest was invariably linked by Southerners with miscegenation. For Quentin, it is the screen that will allow him to "register" blackness in the narrative without "articulating" it. Werner Sollors discusses and documents at length the "longstanding tradition of fusing the representation of incest and miscegenation" in Southern thought and literature, as well as in the literatures of Europe and Latin America.[22]

As Sollors points out, incest and miscegenation have been considered the extreme models of endogamy and exogamy: incest as too close and miscegenation as too distant for society's acceptance. Both have been regarded as serious moral (and biological) transgressions and yet as compelling desires that require great self or social control. Despite their apparently complete opposition, the two impulses were commonly connected in Southern thought by both proslavery and antislavery proponents.

For the antislavery position, incest was the greater crime; miscegenation (assumed to take place generally between white masters forcing themselves upon black slaves) is a sin because it can lead to incest between whites and their own mulatto children. For the proslavery position, miscegenation and incest were equal sins, although in Henry Hughes's frequently quoted, but not unique, pronouncement, incest seems merely a metaphor for the more dire race-mixing: "Hybridism is heinous. Impurity of races is against the law of nature. Mulattoes are monsters. The law of nature is the law of God. The same law which forbids consanguineous amalgamation forbids ethnical amalgamation. Both are incestuous. Amalgamation is incest."[23]

In *Absalom, Absalom!* the problem of incest is the core of opposition between Henry and Bon, Quentin and Shreve, for the bulk of the boys' narration. Ultimately, however, like Sutpen's diabolism for Rosa or Bon's inscrutable fatalism for Compson, incest becomes the "safer" sin for Quentin and, it turns out, for Shreve: an opportunity for them to participate vicariously in a love affair in which innocent brothers and sister are doomed by incomprehensible parental conflict. Quentin plays Henry's role of protecting Judith from Bon and Shreve plays Bon as the mysteriously rejected son pursuing recognition and incestuous love. Although in heated debate as to which brother is the more justified, Quentin and Shreve both project their chosen alter egos as performing acts of honor and love that conceal the race issue. Nevertheless, at the end of chapter 8, Quentin and Shreve decide that incest would not have been a sufficient motive for murder, leaving them no alternative than to release what has all along been the implicit underside of incest, miscegenation, as the major cause.[24]

Along with the incest, a second motive arises in Quentin's and Shreve's narration—which will also be put aside once the miscegenation surfaces. With Shreve's (and apparently Mr. Compson's) quick acceptance of Quentin's "discovery" that Charles Bon, Henry, and Judith are siblings, the narrative begins dealing not only with the love of brother and sister, but also the love of brother and brother. Earlier in the novel, Mr. Compson, not yet knowing of the blood tie, has already raised the friendship of Bon and Henry to an erotic level, consistent with his fascination with Charles as a man of sinister sophistication: "'It was because Bon not only loved Judith after his fashion but he loved Henry too and I believe in a deeper sense than merely after his fashion. Perhaps in his fatalism he loved Henry the better of the two, seeing perhaps in the sister merely the shadow, the woman vessel with which to consummate the love whose actual object was the youth'" (85–86).

Whether influenced by Compson's reading (which is the most unambiguous reference to homoeroticism in the novel) or whether building upon an erotism of their own already present in *The Sound and the Fury*, whether in the intensity of historical recreation they are replicating Henry and Charles Bon or whether they are imposing on them their own sexual desires, there is clearly a buildup of sexual energy between Quentin and Shreve as their narrative progresses.[25] A number of Faulkner critics have identified important, previously neglected textual evidence of this erotic relationship, ranging from explicit scenes of the boys' rapt attention to each other to possible sexual overtures by Shreve: "They stared at one another . . . not at all as two young men might look at each other but almost as a youth and a very young girl might out of virginity itself" (240); Shreve sits shirtless in the zero temperature of New

England winter: "from the waist down the table concealed him; anyone entering the room would have taken him to be stark naked" (177).[26]

The crucial issue here is not simply the presence of the homoerotic material, but its function in the novel. Like the incest, the homoerotic is closely tied to race, and in fact is operating as still another screen for a black presence in the history. Siobhan Somerville makes a persuasive, well-documented argument linking the attention to sexual difference and to race difference in the late nineteenth century: "it was not merely a historical coincidence that the classification of bodies as either 'homosexual' or 'heterosexual' emerged at the same time that the United States was aggressively constructing and policing the boundary between 'black' and 'white' bodies."[27] Rather than parallel or analogous acts of differentiation, these attempts at strict classification were "deeply intertwined," constituting an important "historical construction of intersections . . . at a particular cultural moment" (8).

One consequence of that construction was the emergence of two sexual object choices—interracial heterosexual and homosexual—that were regarded as pathological, both reflecting what one commentator on miscegenation called a "'disharmony of physical, mental and temperamental qualities,'" and another on homosexuality called "'a sign of degeneracy . . . a sad, deplorable, pathological phenomenon'" (30–31). The union of the two pathologies is evident in a certain interdependency of strategies of proof: "Sexologists and others writing about homosexuality borrowed the model of the racially mixed body as a way to make sense of the 'invert,' an individual who appeared to be neither completely masculine nor completely feminine. Finally, racial and sexual discourses converged in psychological models that understood 'unnatural' desire as perversion." Particularly important for the homoerotics of *Absalom, Absalom!* is that "the proximity of 'white' and 'colored' bodies under segregation elicited expert scrutiny and provided a visual marker of transgressive sexual desire" (37).

In detailed readings of James Weldon Johnson's *The Autobiography of an Ex-Coloured Man* and Jean Toomer's *Cane* and other stories, Somerville emphasizes the act of "passing" in a heterosexual relationship as a marker of a concealed homoeroticism. In *The Autobiography* "the pursuit of interracial (heterosexual) marriage is hardly the main trajectory of desire in this text. In fact, it is both integral to, and subordinated by, another form of desire figured as 'perverse' that shapes the ex-coloured man's narrative, that of male homosexuality." The upshot is that "interracial heterosexual desire functions in the text as both an analogy to homosexual object choice and a screen through which it can be articulated" (111–12). As Somerville demonstrates, the "ex-coloured man's" deepest erotic relationship is with his wealthy white male patron.

Somerville makes a similar argument using some of the stories of Jean Toomer, which are linked with Johnson's novel through "the ways in which the construction of the racially ambiguous male body as a simultaneously sexually suspect body has been deployed" (134). Again, with Toomer as well as Johnson, the originality of Somerville's argument is her refusal "to see race and sexuality as metaphoric substitutes," but rather to demonstrate "the ways in which racialization is constitutive of sexuality, and vice versa, in specific historical contexts" (165).[28]

Absalom, Absalom! shares this historical context, incorporating what in the immediately preceding decades had become regarded as twin pathologies of the homosexual and the interracial heterosexual into its probe of the motives behind murder in 1865. There is, however, a major difference in how these pathologies relate to each other. In the Johnson and Toomer texts, as well as in Nella Larsen's, the act of passing and its implied heterosexual miscegenation is what Somerville designates as a screen for homosexuality, inter- or intraracial. In *Absalom* the relationship is reversed. Homosexuality is the visible marker, coming to the surface of the text as early as Mr. Compson's narration in chapter 4 and continuing in Quentin's and Shreve's narration in chapter 8. Charles Bon is not "passing" in the text until page 283, when, according to Quentin and Shreve, Sutpen reveals Bon's racial identity to Henry. For most of their narrative Quentin and Shreve and therefore the characters with whom they identify—Charles and Henry—repress that identity. In their account, Bon does not know of his mother's blackness or possible misdeeds until the final disclosure: "'*I will not even demand to know of him what it was my mother did that justified his action toward her and me*'"; "'he had stemmed from the blood after whatever it was his mother had been or done had tainted and corrupted it'" (261, 265).

In giving voice to the novel's homoeroticism, critics have argued for its priority over miscegenation as the reason Henry kills Bon. Perhaps the most influential critic here is Noel Polk, who claims that Quentin and Shreve play the "race card" at the end of *Absalom, Absalom!* "not because other explanations for Henry's murder of Bon would not do but rather because the other explanations are rife with issues that Quentin and Shreve do not want to deal with directly. Race is, in *Absalom* and in Faulkner generally, a mask for very serious matters of sexuality and gender."[29] The question as to whether homosexuality or miscegenation is the screen in the novel is not easily answered, although it is important to recognize the possible impact of both on Faulkner in the 1930s. To distinguish, as Matthew Vaughn does, between miscegenation as "the openly reviled taboo" and homosexuality as "the unspeakable taboo," and thus to judge that "gay male desire" is a "greater threat" than miscegenation is difficult to verify historically or in the text.[30]

If the novel establishes a priority, I believe it does so through the means fundamental to its existence as a novel, namely, its narrative order. From chapter 1 to the last few pages of chapter 8, *Absalom, Absalom!* moves as a coherent succession of narrative screens, selected by narrators according to their particular needs, biases, and personal experiences—perceptive enough and honest enough to imply, but not fully express, what remains resonant but hidden. That succession of screens ends with the final scene of chapter 8, when the blackness of Charles Bon comes forth, unequivocally, for the first time.

Quentin and Shreve have built their bridge to that blackness through the motives of incest and homoeroticism that precede it in the narrative. It is not the miscegenation (unmentioned up to this point) that screens the homoeroticism, but the reverse. The boys abandon both the incest and homoeroticism with their cooperative decision—for some time now "it did not matter . . . which one had been doing the talking" (267)—that Henry would finally tell Bon to write Judith, which is his implicit consent that they marry: *"and Bon: . . . 'Do I have your permission, Henry?' and Henry: 'Write. Write. Write'"* (279). The fear of incest yields in Henry's mind to the precedence that "kings have done it! Even dukes!" (273), perhaps to his own incestuous desires vicariously satisfied, or possibly to his resistance to his father's refusal to explain his rejection of Bon's mother, as if patriarchal position itself were sufficient justification. Quentin's own struggle for autonomy parallels (at once dependent upon and responsible for) the same struggle in Henry, who defies the father on behalf of the brother.

Moreover, Henry and Bon agree that Bon should pursue the marriage that relinquishes homoerotic desire. Charles as husband to Judith will not be Charles as sexual partner with Henry. In Shreve's droll palatal imagery, champagne and whiskey (paternal recognition and fraternal homosexual consummation?) yield to the sherbet of Judith: "'you find that you don't want anything but that sherbet and that you haven't been wanting anything else but that and you have been wanting that pretty hard for some time'" (258). Forgoing each of these explanations for the murder of Charles Bon—prevention of incest or anger over sexual rejection—Quentin and Shreve move toward the history no one in the novel, including themselves, has been willing to see.

Events following Henry's discovery of his brother's and his possibly potential lover's blackness, such as Bon spreading his cloak over Henry's shoulders, or Henry "panting" and "trembling" (286) when he realizes that Bon still plans to marry Judith, or Bon offering his pistol "by the barrel, the butt extended" to Henry to prevent him from that marriage—they have been read as signs of a still vibrant and unresolved erotic passion between them and between Quentin and Shreve. But they are also the signs that another passion, one that has sundered the South for generations, has once again come into play. It has been the cause of murder before, and it will again. Neither the love Charles and Henry feel for one another, nor, as becomes clear in chapter 9, the love that has enabled Quentin and Shreve to arrive at the climactic scene itself, can overcome that passion of racial hatred. *This is what it's like there. This is what they do there.*

With the (re)emergence of that intolerable truth—in 1865, in 1910, in 1936—of Southern history, the remarkable cooperative telling of Quentin and Shreve falls victim to its own achievement. The truth they have won brings them once more to the historical fact of murder. In chapter 9 the boys descend into their own version of that conflict: the mean-spirited charge and countercharge, rebuke, vulgar summary that ensues for the remainder of the novel. Even as Shreve confesses not only his need to understand the South, but his envy of it, he cannot resist mocking Quentin's Southern plight: "'so that forever more as long as your children's children produce children you wont be anything but a descendant of a long line of colonels killed in Pickett's charge at Manassas'" (289). Quentin's entire thrust in the novel has been to establish himself as far more than that descendant, indeed a new voice in the history, unearthing long buried information. Small wonder, then, that he quickly rejoins, "'Gettysburg. . . . You can't understand it. You would have to be born there,'" thus dismissing Shreve's impassioned contribution to the narrative they have just completed.

Gone now are the imaginative flights of chapter 8: spring replacing winter as Bon and Judith stroll in the Sutpen garden (236), Bon saving Henry's life rather than the reverse (275), Eulalia's lawyer arranging for Bon to attend the same university as Henry (249–52)—all those events and "people who perhaps had never existed at all anywhere" (243). They dissolve into Quentin's strictly factual account of his direct encounter with the past, the primal scene: Henry Sutpen himself, effectively mute, the living corpse of history still waiting for the articulation of its meaning. From that scene the story has come full circle, through one narrative exploration after another, only to return to the blackness of the first catastrophe, restored to life by a creative union that, by virtue of its breakthrough, cannot escape the second.

Blackness invades this collaboration between white Harvard freshmen: the Canadian who numbers the "niggers" it takes to do away with one Sutpen, who taunts the Southern white boy with the threat that eventually the whole North American white race will be "passing," consumed by hidden miscegenation; the Southerner who hysterically denies

that he hates the Southern history of repressed blackness because he
cannot accept the truth he has finally told.[31]

○ ○ ○

The story of just *how* truth is told in *Absalom, Absalom!* is Faulkner's
most significant excursion into the nature of historical exploration, and it
is crucial to his contribution to the issue of race in the South. The theory
of history basic to the novel is dramatically apparent in the difference
between the two accounts of Charles Bon's racial identity, one at the end
of chapter 8 and one in the chronology. The accounts are in agreement
in terms of the essential information disclosed—Charles Bon's mother
was part black—but two entirely different modes of knowledge are
being employed in its delivery. In the chronology of the novel we read:
"1831 Charles Bon born, Haiti. Sutpen learns his wife has negro blood,
repudiates her and child" (305). As a statement of novelistic fact, this is
incontestable. Whether it comes from the omniscient narrator, who has
given us nine chapters, or directly from the author, William Faulkner,
who puts his name on the front page of the novel and on its end-paper
map as "sole owner and proprietor" (315), it is information we have no
warrant to dispute. The narrators within the novel—and we always know
when they are telling the tale—often speak in the interpretive mode, but
the omniscient narrator is always clear on the difference between what
is happening and what *might* be. Charles Bon's bloodline is a fact more
authoritative than eyewitness or circumstantial evidence of an actual historical event, for it exists as decree by the inventor of its world.

The preceding nine chapters of the novel, however, while in agreement with the chronology with regard to Bon's part blackness, do not
claim the same kind of authority. What the chronology flatly affirms is
revealed in chapter 8 as an almost mystically conjured scene, cooperatively experienced by Quentin and Shreve. While we know from Quentin's grandfather that Sutpen did meet with Henry in a Confederate
bivouac in 1865 (221–22), he says nothing—apparently knows nothing—
of what actually took place at that meeting. In short, there is no firsthand
account, no written document, not even, as Mr. Compson earlier puts
it, "a few old mouth-to-mouth tales" (80), that can testify to the content
of that conversation. According to the omniscient narrator, Quentin and
Shreve (figuratively? telepathically?) transport themselves from their
Harvard dormitory in 1910 to a Confederate bivouac in "Carolina" in
the winter of 1864. Unfolding before them, without historical source and
yet apparently without doubt, is the explanation they and the chronology
believe. What the chronology claims unequivocally, however, its product
shed of the process of discovery, the scene in chapter 8 confirms entirely

on the manner of its arrival: the cooperative vision itself as the validation of the truth it tells. The question the novel raises, therefore, is not what we believe but on what grounds we choose to believe it.

A few pages into chapter 8 Quentin and Shreve, we are told by the omniscient narrator, begin a process of alternate telling that passes almost imperceptibly into simultaneous speech or thought, as if identity itself becomes indeterminate, vanishing into a collective vision. Although the process of telling takes the form of a debate—primarily over the question of whether Bon's love for Judith is anything more to him than a form of extortion, a way of gaining recognition from his father—and although, throughout the chapter, Shreve is the primary fabricator of new, often quite fanciful additions to the story, Faulkner emphasizes the cooperative character of the narration: "it might have been either of them and was in a sense both: both thinking as one, the voice which happened to be speaking the thought only the thinking become audible, vocal; the two of them creating between them, out of the rag-tag and bob-ends of old tales and talking, people who perhaps had never existed at all anywhere" (243).

Ten pages later, even as that debate continues to rage—"'But it's not love,' Quentin said"; "'That's still not love,'" (258, 263)—"it did not matter to either of them which one did the talking, since it was not the talking alone which did it, performed and accomplished the overpassing, but some happy marriage of speaking and hearing wherein each before the demand, the requirement, forgave condoned and forgot the faulting of the other" (253).

The approach to the crucial scene in which Henry finally agrees to the marriage is performed, knowingly, by both boys, in apparent conjunction with Henry and Bon as well, "two, four, now two again, according to Quentin and Shreve, the two the four the two still talking," until the scene opens, parenthetically, in the italics of collective vision: "(—*the winter of '64 now, the army retreated across Alabama, into Georgia; now Carolina was just at their backs*" (276). The ensuing passage climaxes in Henry's statement to Bon, "*Write. Write. Write*'" (279), and concludes in the Confederate encampment just before Sutpen will reveal Bon's racial background to Henry. Shreve interrupts the italicized scene to return to the night, back in September, when Quentin and Miss Rosa went out to Sutpen's Hundred. His sole purpose is to insist, as if the fullest meaning of what will follow depends on it, that Clytie "'didn't tell you in so many words . . . didn't tell you in so many words . . . she didn't tell you . . . and she didn't tell you in the actual words. . . . [N]evertheless she told you, or at least all of a sudden you knew'" (280). Implicitly: and I know too, and now we're both going to know, together.[32]

All talking ceases. "They were both in Carolina and the time was forty-six years ago" (280), and the cooperative italics begin again: *"bivouac fires burning in a pine grove, the gaunt and ragged men sitting or lying about them."* But who is telling? Immediately prior to the scene, we learn that this climax about to come is not told by anyone: "He [Shreve] ceased again. It was just as well, since he had no listener. . . . Then suddenly he had no talker either." Now all the screens are being lifted. Even the omniscient narrator disappears. For the first time in the novel, narration comes as if it were *unsourced*, as if we were being presented with knowing released of everything that customarily controls it: the artifice of a voice (omniscient narrator or character) shaping what it sees into sound, the artifice of interpretation already coded by the values, the hierarchies, the exclusions that regulate expression, the artifice of narrative delivery itself. The scene comes to us not as conceived by Quentin and Shreve but as *witnessed*.

At its center Sutpen at last plays his "trump card," destroying his design as the price of purifying it: *"He must not marry her, Henry. His mother's father told me that her mother had been a Spanish woman. I believed him; it was not until later after he was born that I found out that his mother was part negro"* (283). This time, however, unlike earlier versions when Miss Rosa and Mr. Compson play their own trump cards against Clytie and the octoroon mistress, the trump does not dismiss the black man but acknowledges him. Charles Bon names *himself*, deliberately evoking the white man's greatest fear:

—*You are my brother.*
—*No I'm not. I'm the nigger that's going to sleep with your sister.* (286)

No longer the subhuman to be dismissed by epithet, to be declared invisible, Charles Bon demands recognition even if it is to be confirmed by a bullet: *"You will have to stop me, Henry."*[33]

This claim of Charles Bon's black heritage has the least support of any of the prior explanations for his murder. Clearly none of the explanations is indisputable—hence the continuing quest to discover motive—yet the ones that precede have at least a degree of empirical grounding. Miss Rosa has her shocking experience with Sutpen as evidence of the ruthlessness and capriciousness that would make him capable of forbidding Judith's marriage to Bon "without rhyme or reason or shadow of excuse" (12). The octoroon mistress, whose relationship with Bon Mr. Compson stresses in the first part of his account, visited Bon's grave in Jefferson, where eventually her child, Charles Etienne, is brought to live. That Bon's involvement with her would have created a problem for

Sutpen and Henry is certainly plausible (in Faulkner's story "Evange-line," written in 1931, it is *her* part-blackness that causes Henry to kill him).

Even Quentin's contribution that Bon was Sutpen's son has a stronger basis than the revelation of his blackness. When asked by Shreve how Mr. Compson suddenly appears to know that fact, Quentin responds that he told him, "'The day after we—after that night when we—'"; and Shreve fills in, "'Oh, . . . After you and the old aunt'" (214). Later Shreve adds, "'you wouldn't have known what anybody was talking about if you hadn't been out there and seen Clytie'" (220). No other evidence is given, just "seen Clytie." And yet Shreve's matter-of-fact acceptance of Quentin's statement, as well as Mr. Compson's unhesitating shift from the threat of bigamy to the threat of incest on the basis of it, adds to the sense that something other than pure fabrication is involved, although precisely what it is is left extremely vague. The revelation at the close of chapter 8, however, is absent of even an attempt at factual support, as Shreve emphasizes in his reiteration of the fact that Clytie "'didn't tell you.'"[34]

* * *

In order to render in fiction passage from the repressed fact of African American presence to its revelation, Faulkner brings to the historical novel one of the fundamental lessons of modernist thought, namely, the need to attend equally to the "who" of knowing as well as the "what." All four narrators of *Absalom, Absalom!* bring to their telling an extraordinary empathy with the people they focus on, so much so that it is at times difficult to differentiate between their identities. Miss Rosa's powerful sexual sensibility and Mr. Compson's deep cynicism are sufficiently engaged to make the Thomas Sutpen or Charles Bon of their narrations seem as much projections of their desires as objects of historical speculation. Ultimately, however, they withdraw from the growing proximity of "who" to the remoteness of "what," as the possibilities of Sutpen's "blackness" or the Creole Charles Bon's sacrifice for love and honor warn the narrators away from identifications too dangerous to contemplate. Quentin and Shreve, however, follow their empathy with Henry and Bon to full identification, "since both of them were Henry Sutpen and both of them were Charles Bon, compounded each of both yet either neither" (280). They complete the historical demand for an epistemological and moral leap.

In 1935, at the very time Faulkner was writing *Absalom*, R. G. Collingwood was preparing the series of lectures that would eventually be published as *The Idea of History*. As if describing the identifying acts of Quentin and Shreve, Collingwood characterizes the historian as one who "is a part of the process he is studying, has his own place in that process, and can see it only from the point of view which at this present moment he occupies within it."[35] Above all, writing history involves what Collingwood calls a "re-enactment of past experience": "To the historian, the activities whose history he is studying are not spectacles to be watched, but experiences to be lived through in his own mind; they are objective, or known to him, only because they are also subjective, or activities of his own." Historical knowledge is not merely to know "what mind has done in the past . . . it is the redoing of this, the perpetuation of past acts in the present."[36]

Quentin's and Shreve's move to a factually questionable conclusion that Charles Bon was part black also invites comparison with a similar but more radical understanding of the "who" of knowing than Collingwood's. Nearly a century earlier, Kierkegaard sees the task of the historian as the act of becoming "contemporary" with the past, of standing to it as the necessary and only arbiter of its truth: "That which has actually happened (the past) is still not, except in a certain sense (namely in contrast to poetry), the actual. The qualification that is lacking—which is the qualification of truth (as inwardness) and of all religiousness is—for you"[37]

Kierkegaard's concern is not with the historian in general, but with the "person . . . [who would] become a Christian,"[38] and the history he considers is the divinity of Jesus Christ, the only evidence of which lies with his human experience on earth. Jesus's truth is not what biblical history authorizes, what witnesses past and present testify, or what the historical triumph of Christianity confirms. For those who wish to know the truth, such "evidence" only conceals the known facts of Jesus's life on earth: the human being who consorts with the lowly, preaches what has been written, and dies on the cross. Jesus as the human/god is the one who must be sought, but he lives only beneath what "for you" are the screens that hide that impossible truth: "from glory he has not spoken a word."[39]

In *Absalom* the past of Southern history lies concealed by the multiple screens Quentin and Shreve have inherited or create themselves. Like Kierkegaard's "Christendom," as opposed to "Christianity,"[40] that past has degenerated into a more preferable yet still anxiety plagued rationale for another "impossible" truth—not the truth of the human/god but the truth of the African American. The difference between the fact of the chronology of *Absalom* and the fact of chapter 8 is that the former is outside the realm of Kierkegaard's "for you," while the latter is entirely within it. That is, "1831 Charles Bon born, Haiti. Sutpen learns his wife has negro blood, repudiates her and child" is the *known* that is the great *unknown*, the known that is not taken in, not felt on the pulses, not *imagined*, and therefore not truly believed. This is the fact that Quentin and Shreve draw forth, providing authority solely through their action of becoming contemporary with it. They tell the truth the past has refused to know about itself.

Despite the emergence of truth through what Kierkgaard would call a leap, the tragedy of *Absalom, Absalom!* is that Quentin and Shreve, immediately following their great breakthrough, repeat the murder and the motives they have unearthed rather than resolve the fatal division from which those motives have sprung. This is the impasse that Faulkner himself was never able to break through; he diagnoses the disease but never fictionally envisions the implementation of its cure. Edouard Glissant finds in Faulkner a tragic vision unique in that it cannot conclude with any degree of tranquility. The sins are acknowledged, the great war has been bravely fought to its necessary defeat, "yet equilibrium has not been restored," there is no "redemptive effect."[41] The wisdom gained cannot conceive of a different outcome.

The conclusion of *Absalom, Absalom!* is implicit from the outset in Faulkner's choice of his principal historian, whose suicide already circumvents his breakthrough. Faulkner experimented with other narrators, first "Don" and "I," then "Chisholm" and "Burke."[42] He justified his introduction of Quentin Compson in a letter to his editor by saying he needed his "bitterness" toward the South "to get more out of the story than a historical novel would . . . [:] To keep the hoop skirts and plug hats out, you might say."[43] But Quentin's bitterness is more than a fictional tactic; it underlies and renders not irrelevant but impotent the novel's great dramatization of historical understanding. Faulkner can voice the truth this novel realizes only through a narrator who has already suffered the disastrous consequences of the South's failure to do just that.

NOTES

1. William Faulkner, *Absalom, Absalom!*: The Corrected Text, ed. Noel Polk (1936; New York: Vintage International, 1990), 198. Further references are to this edition and will be cited in the text.

2. Toni Morrison, *Playing in the Dark: Whiteness and the Literary Imagination* (New York: Vintage Books, 1993), 25, 38, 66.

3. William Faulkner, *The Sound and the Fury*: The Corrected Text, ed. Noel Polk (1929; New York: Vintage International, 1990), 294.

4. William Faulkner, *Light in August*: The Corrected Text, ed. Noel Polk (1932; New York: Vintage International, 1990), 138.

5. Barbara Ladd, "Race as Fact and Fiction in William Faulkner," in *A Companion to William Faulkner*, ed. Richard C. Moreland (Malden, Mass.: Blackwell Publishing, 2007), 133–47.

6. Ralph Ellison, *Shadow and Act* (New York: Signet, 1966), 59.

7. Richard Poirier, *A World Elsewhere: The Place of Style in American Literature* (New York: Oxford University Press, 1966).

8. "Evangeline" was rejected by two periodicals in 1931 and remained unpublished until 1979. See *Uncollected Stories of William Faulkner*, ed. Joseph Blotner (New York: Vintage Books, 1981), 583–609.

9. Joel Williamson, *The Crucible of Race: Black-White Relations in the American South since Emancipation* (New York: Oxford University Press, 1984), 459. Further references are to this edition and will be cited in the text.

10. Richard Wright, *Black Boy* (1945; New York: Harper & Row, 1966), 190.

11. Neil R. McMillen, *Dark Journey: Black Mississippians in the Age of Jim Crow* (Urbana: University of Illinois Press, 1989), 236.

12. Richard Gray, *Writing the South: Ideas of an American Region* (Cambridge: Cambridge University Press, 1986), 146

13. *I'll Take My Stand: The South and the Agrarian Tradition*, By Twelve Southerners, ed. Louis D. Rubin Jr. (1930; Baton Rouge: Louisiana State University Press, 1977), 14, 62. Further references are to this edition and will be cited in the text.

14. For a comprehensive account of some 1930s texts and cultural shifts emphasizing the existence of African American agency in the South, see Charles Hannon, *Faulkner and the Discourses of Culture* (Baton Rouge: Louisiana State University Press, 2005).

15. Joel Williamson, *Faulkner and Southern History* (New York: Oxford University Press, 1993), 64–71. See also Joel Williamson, "A Historian Looks at Faulkner the Artist," in *Faulkner and the Artist: Faulkner and Yoknapatawpha, 1993*, ed. Donald M. Kartiganer and Ann J. Abadie (Jackson: University Press of Mississippi, 1996), 3–21.

16. Adding to the tension apparent in Faulkner's life and fiction is his February 1931 letter published in the *Memphis Commercial Appeal* virtually defending lynching—"But there is one curious thing about mobs. Like our juries, they have a way of being right"— that appeared shortly after the publication of "Dry September." See Neil R. McMillen and Noel Polk, "Faulkner on Lynching," *Faulkner Journal* 8 (Fall 1992): 3–14.

17. That Clytie, also of his blood, presents no such problem for Sutpen is owing to her sex and her already enslaved status.

18. Joel Williamson, *New People: Miscegenation and Mulattoes in the United States* (New York: New York University Press, 1984), 108.

19. By 1900, as Joel Williamson has pointed out, blacks forced off their land and wandering "loose" were regarded as potentially dangerous, particularly those whose blackness might be "invisible": "The identification of newcomers in a community was always important to them, but as blackness disappeared beneath white skins and white features, it became vastly more so" (*New People*, 103).

20. Barbara Ladd, *Nationalism and the Color Line in George W. Cable, Mark Twain, and William Faulkner* (Baton Rouge: Louisiana State University Press, 1996), 24.

21. Faulkner's awareness of the Mississippi attitude toward French Creoles is evident in his short story "Elly," originally called "Selvage," published in 1934. The story concerns a young woman's affair with Paul de Montigny, who is suspected of being part black by several characters in the story. The name and the man's origin in Louisiana, as Theresa M. Towner and James B. Carothers comment, are a "coded reference to indeterminate racial identity" in Faulkner. See *Reading Faulkner: Collected Stories* (Jackson: University Press of Mississippi, 2006), 116.

22. Werner Sollers, *Neither Black nor White yet Both: Thematic Explorations of Interracial Literature* (New York: Oxford University Press, 1997), 287. See especially chapter 10, "Incest and Miscegenation" (285–335).

23. Henry Hughes, "Treatise on Sociology," in *The Ideology of Slavery: Proslavery Thought in the Antebellum South, 1830–1860*, ed. Drew Gilpin Faust (Baton Rouge: Louisiana State University Press, 1981), 298.

24. Interestingly enough, the relationship between incest and miscegenation that evolves just below the surface in *Absalom* exists in *The Sound and the Fury* as well. As elsewhere in Faulkner (especially *Light in August*), sexuality is itself "black," as indicated in the earlier novel by Quentin's way of characterizing Caddy's sexual experiences: *"Why must you do like nigger women do in the pasture the ditches the dark woods hot hidden furious in the dark woods." (The Sound and the Fury*, 92). With sexuality as black, it is a logical step to see it as inherently miscegenative when whites engage in it, as revealed in Quentin's figuring of Dalton Ames as Othello: *"he had been in the army had killed men . . . with one hand he could lift her to his shoulder and run with her running Running . . . running the beast with two backs."*(148). (In *Othello*, Iago addresses Brabantio: "I am one, sir, that comes to tell you your daughter and the Moor are now making the beast with two backs" [I, i, 118–20]). Moreover, the incest that Quentin chooses to screen that blackness as the more tolerable violation is imaginary. He vacillates between one absurd claim—*"you thought it was them but it was me listen I fooled you all the time it was me you thought I was in the house*—and another: *"Ill make you say we did Im stronger than you I'll make you know we did" (149)*. His aim, similar to the practice of the narrators in *Absalom*, is to transform Caddy's real sexual experience into an incestuous union that, wholly imaginary, annuls that experience even as it exploits its power.

25. For an intriguing account of the "homoerotic urge and the fear of homosexuality" that exist in Quentin and Shreve in *The Sound and the Fury*, see Noel Polk, "How Shreve Gets into Quentin's Pants," *Faulkner and Welty and the Southern Literary Tradition* (Jackson: University Press of Mississippi, 2008), 29.

26. Among the more recent critics who have emphasized the homoerotic elements in the novel are Noel Polk, *Children of the Dark House* (Jackson: University Press of Mississippi, 1996), 137–41; Norman W. Jones, "Coming Out through History's Hidden Love Letters in *Absalom, Absalom!*,"*American Literature* 76 (June 2004): 339–66; Betina Entzminger, "Passing as Miscegenation: Whiteness and Homoeroticism in Faulkner's *Absalom, Absalom!*," *Faulkner Journal* 22 (Fall 2006–Spring 2007): 90–105; and Matthew R. Vaughn, "'Other Souths': The Expression of Gay Identity in *Absalom, Absalom!*," *Mississippi Quarterly* 60 (Summer 2007): 519–28.

27. Siobhan Somerville, *Queering the Color Line: Race and the Invention of Homosexuality in American Culture* (Durham: Duke University Press, 2000), 3. Further references are to this edition and will be cited in the text. Also see Ellen Crowell, "The Picture of Charles Bon: Oscar Wilde's Trip through Faulkner's Yoknapatawpha," *Modern Fiction Studies* (Fall 2004): 595–631, for a reading of Wilde and Charles Bon in terms of homosexuality figured as racially black.

28. Somerville notes a similar dynamic in Nella Larsen's *Passing*, as the situation of Claire Kendry's marital passing contributes to an intraracial sexual attraction between Claire and Irene Redding (145).

29. Polk, *Children of the Dark House*, 139.

30. Matthew Vaughn, "'Other Souths': The Expression of Gay Identity in *Absalom, Absalom!*" (524). Entzminger concurs, claiming that Quentin and Henry "divert their attention away from their homosexual desires onto a more open topic for their time and region: the taint of black blood" (90). Jones combines homosexuality and race, arguing

that the novel's great originality lies in its effort to put forth a "coming-out historiography" in defiance of "the official histories," the greatest danger to which is "the shadowy specter of an interracial gay romance" (361). Black male/white female miscegenation is apparently part of the "official" history and therefore much less of a threat.

31. Quentin's shaking "violently and uncontrollably" (288) in his bed at the beginning of the chapter, echoing his earlier response to his encounter with Henry (narrated later in the chapter), has also been read as a scene of "orgasmic ecstasy" (Entzminger 103), "the roommates' sexual climax result[ing] from their narrative climax, their joint storytelling" (Jones, 345). I suggest that the dissolution that characterizes all of chapter 9 implies trauma rather than ecstasy, a response to the shock of historical discovery at the end of chapter 8, which threatens Quentin's entire moral identity.

32. Ostensibly what Clytie is not telling Quentin is that Henry Sutpen has returned, but Shreve's obsessive repetition suggests that he is talking about the larger secret of why the murder itself took place.

33. Among recent interpretations of Quentin's and Shreve's cooperative telling is Joseph Urgo, "*Absalom, Absalom!* The Movie," in *William Faulkner: Six Decades of Criticism*, ed. Linda Wagner (East Lansing: Michigan State University Press, 2002), 293–310, who reads the formulation of this scene and the novel as a whole as Faulkner's portrayal of the process of movie making (much of the novel was written while he was working in Hollywood), especially the emphasis on creation as a series of collaborative efforts. Jones, in keeping with his emphasis on the homoeroticism of Quentin and Shreve, characterizes their collaboration as "the orgasmic eroticism of Shreve's and Quentin's commingled storytelling" (343); "Telling history becomes a mode of sexual expression for Quentin and Shreve" (345). Jones reads chapter 9 as a "sexual climax result[ing] from their narrative climax" (345).

34. Attempts to determine just how Quentin "finds out" that Bon is part black seem to me to miss the largest point of the novel, which has to do with historical knowing as not being simply a matter of ascertaining fact. The argument of this paper is that Quentin, like the other Southern narrators, already "knows" the motive for Bon's murder but, until the end, is unable to possess it as the core of his own reality.

35. R. G. Collingwood, *The Idea of History* (1946; New York: Oxford University Press, 1956), 248. For further discussion of Faulkner and Collingwood see Richard Gray, *Writing the South*, 182–83; and *The Life of William Faulkner: A Critical Biography* (Oxford: Blackwell, 1994), 208–9; and especially John Padgett, "War and History in the Fiction of William Faulkner" (PhD diss., University of Mississippi, 2004), 265–71.

36. Collingwood, 218.

37. Soren Kierkegaard, *Practice in Christianity*, ed. and trans. Howard V. Hong and Edna H. Hong (Princeton: Princeton University Press, 1991), 62–64.

38. Ibid., 63.

39. Ibid., 24.

40. Kierkegaard, *Philosophical Fragments/ Johannes Climacus*, ed. and trans. Howard V. Hong and Edna H. Hong (Princeton: Princeton University Press, 1985), 220.

41. Edouard Glissant, *Faulkner, Mississippi*, trans. Barbara Lewis and Thomas C. Spear (Chicago: University of Chicago Press, 2000), 97.

42. See Joseph Blotner, *Faulkner: A Biography*, 2 vols. (New York: Random House, 1974), 1:828.

43. *Selected Letters of William Faulkner*, ed. Joseph Blotner (New York: Random House, 1977), 79.

Reading "Red Leaves":
Mouths, Labor Power, and Revolutions

RICHARD GODDEN

Not knowing where to begin, I shall begin in a mysterious place: in a barn loft contemplating a lactating breast. As Issetibbeha's body servant, hidden, waits for the death of his master (his waiting itself a mystery), he hears drumming from the creek bottom near the slave quarters: "The only fire there would be the smudge against mosquitoes where the women with nursing children crouched, their heavy sluggish breasts nippled full and smooth into the mouths of men children; contemplative, oblivious of the drumming, since a fire would signify life."[1] Mouths, full, empty, closed, open abound in Faulkner's "Red Leaves" (1930), the condition of their teeth, gums, tongues, and saliva severally specified, yet few of them are more problematic than those of the "men children" in the slave's fantasy. The exclusion of "female children" from the breast begs an unanswerable question, in order, I would suggest, to set the term "male" in antonymic relation to the preferred word, "men," thereby ensuring appreciation of the contradictions within the phrase "men children." That "men," who are not "children," may suckle (in the mind's eye of the slave), latches adults and infants alike onto the breasts. "Men" consequently operates as split signifier, yielding a divided referent and a divided addressee.[2] Whatever the proliferation of semantic options, the provision of the milk itself brooks no obstruction, since the breasts are "nippled full and smooth into . . . mouths." But the erectile detail, modified by the presence of the term "men," tends simultaneously to erotic and nurturing functions.

The lactate itself proves equally duplicitous since the sentence containing it makes reference to an alternative and poisonous feeder, "the only fire there would be the smudge against mosquitoes." The insects, apparently little more than an element in the mis-en-scene of a hungry man's fantasy, once set against that hungry man's proclivity for eating or recalling the eating of filth, exceed the limits of casual realism. Within a page, and still in the barn loft, the slave will detail the remembered catching and consumption of a rat, this when he was a boy and "spoke then only his native tongue" (119). To the rat he immediately adds a cottonmouth, killed and "eaten . . . save the poison head": "save," here meaning "except," also means "kept," since the slave weaves the skull into an "amulet" with a "mother-of-pearl lorgnon" (a single or double eyeglass, brought back by Issetibbeha from Paris). "Pearl" forms in the roof of an oyster's shell, which oyster is little more than a sucking mouth. The phrase, "mother-of-pearl," occurring four lines after "native tongue," and in the context of maternal nurture, prompts a transposition, whereby "native tongue" becomes "mother tongue," even as the slave's "cottonmouth" semantically stretches to embrace the possibility of "poison" and a certain "dryness of the mouth."

I would stress that my semantic redistribution takes its precedent from Faulkner's usage, as that usage extends from a fantasy concerning the filling of a problematic mouth with problematic milk. Witness "the only fire there would be the smudge against mosquitoes": the noun "smudge," an archaic American term, refers to "a fire in a tent or small enclosure" (as in, "to fill with smoke from a smudge" [1891]). But since an archaism is likely to generate hesitations, and consequently to create a temporary vacancy in meaning, its context may hasten to fill that space. "Smudge," more conventionally heard as a verb, means "to soil, stain, blacken, smirch," "to mark with a dirty smear," or "to rub out," all apt variants in the presence of mosquitoes. A smeared insect, having fed, will leave a smirch. Already stained by the smoke from a smokey fire, the milk in the slave's fantasmic mouth absorbs the merest whim of blood. Blood, ash, and milk constitute an excessive and filthy ingestion, which remains, I would suggest, semantically indigestible. Having traced the textual production of an excessive fluid, I remain all but at a loss as to its function. My confusion results, in large part, from the capacity of the milky image to fuse nurture and erotics, so that the offending "smudge," realized by the associative networks that flow into it, refers simultaneously to the abrupt termination of a feeding insect, and to the "nudge" of an infant (or man) who "nuzzles" a breast, "nippled full and smooth." You may fairly object that I make much of little; to which I would counter that the excess devolves from Faulkner and inheres in his choice of the mammalian image—an odd choice given the slave's condition: long without food (121), and due to be put into the earth to serve, in perpetuity, the master whom he has served for twenty years. What, to co-opt a phrase from As I Lay Dying (also from 1930) are these "mammalian ludicrocities"[3] doing in this place and at this time?

The nature of the slave's service may be thought to speak to the fantasmic mouth. The slave, it seems, "held the pot" for Issetibbeha, and "ate of his food, from his dish" (115) for twenty years. Issetibbeha had good reason to use a long-term food taster: his father, Ikkemotubbe's

"Manship," depended upon the sudden and unexplained deaths of an uncle and a cousin (106), both having better claims to ascendancy. In "The Bear" (1942) Faulkner will elaborate; Ikkemotubbe returns from New Orleans with poison in a snuffbox, demonstrates the efficacy of the powder on puppies, and thereby provokes the abdication of those who stand between him and authority.[4] By implication, Moketubbe models his ascent on that of his grandfather, poisoning his father over the matter of the red shoes. Moketubbe's "crime" (Faulkner's word, 125) remains undetected only because no one cares to detect, but crucial clues litter the text, chief among them, a snuffbox of which two mentions are made within the story: the slave is hunted by two Indians, "both squat men, a little solid, burgher-like, paunchy, with big heads" (100). Three Baskets can be distinguished from Louis Berry by age and in that, "clamped through one ear . . . [he] wore an enameled snuffbox" (101). His choice of personal decoration appears merely eccentric until, during the account of Issetibbeha and his son's largely tacit dispute over ownerships of the red shoes, and as a preface to Issetibbeha's sanguine utterance, "a man cannot live forever" (110), we learn that Issetibbeha used snuff. Details are provided, "a white man had shown him how to put the powder into his lip and scour it against his teeth with a twig of gum or of alphea" (109). Within half a page, Issetibbeha is dead: "he lived for five years longer, then he died. He was sick one night . . . he died before noon" (110). Berry and Basket choose not to discuss the manner of the death; better, they decided, to "think nothing" than to announce what they think (111). But since the victim had a food taster, and the "crime" an oral precedent, what went from the victim's pot to his mouth should not have killed him; the snuff, presumably untested by the taster, might well have been polluted with the residues of Ikkemottube's powder or example. The perpetrator of the crime remains a mystery, whose clues can be read severally. Did Moketubbe suborn Basket? Did Basket act independently of the slave whose task it was to protect Issetibbeha's mouth? Whoever did what, it seems likely that poison was put to lip and "scoured against . . . teeth with . . . gum." The mouth again; again, in all its specifics, a quasi-criminal locus of desire, pollution and the indigestible.

But why does the slave wait, and why does he imagine breast feeding as he waits, watching not simply "Issetibbeha's dying" (116), but for a further twelve hours recording preparations for the feast attendant on the burial? Given that he knows that the Man is dying, and that he is to be buried with him, lingering seems a bad move. He should be running as far and as fast as he can. We will witness his eventual run, noting perhaps that he runs with his "mouth closed . . . his broad nostrils bellowing steadily" (120); certainly observing that he runs not in a straight line, but in a circling fashion and for six days. Since he knows the land, having "hunted it often with Issetibbeha" (120), we can only assume that the body servant cannot, in some sense, quit his master's body. The suggestion that the manner of his protracted wait and incompetent run expresses grief appears on the surface incredible. Why should a slave mourn his master? My question elides a murder mystery with a mystery deriving from the political economy of slavery, by way of the strange nature of mourning. Nor should we forget the mouth and what is put into it.

When, on the morning of the second day of his vigil, the slave sees the doctor emerge from the steamboat "where Issetibbeha lay dying," and at this juncture lies dead, "he [the slave] found that he was still breathing and it seemed strange to him that he still breathed air, still needed air" (119). Earlier, at the outset of his first day hidden in the barn, and prior to the death, on seeing the same doctor emerge "to set fire to two clay-daubed sticks" (118), the slave had concluded, "'So he is not dead yet'":

> he could hear the two voices, himself and himself:
> "Who not dead?"
> "You are dead."
> "Yao, I am dead," he said quietly. He wished to be where the drums were. He imagined himself springing out of the bushes, leaping among the drums on his bare, lean, greasy, invisible limbs. But he could not do that, because man leaped past life, into where death was; he dashed into death and did not die, because when death took a man, it took him just this side of the end of living. It was when death overran him from behind, still in life (118–19).

Faced with this difficult material, I am inclined to draw a line (let the line be called 'Life' or 'L') and to situate death (D) and the slave (S) at various and moveable points on that line, describing arcs or parallels as S leaps D, or D overruns S. My hypothetical diagrams are silly. But I would defend my initial diagrammatic impulse as one that catches the tenor of the slave's performed projection of his own dying. The slave, who is about to run, concentrates his life into a line, along which he will run a footrace with death; each runner will variously "leap past," "dash into," or "overrun" the other. Who outruns whom, and in what manner, matters less than the way in which lines allow me to mime the contraction of the slave's predicative attention to the phenomenology of his own dying.

F. W. J. Schelling on the creative power of the performative utterance may provide a useful gloss. A performative, care of the philosopher J. L.

Austin, is a form of speech that acts, and consequently cannot be thought of as just saying something. "I declare you man and wife," in the marriage service, is performative; Jason Compson's reiterated, "I say. I say" seeks to insist upon the performativity of his every word (he means, "I do. I do"). Schelling identifies, within the performative, "a contraction . . . a kind of withdrawal of the subject into itself, its pure self-positing in a form of negation of all [alternative] predicative determination[s]."[5] Schelling's "contraction" amounts to the formation of "the act" within, and presupposed by, the performative utterance. Seeking to clarify Schelling's difficult formulation of the doing within the uttering, Eric Santner (aptly for our purposes) likens the contraction to the concentration of a runner just prior to a race, "Before leaping from the block, the runner [here, the slave] . . . in a sense contracts his 'being,' in order to be able to extend himself into the space of his own activity [running]."[6] Imagine that a line, in its full length, is compacted into the point at which the initiating pen presses on the page; such is the slave's contraction. At which point, Faulkner's free indirect narration all but accords with the slave's perceptual mechanisms the better to dramatize the fusion of his corporeal and mental excitement; the slave's body (which "leaps," "dashes," is "taken" and "overrun") secretes an abstraction, a mental geometry of points and parabola ("past," "into," "just this side of," and "from behind"). What remains remarkable, therefore, is that even as he contracts towards Schelling's "pure self-positing," the slave divides. For all his concentration, he is two: his death and himself. Two address him in whispers from his own mouth, "himself and himself," "You are dead.' 'Yao, I am dead.'" In what sense does the body servant, "still in life," die because the master is dying? Or, why, when the master ceases to breathe, does the slave find it strange that he "still needed air" (119)? Note that even as he sketches his own struggle with death, he cannot effectively separate himself from death's instance and exemplar, Issetibbeha. The slave seeks to imagine himself as darkness leaping out of darkness into the sound of drums, drum and dance having long been expressive of slave resistance,[7] but as he leaps he passes "invisibly" into the generic term "man," where, inextricable from his service to "the Man," he must leap and dash in the company of the master.

Perhaps "the thin whisper of rat feet" (119) carries the slave in memory from the enclosed space of the barn loft to the enclosed space of the middle passage in search of a singular death (free of the master). Slave historians describe slavery as a condition of "natal death," insofar as masters, investing in human property, sought to render that property readily pocketable. Slaves were, accordingly, renamed at purchase and denied marital or familial links; that is to say, they were made "socially dead,"[8] becoming the saleable things that they were deemed to be (chattels). Issetibbeha's slave has no name; his anonymity speaks to his lack of property in himself (the proper name). Yet in recalling his "ninety days in a three-foot-high 'tween-deck" (119), and subsequent incarceration in a stable, prior to sale, he retains a first and extended "natal death," a death belonging to himself alone, or at least in no sense to Issetibbeha. I add, simply as a reminder of the wider concern of "Red Leaves" with mouths and feeding, that the slave's recollection centers on the catching and consumption of a rat. Since "caught" and "ate" occur in a single sentence and without an intervening "kill," we may at least surmise that the rodent was put living to the mouth's first bite. A living rat and bloodied milk to a hungry man . . . sweet filth or filthy sweetness? And since the sustenance is imagined by a slave dedicated to his master's body (one who "held [his] pot" and "ate . . . from his dish"), as that body dies (a slave whose every expectation is to die with that body), one must surely ask, into whose mouth does the slave place the fantasmal food?

Faulkner's curiosity as to the slave's curiosity, over the exact moment of his own death in relation to Issetibbeha's dying, speaks to the accuracy of Hegel's preoccupation with a similar transposition. In his canonical chapter, "Lordship and Bondage," from *The Phenomenology of Mind*, Hegel argues that such is the dependency of the bound man on he who binds (and vice versa) that each potentially contains the other in disguised form. Masters, as bodies made by slaves, prove liable, for Hegel, to the recognition that the independence of their mastery depends upon the labor of the bound man. Or, as Hegel has it: "Just when the master has effectively achieved lordship, he really finds that something has come about quite different from an independent consciousness. It is not an independent consciousness but rather a dependent consciousness that he has achieved."[9] Understandably, that recognition, tantamount to the insight that slave owners are blacks in white face (or, here, in "red" face), may prove unpalatable, not least because it involves a species of dying— the death of the master's view of himself as an "independent consciousness." Few masters choose to die for such recognition. But what of the slave, within Hegel's model? After all, Faulkner's "Red Leaves" is preoccupied within the viewpoint of the slave. For Hegel, the bound man, as the recipient of a "social death" (as, that is, "one whose essence of life is for another"[10]), holds in his hands contradictory and saving evidence. In Hegel's terms, contemplating that into which he has placed his labor, the slave may recognize that the very things made by his hand—since the making of them delays the master's gratification—constitute grounds for his own independent existence (and consequently for the negation of his own prior negation by the lord): "shaping and forming the object has . . .

the positive significance that the bondsman becomes thereby the author of himself as factually . . . self-existent."[11] Such a moment is uncomfortable in that it requires that the bound man experience both the death of his dependent self and the emergence of an independent self: "Precisely in labor, where there seems to be some outsider's mind and ideas involved, the bondsman becomes aware, through the rediscovery of himself by himself, of having and being 'a mind of his own.'"[12] Since Hegel's slave in effect learns revolution in and from his own hand, that hand as the instrument of recognition through labor, causes the slave no end of trouble. Hegel speaks of "quaking" and "complete perturbation" as the bound man "melts to [his] innermost soul" and "trembles throughout [his] every fiber"[13] precisely because he recognizes his labor power for what it is—both an extension of his own mind, and the substance of his master's mastery. Here, the death of the slave's prior death at the hand of the master, and of the master's subsequent death at the hand of the slave, are coterminous and simultaneous, and all within a "tremble."

Issetibbeha's slave "held [the Man's] pot" and "ate of his food from his dish" for twenty years, a task deemed by Basket a life of soft service "in the shade," a life that warrants the willing repetition of that service in perpetuity (114). Seen from Hegel's rather than Basket's perspective, the food, carried first to the slave's mouth and only then to the mouth of the master, constitutes a congealed form of the slave's labor power. In that he serves as a body servant, Issetibbeha's slave "author[s] . . . himself" as an "independent being" even as he looks upon and recognizes that which his labor has literally authored and preserved, the fed and portly body of Issetibbeha (113). At the risk of glossing my own gloss: the slave lives after the master's death (and against his own expectation) because he reads the liberatory message placed by the work of his own hands into the body of his master. But he lives for only six days—an abbreviated freedom—during which he runs *around* rather than *away from* his master's body. Moreover, his peers consider him dead, and he shares their belief: standing briefly "in the drifting smudge," he concurs with the judgment of his headman, "'The dead may not consort with the living; thou knowest that.' 'Yao. I know that'" (122).

How can I read a revolution into such subservience to his master's will and body? On the third day of his run, the slave is bitten in the forearm by a cottonmouth; touching the head of the snake, he watches it "slash him again across his arm, and again, with thick, raking, awkward blows. 'It's that I do not wish to die,' he said. Then he said it again—'It's that I do not wish to die'—in a quiet tone, of slow and low amaze, as though it were something that, until the words had said themselves, he found that he had not known, or had not known the depth and extent of his desire"

(124). The contradiction is absolute: inviting death by poison, the slave twice denies the death that he invites, in effect insisting that he will die in order not to die. The bitten limb shrinks to that of a child (127), and the slave requests a hatchet so that he may "chop the arm off" (127). His pursuers deny his wish but take his point, noting that to send Issetibbeha "one who will be of no service to him" would be to turn Issetibbeha's postmortem eternity exactly upside down; as Berry says, "Issetibbeha himself would have to nurse and care for" such a servant (127). Ergo, the master will be the slave and the slave would be the master, in perpetuity. The slave finds "the depth and extent" of his revolutionary "desire" in the moment of the bite, as, presumably, the poison enters his flesh. The desired bite elicits "amaze[ment]," not least because the mouth works of the biter and the bitten mirror one another, in that each repeats "again . . . and again," "again"; as the snake strikes "sluggish[ly]" so the slave speaks "slow[ly]." Faulkner's prose scrupulously records what might be taken for a transfer of emissions—poison in, language out. Moreover, the words "[un]known" until the bite, "[say] themselves," all but displacing agency from the utterer. Who then utters; or, better, what within the slave speaks in riddles and contradictions?

I am left, impossibly, with the poison itself. As I hesitate, mystified, so the context of the bite provides glosses and inferences in the form of an alternative and equally problematic piece of mouthwork. The paragraph recording the slave's encounter with the cottonmouth departs from an account of his eating ants from a log; he has, we are told, "eaten nothing else all day": "He caught them and ate them slowly, with a kind of detachment, like that of a dinner guest eating salted nuts from a dish. They too had a salt taste, engendering a salivary reaction out of all proportion. He ate them slowly, watching the unbroken line move up the log into oblivious doom" (124). Elements of the passage of ant to mouth replicate the earlier passage of milk to mouth or mouths: both are "salivary," the former care of "salt," the latter care of lactate; both induce a species of reverie, the nursing mothers are "contemplative" (118), the feeding slave is "detach[ed]"; each implies the presence of mysterious cofeeders, the nipples "full and smooth" enter the mouths of "children" *and* "men," while the slave who eats like a "dinner guest" may be presumed to eat in as yet unidentified company. Once the two passages are set paratactically side by side (without explanation for their conjunction), the phrase "out of all proportion" resonates, begging the question, "Out of all proportion to what?" Presumably, to the size and number of the ants ingested, but in the absence of proffered explanation, the end-stopped disproportion retains elements of the interrogative. Since the passage positions the slave as the "doom" of the ants, in a story where the Indian master took as his generic name "Doom," part of the feeding slave's saliva induced "detachment" may stem from his giddy reorientation: as he feeds, he who is hunted becomes the hunter, and so merits a fragile attribution of the master's name. The lower-case "d" (of "doom") will, within ten lines, assume an implied upper-case form, as the slave claims descent from a cottonmouth whom he calls "Olé, grandfather" (124). In "Red Leaves" a snake addressed via a Chickasaw term takes its place (however briefly), within a Chickasaw genealogy, playing grandfather to "the Man," otherwise known as *du homme*," pronounced "Doom" (105). The doomed man, furthermore and with equal necessity, plays Adam, the most doomed of men, doomed by a snake. Although Issetibbeha bore the name (the Man), the nomenclature was first applied to his father (Ikkemotubbe), who therefore stands as the initially "doomed man," or dead ringer for Adam. In the slave-supplied context of a cottonmouth declared grandfather, the snake (care of the mouthwork of the slave) proves to be God: He who fathered the Man (Adam or Ikkemotubbe) and grandfathered the Man Issetibbeha, only to poison the direct descendant of the Man through the forearm and withered hand of an anonymous slave.

My reading grants a layered and positively Hegelian irony to the slave, by means of which, even as he provokes the deformation of his arm (the instrument of labor), he recognizes that in order "not . . . to die" (as an "independent consciousness") he must die first (as a "dependent consciousness"), doing so, moreover, by poisoning himself in a manner that will poison a limb of the very tree that he (and his class) have sustained. V. N. Volosinov, the Russian linguist, in his work on Freud, defines irony as "conditioned by a social conflict," insofar as it involves "the encounter in one voice of two incarnate value judgements and their interference with one another."[14] His definition fits the taste of the repeated utterance, "It's that I do not wish to die," as it emerges in "slow and low amaze" to form a "deep and extensive" "desire" from within the slave's saliva-soaked mouth. The "[dis]proportion" here is that of immanent revolution, since the phrase "Olé, grandfather" proposes to bring down the very family tree that it inaugurates, by setting poison at its root and head. Quite suddenly, the slave's amulet, worn close to his groin during the chase (119), takes on disproportionate implication: consisting of a cottonmouth skull and half an eyeglass, the bangle effects a magnification of the "poison head" (119). Yet even as I extend the implications of "poison" and "Olé" towards a political potency that recasts the term "Red," in "Red Leaves," so I encounter an apparently insurmountable block to a radical reading: if the slave poisons Issetibbeha through his own body, that body must in some sense contain the body of Issetibbeha, a body that the slave therefore preserves as much as he assaults.

In "Mourning and Melancholia" (1917) Freud argues that melancholics, unable to accept and mourn the loss of a loved person or idea, unconsciously take the lost thing that they cannot lose into themselves, thereby preserving it.[15] The French psychiatrists Nicolas Abraham and Maria Torok elaborate, suggesting that melancholics swallow grief, in an act of "incorporation" whereby their "inexpressible mourning erects a secret tomb" within them.[16] As crypt carriers, melancholics grieve without grief. Abraham and Torok add that for those who come to analysis sick with unresolved mourning, "everything unfolds as though a mysterious compass led them to the tomb wherein the repressed problem lies."[17] I hesitate to bring Faulkner's slave to the couch, but too much fits to be ignored, not least the subject's "mysterious" and tortuous circling back to the tomb of the master. As one who, for twenty years, has served Issetibehha's body and been subject to his will, the slave may well find it impossible to let that will and body go. So read, the body servant becomes a political melancholic who cannot complete a revolution because he loves the very body that he would cast down.

The continued presence of the master within the slave accords therefore with both Freudian and Hegelian models, but more importantly finds expression throughout Faulkner's story. Briefly to backtrack: the slave runs, unable quite to quit the master's body since the binding body retains him as an extension of its will. The slave refrains in greater part from sustenance, denying succor to the master he contains. Or, when he feeds, whether in reality or imagination, he places varieties of filth into his own and so into his master's mouth, seeking to nurture *and* to sicken. To mutilate himself is to mutilate the master. To withhold food from himself is to starve the master. To eat ants is to induce a "salivary reaction out of all proportion" because the saline spit (like the milk before it) flows simultaneously into two mouths, the encryptor and the encryptee.

Early in the story, the narrator attempts to figure the interanimation of binder and bound. Basket and Berry enter a communal hut in the quarters where they encounter a smell that they call "black man's fear" (102), though they struggle to distinguish it either from their own fear ("Your fear has an odor too" [102]), or from the stench of the master's decomposing body. The smell of black sweat induces the hunters to a suspect that the collective body of black labor—a body they suppose to "like sweating" (107)—through the medium of its very sweat or labor power is "thinking something . . . knowing something . . . hiding [something]" (103): "The smell of them, of their bodies, seemed to ebb and flux in the still hot air. They seemed to be musing as one upon something remote, inscrutable. They were like a single octopus. They were like the roots of huge tree uncovered, the earth broken momentarily upon the writhen, thick, fetid tangle of its lightless and outraged life "(102–3). Two similes laid side by side effectively constitute a metaphor, allowing octopus tentacle and arboreal root to indulge what Paul Ricoeur might call a "semantic impertinence." Reading through Aristotle on metaphor, we may see the likeness within the difference, and in so doing tend to press root (tentacle) and branch ("leaves") towards a tense inseparability (or "predicative assimilation") that confronts a revolt of the roots as they, uncovered, "writhe" to topple the very tree that they support.[18]

The figure takes on further resonance once understood as the internal source for Faulkner's "impressionistic" title, a title Joseph Blotner simplifies with his claim that it "refers to the Indians."[19] Blotner's observation derives from Faulkner's own commentary: "It was the deciduation of Nature which no one could stop that had suffocated, smothered, destroyed the Negro . . . [adding later] . . . . The red leaves had nothing against him [the runaway] . . . they probably liked him, but it was normal deciduation which the red leaves, whether they regretted it or not, had nothing more to say in."[20] "Deciduation" is a curious and repeated choice: "deciduous" refers both to the leaves and to parts shed by animals (deer horns and baby teeth are, like leaves, "decidua"). The verb "to deciduate" has (since 1783) meant the tearing away of fetal from maternal tissue at parturition, whereby the body of the mother forms part of the placenta that once enclosed the child. Faulkner's choice affirms the corporeal inseparability of root (slave) and leaf (master), but does so to invert the distribution of power within the arboreal figure for codependency upon which he comments. "Tentacles" "suffocate . . . smother . . . [and] destroy" rather more effectively than do "leaves"; moreover, their "writhen" and maternal "tangle" carries me, via metaphoric logic, towards a connotative network in which sucking tentacles, requiring a salt solution (the sea), meet saline saliva (124) in the suckling mouths of "men children" (118) latched onto those black breasts from whose mystery I started. I lack time and patience (yours), to annotate this extraordinary "tangle" of whispers, save to say that it begs at least one question: why, in 1930, should Faulkner be so interested in a tangled meeting of the mouths and bodies of binder and bound? My answer will involve the briefest of historical interludes, for whose reductions I apologize.

※ ※ ※

J. R. Mandle, historian of African American labor in the South, insists that, until the New Deal, Confederate defeat and the Emancipation Proclamation of 1863 notwithstanding, black labor in the plantation South remained bound, or more accurately, "not slave/not free,"[21] care of systemic debt peonage. As W. E. B. Du Bois put it in 1935, at the close of the Civil War, "the slave went free; stood for a brief time in the sun; then moved back again toward slavery."[22] By 1930, with out-migration from the region slowed by the Crash and incipient Depression, Southern black agricultural workers remained tied to the land by what the historian Jonathan Wiener calls "involuntary servitude."[23] Inflected through Hegel, such ties bind the laboring body to the body of the labor lord, in a relation whose archaism grew apparent during the early '30s. Dependency, an increasingly unproductive form of labor relation, awaited the influx of federal funding associated with the Agricultural Adjustment Program (1933–38) that would finally expel the tenancy from the labor lord and his land. Structurally unbound, black labor might or might not "tremble" in Hegelian fashion, but there is little doubt that it knew in which migratory direction to turn. Small wonder if Faulkner's slave, held in the earliest phase of plantation production and perceived (circa 1930) prior to the New Deal's externally enforced labor revolution, lacks an equivalent sense of direction. Rather, he runs in circles and enacts a necessarily impaired revolution. Caught between feeding and poisoning his master, he exhibits all manner of "morbid symptoms": the phase is Gramsci's and is drawn from his definition of "interregnum," a term relevant to "Red Leaves" insofar as Faulkner sets the story literally between two reigns (those of Issetibehha and Moketubbe) and writes it between two economic regimes: from the extraordinarily extended last days of the premodern plantation, he conjures the first days of that system, even as that system invites revision. Here is Gramsci on the "interregnum," whose crisis consists "precisely in the fact that the old is dying and the new cannot be born: in this interregnum a great variety of morbid symptoms appear."[24]

Yet "Red Leaves" addresses red-black, not white-black, relations and does so at a nonspecified but early nineteenth-century phase of plantation development, rather than at a moment when falling cotton prices and redundant tenants exposed the system's limitations. I am very aware that, throughout my essay, I have been treating "master" and "slave" as structural rather than ethnic terms. I have done so because, persuaded by the considerable scholarship of Patricia Galloway and Robert Dale Parker[25] (among others), I cannot read Faulkner's Chickasaws as Mississippi's Chickasaws. Nor, however, am I persuaded simply to recast them as celluloid red men.[26] Rather, I would claim that the redness of the red leaves allows Faulkner to posit a time at which the regime of accumulation associated with labor "confinement," first as chattel then as peon, was new; that is, when its elements, "bound labor power," "dependency," "the master's mastery," and "the bound man's tremble" had not coalesced into fixed forms and when, therefore, its structural mechanisms might better be made strange, released from the dailiness of an every day that extended from 1850 to 1933.

Witness Basket's and Berry's debate about black "sweat" as taken up by the tribal conclave, under the heading "the Negro question" (106). For the red discussants, slaves exist primarily to yield "sweat," which on all counts retains its natural qualities as that which (variously) "smells" (103), "opens the pores" to night air (107), and gives to black flesh a "bitter taste" (101). The last item shifts the debate: since sweat-affected meat (unlike that of other stock) cannot be used to satisfy need, it does not serve as a "use value"[27] in the matter of hunger (101, 106–7). Killing to reduce numbers is not an option, since to kill without eating has no purpose or use. The question "What for?" (107), applied to the sug-gested cull, elicits first silence and then the troubling notion of "value" ("They are too valuable"). At which point, the Indians, who have no concept of "work," "labor power," or "value," recognize the enormity of the problem—the problem of their own protracted entry into the market place:

> "We must do as the white men do." . . .
>
> "Raise more Negroes by clearing more land to make corn to feed them, then sell them. We will clear the land and plant it with food and raise Negroes and sell them to the white men for money."
>
> "But what will we do with this money?" a third said.
>
> They thought for a while.
>
> "We will see," the first said. They squatted, profound, grave.
>
> "It means work," the third said. (107)

Faulkner's comic timing mimes the emergence of intellectual from manual labor, among a group who do not even start from a concept of manual labor. "Sweat" becomes "work," which becomes "money," which requires further "sweat" so that increased labor power may generate additional capital, which capital tugs a "plantation" from a "forest," prior to linking that plantation to Paris, via New Orleans, as Ikkemotubbe puts forty purpose-bred slaves into his pocket and departs Mississippi for the global economy. For none of which abstractions or places do Faulkner's Indians have adequate concepts, though they will develop them, albeit inadequately—which is Faulkner's point in designing his Indians.

What Basket says of slaves might equally be said of the red leaves, "They are like nothing in this sensible world" (101). "Sensible" should be heard as a pun containing two unconnected meanings: "sensible" as "reasonable, a judgment marked by good sense"; "sensible" as "pertain-ing to the senses and so to sensation." As in all puns, we do not ask which

meaning is meant, "or go back and forth between two alternative perceptions [rather] . . . we recognize both meanings at the same time."[28] Such
a recognition creates (Ricoeur again) a "semantic impertinence" or clash
and a consequent "conceptual need."[29] The quasi-metaphoric tension
within Basket's choice of word, as that word addresses the translation of
sweat (labor power) into value (money), lends itself to a form of resolution once we realize that there is nothing "sensible" (or reasonable)
about the transformative passage of the "sensible" (or that which pertains to the senses) through the monetary form. When Marx points out
that "circulation sweats money from every pore,"[30] he announces a deep
mystery, a mystery into which Basket's pun stumbles. Marx adds that
"not an atom of matter" remains in a "physical object" if that object is
seen as a commodity or value.[31] From the viewpoint of exchange, matter
as matter ceases to matter because something else matters more. Herein
lies the mystery of "value," a veil through which persons and things pass
to emerge as commodities, or elements in a commodity revolution, the
second revolution to redden Faulkner's "Red Leaves."

Ikkemotubbe returns from Paris with a number of useless artifacts,
chief among them a pair of red-heeled shoes from the court of Louis XV.
Moketubbe will kill for those shoes. Why they matter so much to him
may best be approached via examples of Faulkner's account of what they
do to him.

> The stripling removed the shoes. Moketubbe began to pant, his bare chest
> moving deep, as though he were rising from beyond his unfathomed flesh
> back into life, like up from deep water, the sea. But his eyes had not opened
> yet. (116)

Or:

> He could not wear them very long while in motion, not even in the litter
> where he was slung reclining, so they rested upon a square of fawnskin upon
> his lap—the cracked, frail slippers a little shapeless now, with their scaled
> patent-leather surfaces and buckleless tongues and scarlet heels, lying upon
> the supine obese shape just barely alive, carried through swamp and brier by
> swinging relays of men. (125)

Two bodies would seem to be involved. First, the body the slaves made,
oceanic, saline, apt locus for the octopus of black labor. I would return
you to the disproportionate saltiness of the slave's mouth as he feeds on
ants, but here read through the Indian debate on "sweat." When you lick
sweat, you taste salt. The slave accordingly tastes his own labor power

in his salty mouth, a labor power that he had previously dedicated to the body of his lord, but that (on the brink of appropriating the term "Olé") he now administers to that body as the discomfort of thirst (a revolutionary eucharist). Second, the body according to the red shoes: shoes, brought back from an early European market in luxury goods, which though they never fitted him, Moketubbe first played with aged three; stole and hid, aged sixteen, and murdered for, aged thirty, never having given up trying to put them on. Without the shoes, which take him "beyond . . . unfathomed flesh," he must rise "back into life" through his slave-made body (as though "up from . . . the sea"). The shoes by implication take him to another corporeal place, akin to death (since they appear to be killing him), though much desired.

Marx might caption the red shoes "fetish" and speak of their de- and reincarnation by "value." Indeed, Faulkner's footwear warrants comparison with Marx's table, which wooden thing, as soon as it emerges as a commodity, "transcends sensuousness"[32]: abstracted into price (and, care of price, rendered the abstract equivalent of all other priced goods), Marx's table "evolves out of its wooden brain grotesque ideas, far more wonderful than if it were . . . [to] dance of its own free will."[33] Capital's dancing table is danced towards animate inanimacy by the "will" of value as it subsumes the table into the promise of an equivalence that stops nowhere. The table, as "value" rather than "use," will remain the same yet never be the same again: or, as Derrida puts it, "from the moment [Marx's table] comes onto [the] stage of the market [it] resembles a prosthesis of itself," at once sensuous and nonsensible, materially immaterial.[34]

Faulkner's shoes do not tap on Mokotubbe's distended lap, they do rather more. The phrase "just barely alive" refers initially to Moketubbe's body (possessed by the shoes), but by the measure of that body's "supine and obscure . . . inertia," the shoes appear more animate than their bearer; consequently, they, "just barely alive," enliven his inanimacy, becoming Moketubbe in prosthetic form. Note that the word "desire" bridges section 4 (closing on the slave's encounter with the cottonmouth) and section 5 (starting with Moketubbe's encounter with the shoes). "Desire" seems doubly apt: revolutionary desire on the slave's part, commodified desire on the part of Moketubbe. Note also which part of Mokeotubbe the shoes most effect, aged thirty, unmarried because by implication married to the shoes, which rest "on a square of fawnskin" on his lap: the word "fawnskin," with a "magic" akin to the "necromancy"[35] discerned in commodity by Marx, becomes "foreskin" as the red shoes dis- and reembody Mokotubbe in their form, the form of the commodity.

Two revolutions, neither of them fully realized in 1930 (when Faulkner wrote "Red Leaves"), the first latent in the immanent release of the bound body from the binding labor lord (circa 1933–38); the second immanent in the structurally transformative influx of New Deal funds that were pervasively to substitute wage labor for debt peonage (circa 1933–38). My sense of the story, as formed by revolutions that Faulkner sensed to be immanent, rests on the presence of contradictions: those contradictions, between "use" and "value," slave and master, have most typically surfaced in the story's account of physical experience, of feeding, of sweating, of feet. Yet the mysteries of mouth or breast have been linguistic rather than corporeal; that is to say, a function of Faulkner's language as it materializes body parts. Mouth, breast, foot, foreskin have been attended by a "too much of address" (I borrow the phrase from Eric Santner, from whom I continue to borrow[36]), an address that results in an "excess" whose "insistent unreasonableness" derives from traceable contradictions—contradictions that pitch the reader "among enigmatic messages" whose import remains "indigestible."[37] Filthy milk; talking poison; the "sensible" that is and is not "sensible"; the "tongue" of a "scaled" shoe—each instance gestures towards a surplus of the real within reality, and thereby initiates a sense that the real might have been made a different way: which sense surely *is* the work of revolution, born of contradiction. Herein lies the real mystery of reading, in necessarily Delphic fashion, Faulkner's "leaves," so contrarily "red."[38]

NOTES

1. William Faulkner, "Red Leaves" in *Selected Short Stories of William Faulkner* (New York: Modern Library Edition, 1993), 118. Subsequent references to the story are to this edition and will be included in the body of the text.

2. See Paul Ricoeur, "The Metaphoric Process as Cognition, Imagination, and Feeling," *Critical Inquiry* 5:1, Special Issue on Metaphor (Autumn 1978): 143–59. Ricoeur paraphrases and arguably recasts Jakobson to say, "the supremacy of poetic function over referential function does not obliterate the reference but makes it ambiguous. The double-sensed message finds correspondence in a split addresser, in a split addressee, and what is more, in a split reference, as is urgently exposed in the . . . exhortation of the Majorca story tellers . . . 'it was and it was not'" (153). He adds that "the poet is this genius who generates split references *by* creating fictions. It is in fiction that the absence proper to the power of suspending whatever we call 'reality' in ordinary language concretely coalesces and fuses with the positive insight into the potentialities of our being in the world which our everyday transactions with manipulable objects tends to conceal" (155).

3. William Faulkner, *As I Lay Dying* (New York: Random House, 1990), 164.

4. William Faulkner, *Go Down, Moses* (New York: Random House, 1990), 159–60. In "The Old People" Faulkner revises Ikkemotubbe's family tree, designating Moketubbe his cousin. For the variants of Ikkemotubbe's genealogy through the four Indian stories,

see Patricia Galloway, "The Construction of Faulkner's Indians," *Faulkner Journal* 18:1, 2 (Fall 2002-Spring 2003): 20.

5. I quote from Eric Santner's summation of F. W. J. Schelling's claims concerning "contraction" and the "logic of predication." See Santner, *The Psychotheology of Everyday Life: Reflections on Freud and Rosensweig* (Chicago: Chicago University Press, 2001), 47, note 1. Santner's arguments have been central to the formation of the essay, here and in its conclusion.

6. Ibid.

7. Shane and Graham White, "'Us Likes a Mixtery': Listening to African-American Slave Music," *Slavery and Abolition* 20 (1999): 22–48. I would like to thank Richard Follett for alerting me to the subversive nature of these forms.

8. James Oakes, *Slavery and Freedom: An Interpretation of the Old South* (New York: Knopf, 1990), 7. See also Orlando Paterson, *Slavery and Social Death* (Cambridge: Harvard University Press, 1982), particularly part 1, chapter 2.

9. G. W. F. Hegel, *The Phenomenology of Mind*, vol. 1, trans. J. B. Baillie (New York: Macmillan, 1910), 184.

10. Ibid., 182.

11. Ibid., 186.

12. Ibid., 187.

13. Ibid., 185.

14. V. N. Volosinov, *Freudianism: A Marxist Critique*, trans. I. R. Titunk (New York: Academic Press, 1976), 113.

15. Sigmund Freud, "Mourning and Melancholia," in *The Standard Edition of the Complete Psychological Works of Sigmund Freud*, vol. 14 (London: Hogarth Press, 1981), 243–58.

16. Nicolas Abraham and Maria Torok, "Mourning or Melancholia: Introjection verses Incorporation," in *The Shell and the Kernel: Renewals of Psychoanalysis*, ed. and trans. Nicholas T. Rand (Chicago: Chicago University Press, 1994), 125–38.

17 Ibid., 118.

18. My phrases and argument are drawn from Ricoeur, "The Metaphoric Process of Cognition, Imagination, and Feeling," 144, 148, 153, 155, 158–56.

19. Joseph Blotner, *Faulkner: A Biography*, vol. 1 (New York: Random House, 1974), 663.

20. Quoted by Blotner, ibid., 663–64.

21. J. R. Mandle, *Not Slave, Not Free: The African American Experience since the Civil War* (Durham, N.C.: Duke University Press, 1992).

22. W. E. B. Du Bois, *Black Reconstruction in America, 1860–1880* (New York: Harcourt and Brace, 1935), 30.

23. Jonathan Wiener, "Class Structure and Economic Development in the American South, 1865–1955," *American Historical Review* 84 (1984): 992.

24. Antonio Gramsci, *Selections from the Prison Notebooks*, ed. and trans. Quintin Hoare and Geoffrey Nowell Smith (New York: International Publishers), 76. I should like to thank Nasser Mufti for establishing this connection.

25. Galloway, "The Construction of Faulkner's Indians," 9–31; Robert Dale Parker, "Red Slippers and Cottonmouth Moccasins: White Anxieties in Faulkner's Indian Stories," *Faulkner Journal* 18:1, 2 (Fall 2002–Spring 2003): 81–100.

26. See Peter Lancelot Mallios, "Faulkner's Indians, Or the Poetics of Cannibalism," *Faulkner Journal* 18:1, 2 (Fall 2002–Spring 2003): 143–78. Mallios creates an intriguing argument for why, amongst other things, Faulkner's Indians should be read as movie derived.

27. For Marx's definition of "use value" see Karl Marx, *Capital*, vol. 1, trans. Ben Fowkes (London: Penguin, 1990), 126.

28. Malcolm Bull, *Seeing Things Hidden* (London: Verso, 1999), 25.

29. Ricoeur, "The Metaphoric Process as Cognition, Imagination, and Feeling," 146–47.

30. Marx, *Capital*, 1:208.

31. Ibid., 138.

32. Ibid., chapter 1, section 4, "The Fetishism of the Commodity and Its Secret," 163–77.

33. Ibid., 164.

34. Jacques Derrida, *Specters of Marx* (New York: Routledge, 1994), 158.

35. Marx, *Capital*, 1:169.

36. Eric L. Santner, *The Psychotheology of Everyday Life: Reflections on Freud and Rosensweig* (Chicago: University of Chicago Press, 2001), 32, 37.

37. Ibid., 32, 37, 140.

38. Rather than end in a plethora of theorists, I have displaced my theoretical sources into a final footnote consisting of three epigraphs cast as afterwords. Herbert Marcuse on "contradiction": "contradiction . . . does not displace the actual identity of things, but produces this identity in the form of a process in which the potentiality of things unfold" (*Reason and Revolution: Hegel and the Rise of Social Theory* [London: Routledge, 1973], 124). Walter Benjamin on "revolution" as that which, "blasted out of the continuum of history," constitutes "a tiger's leap into . . . the open air. . . . Where thinking suddenly stops in a configuration pregnant with tensions" ("Theses on the Philosophy of History," in his *Illuminations* [London: Harcourt and Brace, 1969], 261–62). Faulkner's slave, "It's that I do not wish to die" ("Red Leaves," 124).

"Nice Believing": Mystery and Mysteries in *Light in August*

Sean McCann

Midway through *Light in August*, in one of his conversations with Byron Bunch, the Reverend Gail Hightower delivers a passing remark about the distance between his home and the area surrounding Joanna Burden's now destroyed mansion. "I used to walk it myself now and then," Hightower remarks. "It must be about three miles."[1] Though nothing further is said to suggest that the comment is especially significant, the passage might be taken for a characteristically Faulknerian provocation. For, it seems to be one of the devices of Faulkner's characterization to present, without any particular notice, apparent incongruities that bear the potential to reshape our view of a character and sometimes the broader implications of a novel. Consider, for example, the moment when the solitary Anse Bundren touches the face of his wife's corpse, or the scene in *Go Down, Moses* when Ike McCaslin deciphers the record of his grandfather's sins while, as Richard Godden and Noel Polk point out, managing to read right past the evidence of his father's alternative exploitation of slavery for sexual gratification.[2] Or for more obvious examples, think about the way Jason Compson betrays his avowed, ruthless pragmatism by playing the cotton market and hoarding his capital beneath the floorboards, or the manner in which the savvy V. K. Ratliff makes himself a victim to Flem Snopes in *The Hamlet*.

In each of these cases, we are presented with easily overlooked, minor puzzles that lead to the larger enigmas at the core of the novels that contain them. Reverend Hightower's comment presents a similar incongruity. After all, we know not only that Hightower is a profoundly solitary and sedentary man, but that the area surrounding the Burden mansion is "a region of negro cabins and gutted and outworn fields" (287). What would a failed preacher and a figure of Victorian gentility like Gail Hightower—a "hopeless High Romantic," as Harold Bloom describes him—be doing walking out there?[3]

As it happens, there are good symbolic and thematic answers to this question. Like all of the major characters of *Light in August*, Hightower is a marginal figure to the town of Jefferson, and like all but Byron and

Lena Grove his marginality is marked in specifically racial terms. That he has frequented the area of the Burden mansion and will return there later in the novel contributes to establishing that highly charged liminal status and underscores some important concerns of the novel. But, before turning to such thematic and symbolic matters, I think it is worth noting the way that moments like Hightower's comment draw *Light in August* near to the generic orbit of a quite different kind of narrative.

In another type of story, when a character unwittingly indicated that he had spent time near the scene of an important crime, the admission would provide the occasion for extended consideration. The comment would be probed for its consistency with the character's more considered avowals, for what it reveals about his movements and actions, and, most importantly, for what it might illuminate about his motivations and those of other characters. The comment would thus turn out either to be evidence toward a pattern of intended action, one drawing the narrative's apparently disparate events into a meaningful web of causation and significance. Or it would be revealed to be a bit of useless information with no greater import for the story—mere static, as it were, in the narrative system. The process of separating signal from noise, moreover, would provide an illuminating map of broader social action and, still more importantly, the outline of a moral order distinguishing the vicious from the virtuous, the guilty from the innocent.

The genre to which I am referring, of course, is the detective story. And although the observation is perhaps not a profoundly original one, I think it's worth taking note of the extent to which *Light in August* resembles an example of the most widely read genre of narrative fiction of its day.[4] As a number of scholars have recently pointed out, Faulkner, like many of his contemporaries among the era's most ambitious artists and intellectuals, had a lifelong and ambivalent attraction to popular crime narrative. "I read Simenon because he reminds me something of Chekhov," Faulkner remarked to Jean Stein in the 1950s, thereby nicely acknowledging both a taste for the detective story—the evidence for which would later be discovered in the collection of mystery novels found in his library—and the characteristic modernist defensiveness about mass culture.[5] The marks of that ambivalence run all through Faulkner's major fiction, where the investigation of buried crime often provides the occasion and method of narrative invention and where the hermeneutic expectations encouraged by the detective story are both solicited and consistently frustrated.

It may be in *Light in August*, though, that Faulkner most thoroughly mimics and subverts the conventional features of the mystery novel. The narrative hinges of course on the discovery and punishment of murder. Just as in most examples of the detective story, moreover, victim, killer,

and avenger in *Light in August* present a problematic triad of characters whose moral deviance reveals by contrast the outlines of a social
order to which, in varying degrees, they are each foreign. Joe Christmas
resembles a murderer out of the mythology of Southern nightmare, of
course, but he is also a figure who might have walked from the pages of
the pulp fiction he reads and which he appears to confuse with his own
violence. Joanna Burden, too, is cast as someone similar to the victims of
most mystery novels. Like the unfortunate women who fall prey to violence in thousands of crime stories, she is a character whose unorthodox
life and troubling sexual history, along with her pathological entanglement with the killer, place her on the margins of her society and appear
to invite the violence she suffers.[6] Even Percy Grimm—the "boy" with
"that black pistol," as Hightower thinks of him—is not far distant from
the righteous vigilantes who fill the volumes of American crime fiction
(492). The prototypical "saint with a gun" of the hard-boiled crime story
is a heroic figure whose morally ambiguous qualities make him a mirror
to the criminals he subdues, while constraining him to live always on the
border of the community he protects.[7] Grimm, too, is, or wishes to be, a
puritanical avenger—he possesses the "serene, unearthly luminousness
of angels in church windows"—who is ready to surrender "his own life,"
and to take the life of the rival to whom he is intimately bound, "in payment for" that heroic sense of mission (462, 451).

In conventional detective stories, the figures of that moral triad form
the main players of an endlessly flexible mythology of liberal society.
Typically, we first encounter a world where the individual liberties
and commercial networks of market society appear to produce a haz-
ardous, unjust, and coldly amoral universe of individual self-seeking.
Then, through the interactions of the three central figures, we witness
the seemingly worst dangers of that world both dramatized and ritually
excised, so that, by contrast, we may come to a new realization of the virtues of civil society. These include, we are now positioned to appreciate,
not only personal freedom, but the norms of lawfulness, cooperation,
openness, and tolerance that enable liberal society to function without direct coercion.[8] Such qualities are frequently limned in the jovial
friendships or, especially, the marriages of minor characters that often
open and close detective stories. Nothing is more common in detective
fiction than for the hero to rescue some tormented young woman or man
who is thereby freed to wed—marriage functioning in this fashion, as it
often does in American literature, as the paradigmatic example of the
consensual relations prized by liberal society.

Though significantly not in quite the same way, *Light in August* similarly uses murder and execution to reveal to us "the town" of Jefferson as
a collective body and to allow it to transcend the ordinary social friction

of market society. Faulkner's community, it might be noted in this light, first appears to us as a fragmented population of petty, bigoted, antagonistic, and cruel individuals whose worst qualities are a complement of their thorough absorption in commercial society. They are shown to us at the scene of the murder, for example, as a collocation of "parties and groups," among them "casual Yankees," "poor whites," and "southerners who had lived for while in the north" (287, 288). All of them are said to be eager to find in the murder an "emotional barbecue" because, we are told, the mistaken pursuit of vengeance makes "nice believing": "better than the shelves and the counters filled with long-familiar objects bought . . . in order to cajole or trick other men into buying them at a profit" (289). By the end of the novel, however, these unappealing individuals will escape the banality of commercial society to be rediscovered as the "good people" of the town, and they will be endowed, in Reverend Hightower's meditation on them, with formal dignity and perverse beauty. No longer the deracinated factions envisioned at the scene of the murder, they have become a "people" defined by "history, . . . land, . . . [and] environed blood" and, still more, unified by their tragic dedication to the grotesque ritual of lynching—"that which they know on the morrow they will have to do." They are driven, Hightower thinks, *to crucifixion of themselves and one another* and become at the height of their spiritual drama the singers of "a single blended and sonorous and austere cry." Their music sounds to Hightower's ear "ecstatic, solemn, and profound" (367–68, emphasis in original).

I think we should recognize the changed vision of the town of Jefferson that occurs between these two passages as a striking transition and one central to Faulkner's novel. The shift in tone and diction between the two passages should prevent us from conflating, as is often done, the two analyses they propose and should underscore instead the transformation they present. In the difference between them, we move from a vision of banal social competition ("to cajole or trick other men") to one of profound collective identity, from extrajudicial violence viewed as ugly self-delusion (an "emotional barbecue") to lynching imagined as a religious ritual somehow suffered mutually by its perpetrators and victims ("crucifixion of themselves and one another"). More abstractly, the novel takes us from an explicitly sociological frame of analysis to an avowedly spiritual one. That transition, as I will try to explain, is importantly not what occurs in most popular crime fiction. Indeed, it all but directly reverses the logic at the core of most murder mysteries. But the imperfect parallel it presents to the central narrative of the detective story is an illuminating one, and in this light the implications of the popular genre against which *Light in August* is implicitly posed may be worth considering in greater depth.

* * *

The central feature of the murder mystery to note in this context is the way the genre is itself often said to provide a form of ritual gratification that hinges on the recognition and resolution of evil and injustice.[9] Seen in this light, the aesthetic accomplishment of the conventional detective story comes in the way the form allows us to experience a double reorientation of vision—so that we first see ordinary social life displaced by a bleak vision of corrosive social competition, only then in the story's resolution, following the identification and symbolic banishment of the killer, to recognize the norms of cooperation that transcend and constrain criminal appetite. In that same narrative transition, the genre traditionally offers us a highly compressed ideology of history. As scholars like Karen Halttunen have helped us understand, the roots of the modern crime story lie in a gothic imagination that developed alongside the market revolution of the nineteenth century. The gothic, as Halttunen shows, provided the inhabitants of a newly capitalist world with the imagery of passions and pathologies that lay ostensibly buried in archaic depths below and before the self-discipline encouraged by modern commercial life.[10] The detective story in turn repackaged that gothic imagery by casting itself as a narrative of the emergence of liberal society out of the murk of a cruel and unjust past or a dark otherworld. This was, for example, part of the significance of Poe's decision to place Monsieur Dupin in the Paris of the July Monarchy, where his powers of ratiocination enable him to trump the unscrupulous power and court intrigue of the Minister D_. But it is also the premise that encouraged Arthur Conan Doyle to frequently link the crimes of his stories to the deep history of war over the throne (as in "The Musgrave Ritual") or the unsavory practices in the imperial territories or on the American frontier (as in "The Speckled Band" and *A Study in Scarlet*).

All these settings are imagined to be outside the norms of liberal society, and all raise, at a convenient distance, the peril of the cruelty and domination to which liberalism, as thinkers like Richard Rorty and Judith Shklar have argued, is most deeply opposed.[11] The importance of that underlying contrast helps clarify one of the central conventions of the genre. As Carlo Rotella points out, successful crime stories tend "to dig beneath the surface crimes that drive the plot" so as to "unearth deep structural wrongs, an order of violence more diffuse than murder or robbery."[12] In doing so, it might be added, they allow us to imagine ourselves descending into ostensibly buried depths beneath our world, places of hidden cruelty and oppression, so as to reemerge into a condition of greater justice and freedom. To put the point a slightly different way, the gothic imagination, as Haltunnen notes, conceives of the problems of evil and injustice as "mystery"—that is, as an epistemological and moral enigma that presents a challenge to the authority of reason and law. But the detective story is, of course, equally committed to transforming the large mystery of evil into the small, resolvable mysteries of intention and action, into, in other words, the sort of question that could be answered by asking what purpose Gail Hightower had in walking by Joanna Burden's house. Thus, as one aesthetic pleasure of the detective story comes in seeing cruelty and domination brought under control, an inextricable satisfaction comes in seeing the way eerily incomprehensible events, hinting at the influence of supernatural or cultic forces, can be understood through perfectly straightforward empirical explanations. A ghostly hound turns out to be a large dog painted with phosphorous; a locked room can be entered by a trained orangutan.

Seen in relation to these aspects of the mystery genre, *Light in August* looks revealingly both like and, more seriously, unlike the conventional detective story. What better description could there be of Faulkner's repeated archaeological excursions into its characters' pasts than the search for deep crime and the effort to explain it? Indeed, as if to underscore his novel's similarity to the social vision of the mystery novel, Faulkner ends *Light in August* with a deft portrait of the freedoms and pleasures of life in commercial society. Not only do we learn in the book's concluding passage of the way Lena Grove takes pleasure in "just travelling" around the country with her would-be husband, Byron, trailing devotedly after her (506). We hear the story from a travelling furniture dealer who tells the anecdote to his wife amid the apparently mutual satisfactions of their marital bed. With the exception of the story of Rider and Manny in "Pantaloon in Black," this is perhaps the only memorable depiction of wedded happiness and sexual pleasure in all of Faulkner's fiction. As a coda to Faulkner's novel of fateful violence, the concluding narrative highlights the contrast between the comic register of love and mutuality, on the one hand, and the tragic register of coercion and destruction, on the other. In this fashion, it resembles the depictions of marriage or friendship that often end murder mysteries.

But, of course, in most other respects, *Light in August* does not look much like a detective story at all. By contrast to the happy marriages or jovial friendships that conclude many detective stories, for instance, the depiction of the furniture dealer and his wife makes them tangential figures to the main action depicted in Faulkner's novel—even as the dealer himself, remarking that Lena and Byron "must have been" where "they lynched that nigger," returns the central events of the novel to our attention (497). Rather than neatly marking the conclusion of the narrative, that is, the novel's coda underscores the manner in which its core problems can neither be resolved nor ignored. In the conventional detective story, crime and injustice are the subjects of public concern and ultimately of public accord, a quality emphasized by the fact that no significant character will appear in the narrative who is not intensely aware of the murder at the novel's center and who is not directly affected by the story's resolution. For Faulkner's furniture dealer, by contrast, the killings of Joanna Burden and Joe Christmas are matters of indifferent gossip, and yet they are also so important that they are the first things he thinks of when he hears the name Jefferson. Racial violence, the passage implies, is at once outside his range of attention and of fundamental importance to him. And the manner in which he is both affected by and unrelated to the novel's core events can be thought of as typical of the complex construction of Faulkner's novel, which, with its recurrent flashbacks and digressions, and its elaborate formal parallels, constantly suggests and frustrates the impression that it forms an integrated whole. Put simply, the most obvious difference between *Light in August* and the detective story is that Faulkner's novel lacks not only a true detective, but the moral, epistemological, and formal clarity that characterizes the mystery novel. If most popular crime stories work as Rotella suggests—linking surface and deep crimes and using the investigation of the former to create the impression of an aesthetic and conceptual control of the latter—Faulkner's major novels both gesture in this direction and yet appear unable to bring the two frames of present crime and historical injustice into useful alignment.

The imperfect parallel between Faulkner's novel and popular crime fiction can be seen in a more precise fashion, I think, by noting the extensive similarities between *Light and August* and *Knight's Gambit*, one of the two books in which Faulkner made a conscious attempt to write what he called "more or less detective stories" and where he assembled a series of narratives that revealingly skirt without directly taking up the charged issues at the center of *Light in August*.[13] Indeed, on a nearly point-by-point basis, the six stories included in *Knight's Gambit*, which, with the exception of the closing title story were written for massmarket magazines over the course of the thirties and forties, present a revealing countertext to *Light in August*, as if Faulkner were continually returning to the preoccupations dredged up by the novel and handling them in a formally delimited genre toward which he felt both attraction and disdain. Each of the slight narratives in *Knight's Gambit* features a crime investigated by Yoknapatawpha County Attorney Gavin Stevens, and each like *Sanctuary* and *Light in August* makes that crime an index of Yoknapatawpha's troubling integration into the commercial networks of industrial society. ("Someday," Gavin Stevens notes in the course of one investigation, "all the main roads in Mississippi would be paved like the streets in Memphis and every family in America would own a car.")[14] As in *Light in August*, too, Faulkner dramatizes the dangers of urban-ized society by introducing figures whose criminal histories are exacer-bated by mysterious and racially uncertain parentage: Buck Thorpe, for example, a "black-complected" roisterer who "had appeared overnight from nowhere, a brawler, a gambler," and a bootlegger (70, 59). Just as he does by making Byron Bunch a foil to Lucas Burch, moreover, Faulkner answers the dangers of apparent outlanders like Thorpe by placing them in direct counterpoint to poor hill farmers, who assume, by contrast, the qualities of a deep-rooted yeomanry. Indeed, *Knight's Gambit* includes in one such figure—Stonewall Jackson Fentry of the story "Tomorrow"—a character who quite directly rewrites the tale of Byron Bunch. A poor hill farmer forced by necessity to move into town and take employment in a mill, Fentry looks up one day and instantly falls in love with a pregnant young woman who is pretending to "hunt for the husband that had deserted her" (69). His most important difference from Bunch is that Fentry is able to convince his beloved to return to his family farm, where, after delivering her child, she finally marries the stoic farmer on her deathbed and leaves her widowed husband to raise the child on his own.

The most interesting point of comparison between *Light in August* and *Knight's Gambit*, however, may be the two figures who most directly present parallels to the artist himself. As Ross Macdonald once noted, it is among the privileges of the detective story to create in its protagonists a fantasy of the writer as hero—an "equivalent for the artist intellectual" who not only represents qualities the author most admires and wishes he possessed himself, but who is thereby able to present an idealized image of the power of literary intelligence to create meaning out of the apparent confusion of his world.[15] Gavin Stevens fits that part in *Knight's Gambit* all but directly, having stepped forward from the marginal role he first interestingly played in *Light in August*. In that first incarnation, as in his subsequent appearance in *Go Down, Moses*, Stevens is a minor and apparently ineffectual figure, and the small part he plays can be taken to mark the moral triviality of Southern liberalism before the enor-mity of racial injustice.[16] In *Knight's Gambit*, however, Stevens moves into the foreground, where, as the novel's detective figure, he becomes a representative of canniness, intellectual power, and, still more, paternal benevolence. When we first encounter Stevens in *Knight's Gambit*, we are told that he is equally at home "discuss[ing] Einstein with college professors" and in spending "whole afternoons among the squatting men against the walls of country stores, talking to them in their idiom" (16). He is, in short, a figure for the hope that critical intelligence, tolerance, and sympathy can bridge class division and resolve social conflict. Only Stevens, needless to say, fully understands Stonewall Jackson Fentry.

Though he is no detective himself, Gail Hightower represents a distinctly unsuccessful version of the fantasy that Gavin Stevens embodies in *Knight's Gambit*. Faulkner's conception of *Light in August* began with Hightower, and, but for the coda of the furniture dealer's story of Lena and Byron, the novel ends with him as well and with his unique, if finally failed, effort to see the characters and events of the novel in a meaningful and complete pattern. Indeed, in nearly every respect Hightower looks like an unhappy mirror to the Stevens of *Knight's Gambit*. Stevens is confident and voluble in his explanation of crime and its relation to the history of Yoknapatawpha County; Hightower remains confused and unable to articulate his intuitions about violence into a coherent sentence. ("'Why it's . . . . . .,'" Hightower thinks, as he perceives the apparently fateful doubling between Joe Christmas and Percy Grimm, "The one who. . . . . . into the kitchen where . . . . . killed" [492].") Stevens is joined to the hill farmers outside Jefferson by mutual care and respect; Hightower's conversations with Byron Bunch are secretive and finally unrewarding to both men. Though Stevens is, like Hightower, a solitary and eccentric intellectual, his learning is apparently respected by his community. Hightower's taste for Tennyson and his unsuccessful trade as a purveyor of art lessons and Christmas cards reflects, by contrast, as Harold Bloom suggests, an image of effete gentility.

Even Hightower's confrontation with Percy Grimm has a more appealing counterpart in *Knight's Gambit*. Stevens's nephew Chick Mallinson plays in that collection a version of the sidekick role so common in classic detective fiction. He is Stevens's Watson, or better yet the Archie Goodwin to Stevens's Nero Wolfe, the mundane counterpart whose friendship negotiates the hero's relation to ordinary sociability and whose physical prowess complements the detective's cognitive gifts. In *Light in August*, by comparison, the intellectual and the warrior confront each other without any meaningful congress, just as the gentleman and the poor hill farmer are, in the breakdown of the friendship of Hightower and Bunch, finally divided. Strikingly, although he provides them with significantly different class backgrounds, Faulkner underscores the comparability of Chick and Percy Grimm by giving both young men the same sense of martial belatedness. Each experiences "the terrible tragedy," as Faulkner describes it in *Light in August*, "of having been born not alone too late but not late enough" to escape knowledge of a conflict in which he might have proved his manhood (450). Each boy is a would-be soldier angry at being too young to participate in European war, and each as a result is led to take advantage of the same federal military policy. "The

new civilian-military act which save[s]" Grimm in *Light in August*—the
National Defense Act of 1920—is also the legislation that created the
ROTC program in which young Chick participates without satisfaction
in *Knight's Gambit* before he finally enrolls and serves as a pilot during
World War II (*LIA* 450). Unlike Grimm, Chick does not mistake the
"pastless metal lozenges" of the ROTC uniform for the uniforms that
"real officers wore," but he is similar enough to his counterpart that we
might plausibly say Grimm is a would-be Chick who, lacking Chick's
stature as a child of the Southern gentry, also lacks a Stevens to lead him
toward maturity and toward "the realm of valor and risk" Chick desires
and finally achieves (*KG* 133).

In every respect, in sum, *Knight's Gambit* presents a contrast to the
social fragmentation and narrative complexity emphasized by *Light
in August*, providing instead an image of social cohesion—a vision of
Yoknapatawpha County as an "agrarian and equestrian land" in which
minor injustice and social conflict, occasioned especially by the intrusion
of outlanders, can be readily negotiated (113). Even the most apparently friendless and orphaned person in *Knight's Gambit* turns out to
have "inherited [a sense of identity] from the earth, the soil" and to
benefit from a deep bond with Gavin Stevens (35–36). The difference
between the two books in this respect can be understood at one level as
a generic distinction. The difference between the work of middlebrow
commercial entertainment, on the one hand, and the novel of modernist
ambition, on the other, we might say, amounts to the difference between
a text built around the lawyer whose wisdom and intelligence grant him
the ability to mediate a stable society and one featuring a failed minister
whose dissatisfaction is echoed throughout his divided community. Put
another way, it is the difference between a story stressing the moral and
epistemological confidence suited to the detective story and one about
what Hightower calls spiritual "hunger" (488).

° ° °

That hunger, I think it's worth emphasizing, is arguably the central
theme of *Light in August* and a close complement to the novel's other
main preoccupation with racial difference. With the exception of Lena
Grove, all of the main characters of *Light in August* and many of its
minor figures are driven by religious commitment and intense spiritual
yearning. Those qualities surface in the theological musings of Hightower, the brute zealotry of McEachern, the lunatic Calvinism of Doc
Hines, and the racial soteriology passed down from Calvin Burden to his
granddaughter Joanna. Although less directly expressed, they are equally
evident in the ascetic devotion of Byron Bunch and in Joe Christmas's

apparent antinomian determination to invade the house of the lord in order to send his sacrilegious version of the "good news" to Jefferson (325). Not only is the text rife with biblical allusions and with the ambiguous Christian symbolism evident in Joe's name, virtually everyone we encounter in *Light in August* is compelled by an unsatisfied obsession with the sacred.

In emphasizing that theme, Faulkner placed his novel among the broader tendency evident throughout modernist fiction to align avant-garde art with a spiritual commitment that appeared otherwise fading in the modern world. As Pericles Lewis points out, the theme is repeatedly raised in a wide range of novels—by James, Proust, Joyce, and Kafka, among others—that confront disenchanted nonbelievers like Hightower with implicitly premodern religious practices that appear by contrast to remain rooted in folkways untouched by doubt. Much of the pathos of modernist fiction, in other words, hinges on the meeting between disillusioned artists and intellectuals, on the one hand, and religious primitives, on the other. Faulkner's admirer Cleanth Brooks articulated this logic in comments he made shortly after the publication of *Light in August*. "The qualities which art shares with religion," Brooks argued, "are just those which liberal Protestantism through its imitation of science has lost." His remark might be taken to encapsulate all that Hightower, the exemplification of weak art and thin belief, comes to realize he has surrendered.[17]

By the same token, however, Faulkner more directly placed his novel amid the intense religious conflicts that divided American society in the years during which he came to artistic maturity. Brooks's own alignment of art and religion appeared in one entry in that controversy—in an essay lamenting the prospect that "liberal Protestantism" was "secularizing itself out of existence" and urging the nation's religious leaders to discover some of the spiritual enthusiasm that had been displayed in the recently prominent Fundamentalist movement. "Civilizations are founded, not on ethical societies," Brooks urged, "but on religions." He was but one in a trend of modernist intellectuals who, struck by the fervor of Fundamentalism, discovered in its "cruder aspects" marks of an authenticity that seemed all but lost to dominant religious and social institutions and who urged that religious and cultural elites seek to rediscover that authenticity.[18]

The Reverend Gail Hightower, *Light in August*'s intellectual, comes to a similar observation in the ultimate spiritual crisis in which he confronts his own failings and discovers their implicit relation to the patterns of religious violence that result in the murder of Joe Christmas. "He sees himself a shadowy figure among shadows . . . with a kind of false optimism and egoism," and he comes to regard his failing as a minister and husband as typical of a larger crisis of organized religion:

> It seems to him that he has seen it all the while: that that which is destroying the Church is not the outward groping of those within it nor the inward groping of those without, but the professionals who control it and who have removed the bells from its steeples. He seems to see them, endless, without order, empty, symbolical, bleak, skypointed not with ecstasy or passion but in adjuration, threat, and doom. . . . "And I accepted that," he thinks. . . . "Nay, I did worse: . . . I served it by using it to forward my own desire. I came here where faces full of bafflement and hunger and eagerness waited for me, waiting to believe; I did not see them." (487)

For the Gavin Stevens of *Knight's Gambit*, the central question raised by the collection's various tales of crime and justice concerns the ability of the norms of Yoknapatawpha's "agrarian and equestrian" society to accommodate the energies of an increasingly commercialized society—a resolution that, in each case, occurs without difficulty because of Stevens's penetration and sagacity. At least for Gail Hightower, by contrast, the violent events at the core of *Light in August* point to the different problem of his people's unmet spiritual needs. That question positions Faulkner's novel, as it did Cleanth Brooks, alongside a contemporaneous religious controversy toward which it shows revealing ambivalence. For, not unlike Brooks, Faulkner manages in Hightower's eloquent self-condemnation to deftly position himself apart from both the Fundamentalist and liberal strains that contended over the Protestant churches in the 1920s, even as he adopts much of the Fundamentalist critique of organized religion.[19]

In fact, Hightower's meditation subtly combines elements of both liberal and Fundamentalist rhetoric, yet nevertheless gives greater weight to the complaints of the Fundamentalists. On the one hand, for example, Hightower's description of the Church professionals who direct "adjuration, threat and doom" toward their congregants resembles the liberal charge that Fundamentalist religion distorted Christianity by rendering it "scholastic, static, [and] authoritarian."[20] But Hightower's stronger self-indictment, and his disgusted realization of his own "false optimism and egoism," still more nearly echoes the Fundamentalist complaint against the dangers of religious liberalism. Like their enemies among liberal Protestants, the era's Fundamentalists worried that Christian beliefs were being reduced to "empty shells."[21] But the Fundamentalists saw those dangers especially in the way that religious Liberalism allegedly transferred devotion from sacred authority to secular visions of social progress—so that religion became simply another way of describing the human "power of molding situations to man's desire."[22] As Bradley Longfield summarizes the charge, Fundamentalists indicted in liberal Protestantism "a persistent accent on the immanence of God in human affairs, the goodness and value of humanity," and an "evolutionary" view of social progress.[23] Hightower's late discovery that "it was the town he desired to live in and not the church . . . he wished to serve," and his assimilation of this desire to an unjustifiably optimistic and self-centered view of the world, closely resembles the Fundamentalist fear that liberal Protestantism had lost the essential character of religion itself and become, as Cleanth Brooks warned, "merely a sociopolitical program."[24]

By drawing in this manner on the rhetoric of both Fundamentalist and liberal Protestantism, Faulkner in effect allows Hightower in his late moment of conscience to direct a pox toward both houses, even as he gives greater warrant to the complaints of the Fundamentalists. Such an attitude might well have seemed appealing in 1931, when the leaders of Hightower's Presbyterian Church had recently called on a process of bureaucratic negotiation to patch up the bitter disputes that divided them throughout the twenties.[25] In response, the populist fervor that drove Fundamentalism in the twenties would soon shift from the struggles over the Church's national leadership out into local congregations and new, unofficial institutions and unorganized religious practices—spiritual activities of the sort, that is, portrayed by Faulkner in the self-sufficient zealotry of McEachern, the eccentric fervor of Hines, the solitary devotion of Byron Bunch, and the personal torment of Joe Christmas and Joanna Burden.[26] There was good reason at the time, in other words, for a minister like Hightower to suspect that the leaders of both the liberal and Fundamentalist camps in the Presbyterian Church hierarchy had effectively conspired to neglect the popular desires of their congregants and to be sensitive to the fact that alternative religious practices were arising to meet popular demands.

At a deeper level, perhaps, Hightower's hybrid rhetoric in this passage might be taken to imply that in their mutual antagonism each of the major religious movements of the early twentieth century had betrayed a genuine spiritual need by exclusively emphasizing one aspect of Christian tradition—Fundamentalism stressing authority and orthodoxy, and Liberalism preferring *caritas* and brotherhood. Something along the lines of such a complaint might be suggested by the way *Light in August* implicitly juxtaposes the rigid authoritarianism of a believer like McEachern or Doc Hines to the ineffectual pity and half-hearted generosity displayed by Hightower, each figure appearing in turn as an ultimately barren caricature of the belief he professes. It may be more strongly implied by the ways in which, in the epiphany that reveals to him the failure of organized religion, Hightower comes to perceive the authentic spirituality he believes he has lost. Lamenting the mistake he has made in presenting his congregants with the vision of "a swaggering and unchastened bravo killed . . . in a temporary hiatus of his own avocation of killing," Hightower regrets that he failed to offer them "the crucified shape of pity and love" (488). His language here again synthesizes the concerns of Fundamentalists and Liberals. For, it implicitly stresses the inextricability of the *caritas* that liberal Protestantism viewed as the core of Christianity, on the one hand, and the divine wrath and atonement for sin that Fundamentalism worshipped in the crucifixion, on the other. It seems important to Hightower's late revelation, in other words, that Jesus both exemplify pity and love, on the one hand, *and* that he had been crucified, on the other.

The synthesis implicit in his phrasing is especially striking because no issue was more central to the religious battles of the twenties than the apparent conflict between the divine love apparent in the life of Jesus and the divine anger at human sinfulness thought to be sated by his crucifixion. Leaders among the liberal faction worried that Fundamentalists sought to impose "a special theory of the atonement—that the blood of our Lord, shed in a substitutionary death, placates an alienated Deity"—and they worried in particular that the Fundamentalist emphasis on atonement would sacrifice the "magnanimity and liberality and tolerance of spirit" that they thought the true core of Christianity.[27] Fundamentalists and their sympathizers, for their part, worried that Liberals sought "to repeal the old ordinances of sacrifice and ritual."[28] "All that believe in Him," a prominent Fundamentalist leader declared summarizing this central conviction, "are justified on the ground of His shed blood."[29]

Hightower's culminating religious vision appears to combine both these aspects of Christianity—to demand both "liberality and tolerance of spirit" *and* the "ordinances of sacrifice and ritual"—and to suggest that the various professionals of the organized church have abandoned the full meaning of their religion and perhaps that this distortion is typical of the larger fragmentation and spiritual impoverishment of modern society. Shortly after *Light in August* was published, Theodor Adorno described the relation of avant-garde art to mass culture, and the way each bore "the stigmata of capitalism," by referring to the two cultural spheres as "torn halves of an integral freedom, to which, however, they don't add up." Neither high art nor popular entertainment, Adorno stressed, could be legitimately sacrificed to the other, or enjoyed in its own right, or somehow combined without a sense of loss and incompletion that testified to the larger dislocations of capitalist society.[30] In its juxtaposition of a liberal Christianity of pity and mercy and a Fundamentalist religion of vengeance and atonement, *Light in August* similarly provides an account of the division of elite intelligence from popular desire and of their mutual dependence, antagonism, and insufficiency. We encounter in *Light in August* many characters driven by a righteous desire to mete out punishment and a few examples of an ultimately ineffectual willingness to extend pity. But in each case Faulkner appears to emphasize the partiality and inadequacy of the impulse he depicts. Thus, the novel confronts Hightower's failed effort to save Joe Christmas from lynching with the vengeance demanded by Percy Grimm, who in his outrage is said to approach the failed minister with the voice of "a young priest" (464). The abuse and humiliation Hightower suffers in the encounter is cast, moreover, as a justified and fateful devastation of the false pride he later realizes has been the keynote of his life. "There is one thing more reserved for him," we are told of Hightower as the failed minister indulges the sense of "exultation" that he experiences after delivering Lena Grove's child (414, 413). That one thing, of course, is his encounter with the brute reality of racial violence.

Similarly, the novel pairs, as "strophe and antistrophe," Doc Hines's "prophetlike" desire to destroy his grandson with his wife's yearning to save Joe and to nurture the child she confuses with him (376, 371). Their paired visions are described as equally hallucinatory: "something performed in a region without dimension by people without blood" (376). Less directly, the novel implicitly compares McEachern with Joanna Burden, much as it juxtaposes McEachern's violent coercion to his wife's sympathetic enticement. Each welcomes Joe Christmas into his or her home and proves eager, for religiously inspired reasons, to ignore the racial boundaries that organize the society around them.[31] But, despite the contrast between McEachern's punitive Calvinism and Burden's reformist Calvinism, both believers discover not only that their salvific visions cannot affect Joe's fate, but that those very visions lead ultimately to the believers' own death at the hands of the man they would save.

The pattern appears in its most explicit form in the meditation in which Hightower, separated from his Church and hearing its blended voices from afar, contrasts his former congregants' "stern and implacable" devotion to a spirituality of "revenge" with his own wish that they could discover an alternative religion of "pity" (367, 368). Both the Christianity of mercy and the Christianity of sin and punishment appear, here and throughout, as counterparts that, in their division, are also alienated, partial, and inadequate.[32] Interestingly, Hightower's former congregants in their demand for vengeance and Hightower himself in his ultimate, failed attempt to shield Joe Christmas are described in comparable ways. Hightower perceives his former congregants' eagerness to lynch as "terrible, terrible, terrible" (368). But, Faulkner describes Hightower himself with the same term when Percy Grimm invades the failed minister's home. "He too with his bald head and his big pale face streaked with blood was terrible" (464). Both represent a spiritual desperation of sublime extremity.

◦ ◦ ◦

Seen in this light, in short, *Light in August* offers a vision of the fragmentation and impoverishment of religion, and it presents the terrible intensity of its characters' spiritual hunger as both a mark of their desperation and as an example of their yearning for a religious experience of a sort that the modern world appears to foreclose. Viewing Faulkner's novel from this perspective, however, presents a challenge to a predominant understanding of the text. In the view of the novel I have sketched here, *Light in August* turns on a complaint, of a sort common among modernist artists, against the disenchantment of faith and more generally against the social dislocation that accompanied the modernization of traditional society. Emphasizing the distorted forms of religious practice that flourish in modern society generally, the novel directs particular animus toward educated nonbelievers like Hightower whose "egoism" leads them to substitute secular desires for authentic belief.

Perhaps the most common view of the novel, however, takes a contrary stance and reads it as, in effect, an implicit plea for the increased liberalization of Southern religion and of the system of Jim Crow segregation with which religious belief was entwined. "Fundamentalist Protestantism," Daniel Joseph Singal contends, for example, is "the root cause" of the tragic events at the heart of the novel. Charles Reagan Wilson similarly claims that *Light in August* depicts "the pathology of Southern civil religion." In perhaps the most fully considered version of this argument, Leigh Ann Duck asserts that *Light in August* "presents an absolute devotion to a divine authority as both a model and a vector for support of a white supremacist status quo."[33] In effect, such readings seek to align *Light in August* with the secularizing and reformist view of religion proposed by liberal Protestantism and, more broadly, with the type of liberal approach to social injustice that informs the conventional detective story.[34] The problem with religion in *Light in August*, Duck thus explains, is that it interferes with the "empathy," "critical self-awareness," and "rational thought" that should lead the characters "to question racial oppression." Religious belief, she complains, frustrates their ability "to forge a more habitable perspective on life."[35]

And, yet, if the sentiments attributed to Gail Hightower in the concluding pages of *Light in August* are any guide, the people of Jefferson
neither seek nor need habitable perspectives on life. They desire, as
Hightower suggests, a world with bells in its steeples. Nor is it most
accurate to say that Faulkner depicts their yearnings for a restoration of
the sacred as either an ideological support for the institutions of white
supremacy or as a challenge to the institutions of Jim Crow. Indeed,
the one form of conventional Southern religious practice we are curiously never shown by the novel is the use of religious authority to justify
racial subordination or to defend the existing social order.[36] This is not
to say that *Light in August* does not reveal the spirituality it depicts
to be thoroughly enmeshed in and obsessively preoccupied with white
supremacy. It does. But rather than portray religious belief as an ideological justification for a dominant "status quo," Faulkner instead casts
the spiritual hunger of his characters as a desperate response to their
conviction that they live in a society that is at once organized by racial
segregation and yet nevertheless constantly challenged by the problem
that Joe Christmas dramatizes—that racial boundaries are arbitrary and
unreliable. In the lunacy of Doc Hines, in Joanna Burden's theology
of racial uplift, and in Joe Christmas's own antinomian fervor, as in the
implacable vengeance of Hightower's congregants and his terrible pity,
we see people who are tormented by the fact that they live in an interracial society. Their spiritual hunger appears less as a cause or support
of white supremacy than as a consequence of racial anxiety and, in this
fashion, as their response to a society whose instabilities appear to be
intensifying under the increasing pressure of commercial modernization. The implication, in short, is not so much that believers are given to
maintaining the status quo as that the spiritually zealous are desperate
to believe because they have no sense of a secure status quo.

One way to see this aspect of *Light in August* is to return again to a
comparison of the novel and *Knight's Gambit* and to note that, in the
latter, where Faulkner is able to make use of the detective story form,
the issues of racial difference and the problems of racial segregation are
almost entirely absent. "Negroes" and "niggers" make brief appearances
in marginal and servile roles throughout *Knight's Gambit*, but the collection includes no analogue to Joe Christmas, and there is no significant problem of racial conflict or miscegenation raised anywhere in the
volume. It is in this collection of slight detective stories, in other words,
that Faulkner depicts a dominant and stable order of racial supremacy.
To the extent *Knight's Gambit* raises the intimation of what Rotella calls
"deep structural wrongs," the issues all turn around the potential dangers of class tension among whites, especially as reflected in the possible

anger and resentment of the farming poor. But these, Faulkner suggests, are all small matters that can be easily handled through the mediation provided by Gavin Stevens. In *Light in August*, matters are not so
straightforward.

The two texts' different views of Southern society are marked in particular by the two intellectual figures who, in different ways, organize
Knight's Gambit and *Light in August*. For, as the books' resident intellectuals, each provides us with a framework through which we can grasp
the key problems of the texts and through whose conceptual and geographical peregrinations we can map the important terrain they cover.
Over the course of *Knight's Gambit*, Gavin Stevens travels repeatedly
out from Jefferson to the surrounding hill country, in order to meet poor
farmers with whom he feels powerful "sentimental" and customary obligations; there he discovers the descendants of the white "pioneer[s]"
who, he explains, have "founded" Yoknapatwpha County (48). Gail Hightower's sole journeys away from his home take him by contrast, as we
have seen, to the former Bundren plantation—where he is led inescapably to encounter the racially integrated history of slavery. Journeying
back to that area after having successfully delivered Lena Grove's child,
Hightower thinks of himself as a revived man, and he imagines "luck and
life returned to these barren and ruined acres" (406–7). "She will have
to have others," Hightower thinks of Lena and her child. "That will be
her life, her destiny. The good stock peopling in tranquil obedience to it
the good earth" (406). Especially given his previous attempt to assist a
black woman in childbirth, an effort that culminates in the death of the
child and in Hightower's complete alienation from his community, the
vision he indulges here appears to sketch a narrative of historical transformation. With the birth of Lena's child, Hightower seems to envision
the displacement of a violent, conflicted, and death-bound interracial
society by the rise of a new white yeomanry to which his own guidance
will be central. He imagines, that is, something like the world of *Knight's
Gambit* and sees himself in something like the role of Gavin Stevens in
that book.

Significantly, however, Hightower finds himself unable to imagine
that rebirth without also resuscitating in his imagination the slave society at the center of Jefferson's history: "it seems to him that he can see,
feel, about him the ghosts of rich fields, and of the rich fecund black
life of the quarters, the mellow shouts, the presence of fecund women,
the prolific naked children in the dust before the doors; and the big
house again, noisy, loud with the treble shouts of the generations" (407).
Interestingly, Gavin Stevens is said at one point in *Knight's Gambit* to
be "trying to bring the notions of 1860 into the politics of the nineteen

hundreds," an admiring description that refers solely to his courtly sense of honor (41). Hightower threatens to bring another feature of the antebellum plantocracy into the twentieth century, and significantly he seems unable to imagine sexual reproduction without automatically envisioning a fecundity that mingles black and white—the "prolific" offspring of the "quarters" and the "generations" of "the big house." Like nearly every other character in the novel, in short, Hightower finds himself continually reminded that he lives in an interracial world whose permeable boundaries cause him confusion and anguish.

By contrast, such problems are not only absent in *Knight's Gambit*, they are almost directly shunted aside. If, as I remarked earlier, the story of Stonewall Jackson Fentry rewrites the tale of Byron Bunch, it does so nearly explicitly so as to remove the possibility with which sexual license almost always seems to be associated in Faulkner, the peril of miscegenation. When Jackson Fentry temporarily adopts the child of his widow and brings the infant to the hills, he removes the orphan from the urban environment that is so racially troubling in Faulkner's work, and when he is ultimately forced to turn over the child to his wife's brothers, we are informed that those family members have already ascertained that the unnamed woman was previously married—thus removing the possibility that, as with Joe Christmas, his antecedents will be unknown. When we ultimately discover this child has grown to become the problematic Buck Thorpe whom I mentioned earlier, the circle becomes complete. Though Thorpe initially seems, like Joe Christmas or Lucas Burch, a threateningly "kinless" outsider, he is finally revealed to be a person with a deep family past. That this family appears to include only men (a suggestion emphasized by the death of his mother in childbirth) underlines the point. By contrast to *Light in August*, there is no miscegenation in *Knight's Gambit*, among other reasons, because there are virtually no women and almost no possibility of sexual reproduction suggested in the book. The relationship of Jackson Fentry and his adopted child, the lineage of the Thorpe brothers, and the idealized fellowship of Stevens and his nephew Chick are but a handful of the many places in the book where Faulkner imagines familial groupings that somehow manage to include only white men.

The difference between *Knight's Gambit* and *Light in August*, in other words, is not only the difference between middlebrow entertainment and serious art, or between the vision of a coherent culture and the drama of social fragmentation, or between the epistemological and moral confidence of the detective story and the spiritual hunger of the modernist novel; it is also the difference between a world where racial mixture is all but impossible to imagine and one where miscegenation is a constant threat. Only in the former world, it seems, can Faulkner conceive of injustice subject to the kinds of mediation and amelioration that the detective story emphasizes.

In *Light in August*, by contrast, resolution comes only through racial violence, and that violence it is worth emphasizing is presented in strongly spiritual, even cultic terms. It is, of course, the lynching of Joe Christmas that removes him from the world of Jefferson and that, relieving the manifold tensions that energize the novel, makes of him a quasi-deific figure and a totem for a restored racial order. As sacrificial victim, Christmas rises, "soaring into their memories forever and ever" where his presence will underlie all that the people of Jefferson do in the future (465). That totemic role, it should be recalled, is the result of a killing that Faulkner depicts not as an "emotional barbecue" or as the squalid act of brutality we might expect, but as an act of sacred violence in something that resembles a primitive ritual:

> Grimm turned and ran across the yard and into the house where the old disgraced minister lived alone, and the three men followed, rushing in the hall, pausing, bringing with them into its stale and cloistral dimness something of the savage summer sunlight which they had just left.
>
> It was upon them, of them: its shameless savageness. Out of it their faces seemed to glare with bodiless suspension as though from haloes, as they stooped and raised Hightower, his face bleeding, from the floor where Christmas, running up the hall, his raised and armed and manacled hands full of glare and glitter light lightning bolts, so that he resembled a vengeful and furious god pronouncing a doom, had struck him down. (463)

With its commitment to the virtues of civil society, the conventional detective story is driven to convert spiritual mystery into empirical mysteries and to view that transformation as a model for the way that social conflict can be mediated and injustice ameliorated. In *Light in August* Faulkner does something like the reverse, rendering brute murder as a sacrificial rite that resolves for a disordered community and a group of desperate individuals a paralyzing sense of spiritual crisis.[37] If modernity strips the bells from the altars, for the people of *Light in August* racial violence promises to restore them. Seen from this vantage, Faulkner's novel provides a powerful account of lynching not primarily because the novel criticizes intolerance or portrays the limits of bigotry, but because it dramatizes the psychological need and spiritual hunger that legitimized racial oppression. By the same token, it suggests that something more than the virtues of tolerance, openness, and civility honored by liberalism and celebrated by the detective story would be required to challenge the Southern system of white supremacy.

NOTES

1. William Faulkner, *Light in August:* The Corrected Text (New York: Vintage, 1990), 317; subsequent citations given parenthetically as *LIA*.

2. On Anse Bundren's gesture, see Sean McCann, "Does Anse Bundren Love His Wife? Gifts, Promises, and Obligations in *As I Lay Dying*," in *Approaches to Teaching Faulkner's "As I Lay Dying*," ed. Patrick O' Donnell and Lynda Zwinger (New York: MLA Press, 2011); on Ike McCaslin's reading, see Richard Godden and Noel Polk, "Reading the Ledgers," *Mississippi Quarterly* 55 (2002): 301–59.

3. Harold Bloom, *Genius: A Mosaic of One Hundred Exemplary Creative Minds* (New York: Warner Books, 2002), 566.

4. Michael Millgate suggests that *Light in August* resembles "the detective story as intruded on by Greek tragedy." Millgate, Introduction, *New Essays on Light in August* (New York: Cambridge University Press, 1987), 5; Greg Forter considers Faulkner's debt to popular narrative in greater depth in "Faulkner, Trauma, and the Uses of Crime Fiction," *A Companion to William Faulkner*, ed. Richard C. Moreland (Malden, Mass.: Blackwell, 2007), 373–93.

5. Jean Stein, "The Art of Fiction No. 12: William Faulkner," *Paris Review* 12 (1956): 21.

6. See Karen Halttunen, *Murder Most Foul: The Killer and the American Gothic Imagination* (Cambridge: Harvard University Press, 1998), 172–207.

7. William Ruehlmann, *Saint with a Gun: The Unlawful American Private Eye* (New York: NYU Press, 1984).

8. See Sean McCann, *Gumshoe America: Hard-Boiled Crime Fiction and the Rise and Fall of New Deal Liberalism* (Durham: Duke University Press, 2000), 1–38 and, for a related view, Leonard Cassuto, *Hard-Boiled Sentimentality: The Secret History of American Crime Stories* (New York: Columbia University Press, 2009).

9. The ritual features of the detective story, and the depth of its preoccupation with the "conflict between good and evil," were first pointed out by W. H. Auden in his brilliant essay "The Guilty Vicarage: Notes on the Detective Story, by an Addict." *Harper's Magazine* 196 (May 1948), 406–12, 406. Since then, variations on Auden's insight have been repeated many times. See, e.g., David Lehman, *The Perfect Murder: A Study in Detection* (1987; Ann Arbor: University of Michigan Press, 2001).

10. Halttunen.

11. Richard Rorty, *Contingency, Irony, and Solidarity* (New York: Cambridge University Press, 1989); Judith N. Shklar, *Ordinary Vices* (Cambridge: Harvard University Press, 1985), 7–44.

12. Carlo Rotella, *Good with Their Hands: Boxers, Bluesmen, and Other Characters from the Rust Belt* (Berkeley: University of California Press, 2002), 119.

13. *Selected Letters of William Faulkner*, ed. Joseph Blotner (New York: Random House, 1977), 280.

14. William Faulkner, *Knight's Gambit* (New York: New American Library, 1950), 72; subsequent citations given parenthetically as *KG*.

15. Ross Macdonald, "The Writer as Detective Hero," in *Detective Fiction: A Collection of Critical Essays*, ed. Robin W. Winks (Englewood Cliffs, N.J.: Prentice-Hall, 1980), 180.

16. See Noel Polk, "Man in the Middle: Faulkner and the Southern White Moderate," *Children of the Dark House: Text and Context in Faulkner* (Jackson: University Press of Mississippi, 1996), 219–41.

17. Cleanth Brooks, "A Plea to the Protestant Churches," in *Who Owns America? A New Declaration of Independence*, ed. Herbert Agar (Boston: Houghton Mifflin, 1936), 331. Pericles Lewis, "Churchgoing in the Modern Novel," *Modernism/Modernity* 11.4 (2004) 669–94. For a related view of *Light in August* in particular, see Virginia V. Hlavsa,

"The Crucifixion in *Light in August*: Suspending Rules at the Post," in *Faulkner and Religion*, ed. Doreen Fowler and Ann J. Abadie (Jackson: University Press of Mississippi, 1991), 127–39.

18. Brooks, 331, 323, 332; on the tendency of modernist intellectuals during the 1920s to hesitantly endorse Fundamentalist religion against liberal secularism, see William R. Hutchison, *The Modernist Impulse in American Protestantism* (Durham: Duke University Press, 1992), 257–87.

19. See, Bradley J. Longfield, *The Presbyterian Controversy: Fundamentalists, Modernists, and Moderates* (New York: Oxford University Press, 1991).

20. Charles Clayton Morrison, qtd. at George M. Marsden, *Fundamentalism and American Culture*, 2nd ed. (New York: Oxford University Press, 2006), 175.

21. W. B. Riley, "The Faith of the Fundamentalists," *Current History* 26 (June 1927), 437, 435.

22. Brooks, 330.

23. Longfield, *The Presbyterian Controversy*, 19.

24. Brooks, 325.

25. Marsden, *Fundamentalism and American Culture*, 176–98.

26. As Charles Reagan Wilson notes, this tendency was especially pronounced in the South because of the region's prominent evangelical tradition. Wilson, "William Faulkner and the Southern Religious Culture," in *Faulkner and Religion*, ed. Doreen Fowler and Ann J. Abadie (Jackson: University Press of Mississippi, 1991), 21–43.

27. Harry Emerson Fosdick, "Shall the Fundamentalists Win?," in *The Christian Work* (10 June 1922), 717.

28. John Crowe Ransom, *God without Thunder: An Unorthodox Defense of Orthodoxy* (New York: Harcourt Brace, 1930), 35.

29. Riley, "Faith of the Fundamentalists," 435.

30. Adorno to Walter Benjamin (18 March 1936), in Adorno et al., *Aesthetics and Politics: The Key Texts of the Classic Debate within German Marxism* (1977; New York: Verso, 1980), 123.

31. Unlike most other characters, McEachern appears to be aware of, yet indifferent to, Joe's uncertain parentage—saying of Joe that "he will grow up to fear God . . . despite his origin"—and to be committed to a religious ideology that explicitly transcends genealogy (143). "In their rigid abnegation of all compromise," Faulkner says of the embattled McEachern and Joe, they are "more alike than actual blood could have made them" (*LIA* 148). Though it shows him to be brutal, the novel gives us no reason to doubt McEachern's commitment to making Joe a member of his family or to question his apparent belief that religious devotion trumps parentage. Notably, however, Joe appears determined to assert the importance of his uncertain racial origins. Despite arriving at the McEachern farm at the age of five and having lived with the McEacherns for thirteen years, when he meets Bobbi, Joe declares that his name is "not McEachern. . . . It's Christmas" (184).

32. In the tortured defense of lynching that he sent to the Memphis *Commercial Appeal* near the time of the composition of *Light in August*, Faulkner draws on a comparable logic—arguing that lynching is practiced by a "race which holds with the Bible that justice is a matter of violent and immediate retribution on the person of the sinner," but also suggesting that this attitude is somehow consistent with the stance of a "sentimentalist" who regards the minor crimes allegedly committed by African Americans with benign condescension. Both retribution and "sentimentality" appear in this letter as the unjust and distorted (not "balanced"), yet understandable reactions of whites to living in an interracial society that by its nature ("with the population being what it is") is unjust and

distorted. Lynching, Faulkner implies in this letter, is an inevitably failed and exaggerated, but defensible effort to restore justice to an unjust society. "We have been the prey of opportunist and demagogues," Faulkner writes. "Is it strange that at times we take violently back into our own hands that justice which we watched go astray in the blundering hands of those into which we put it voluntarily?" Faulkner to the Memphis *Commercial Appeal* (15 February 1931), repr. in Neil R. McMillen and Noel Polk, "Faulkner on Lynching," *Faulkner Journal* 8:1 (Fall 1994): 5.

33. Daniel Joseph Singal, *The War Within: From Victorian to Modernist Thought in the South, 1919–1945* (Chapel Hill: University of North Carolina Press, 1982), 186; Wilson, "Faulkner and the Southern Religious Culture," 32; Leigh Anne Duck, "Religion: Desire and Ideology," in *A Companion to William Faulkner*, ed. Richard C. Moreland (Malden, Mass.: Blackwell Publishing, 2007), 270.

34. In its generic devotion to enlightenment and liberality, the detective story is typically suspicious of religious and ideological enthusiasm of all kinds, an attitude evident in the frequency with which religious charlatans, unjustified authorities, and fanatical believers provide the genre with its villains. One aspect of its habit of converting spiritual or philosophical profundities into solvable empirical riddles—of transforming mystery into mysteries—is thus its hostility to ideological commitment or profound spiritual conviction. "I . . . [am] against zeal," Robert Parker's detective hero Spenser says in a programmatic statement of a view that runs consistently throughout the genre. "Zeal distorts . . . [people]. Makes the normal impulses convolute. Makes people fearless and greedless and loveless and finally monstrous." Robert B. Parker, *Promised Land* (1976; New York: Dell, 1987), 156.

35. Duck, 272, 275.

36. As Duck acknowledges, "the novel does not present the white church as the dominant source of local racial hatred." Doc Hines, she points out in this context, is presented not as a voice of religious authority but as an overtly eccentric theologian" (275). Hightower's former congregants, it might be added, are shown to be guided in their dedication to lynching not by doctrine or by church leadership, but by popular desire.

37. In this respect, *Light in August* provides a view of lynching similar to the interpretations offered by Donald G. Matthews and by Orlando Patterson. Emphasizing the ritualistic aspects of lynching and its infusion with Christian symbolism (and, in particular, with elements of the tradition of Southern Protestantism emphasizing the centrality of sin and atonement), both Matthews and Patterson argue that for its white practitioners lynching promised not only to maintain racial hierarchy or to create a subjugated labor force of African American workers but to create ritual resolutions to a sense of cultural and spiritual crisis created by the perceived instability of the white South and thus to sacralize the political structure of white supremacy. Donald G. Matthews, "The Southern Rite of Human Sacrifice," *Journal of Southern Religion* (2000), http://jsr.fsu.edu/mathews.htm; Orlando Patterson, *Rituals of Blood: Consequences of Slavery in Two American Centuries* (New York: Basic Civitas, 1998), 169–232.

"To Survive What Looked Out": The Forensic Trail and William Faulkner's *Intruder in the Dust*

Rachel Watson

Describing the role of DNA evidence in the O. J. Simpson case, science historians Anne Joseph and Alison Winter write:

> The various mechanical techniques which transformed the forensic traces in the Simpson case to the positive match had no social agendas or prejudices of their own. The fact that here, at least, one could imagine the evidence being treated in isolation of issues of racial prejudice conferred upon the technique an immense weight of trust and expectation. . . . By alluding to chemical structures, the police, public imagination, and courtroom can step around the troubling and pertinent social issues. The focus is on the trace once it has been removed from the mud, sidewalk, or crime scene and the biological components of the person, also separated from the social context, who left the trace behind. The environment is discarded as unimportant. . . . However, issues of race also operate just as powerfully, precisely *because they are less visible*, in identificatory techniques which are ostensibly color-blind.[1]

The job of Johnnie Cochran et al. then involved relocating forensic evidence to "a contested space rather than an authoritative one" by focusing on the human errors of the police officers and forensic specialists charged with handling and interpreting the biological evidence in its journey from the crime scene to the crime lab. The Simpson defense team, in other words, had to reframe the crime narrative as one composed of elements deeply rooted in the time and place of racially charged 1994 Los Angeles, and not just in the ostensibly timeless discursive world of "science." Though the argument continues as to whether the verdict rendered real justice, the case illuminated a contemporary manifestation of a set of tensions that has its own history. The fantasy of forensic science producing authoritative interpretations in a discursive realm removed from the complexities of history is not unique to modern DNA identifications, but has been key to the power and purchase of the science from its inception, particularly in the United States.

This essay suggests reading *Intruder in the Dust* as a story about hard evidence: how it is recognized, how it works on us, how we feel about it, and how we use it as a category with which to mark and revise our competing desires for "pure" signs of a scientific discourse on the one hand and the messier, contingent signs of the cultural and social world on the other. In the 1930s through the 1940s the cultural status of and connotations around *evidence* itself played a key role in possibilities and strategies for racial progress and the realization of egalitarian, democratic ideals. By thinking about *Intruder in the Dust* as an extended meditation on persuasive forms of evidence and the complexities of interpretation, Faulkner's most serious attempt at detective fiction emerges as an engagement with Americans' evolving interest in forensic certainty, and a belief in the ability of "hard evidence" to render human truth. Though many critics have noted the novel's resistance to federal involvement in Southern problems[2] in its insistence upon a forensic solution, the "facts" of *Intruder in the Dust* actually tell a more ambiguous story. Though Gavin Stevens lectures extensively regarding the Northern threats to Southern ways of life—particularly those posed by modernization and commercialism—for Chick Mallison and Lucas Beauchamp, there is one federally generated "way of knowing" that dramatically elevates the moral possibilities for the entrenched white South: the persuasive powers of unarguable evidence. In this essay I suggest two evidentiary contexts informing the strange pairing of murder mystery and segregation-era moral tale: forensic on the one hand, and sociological on the other. During the 1930s and 1940s these discursive fields posit how "scientific evidence," when read with the proper recognition and interpretation, can be harnessed toward realizing American ideals of individual integrity and equality.

Though frequently and notoriously "cluttered" by the didactic and longwinded speeches Gavin Stevens imparts to his nephew Chick Mallison,[3] the "facts" of the novel's detection plot remain. Set in roughly 1948, the story begins with sixteen-year-old Charles "Chick" Mallison witnessing Lucas Beauchamp, a black man who had saved his life four years earlier, being taken from the sheriff's car into the city jail. Beauchamp, arrested just before the story begins, was found standing over a white man's corpse with a (literal) smoking gun. In jail, Lucas tries to retain Chick's uncle, town lawyer Gavin Stevens. But while Stevens is willing to negotiate on Lucas's behalf, he is unwilling to believe that Lucas could be innocent. Lucas, not interested in pleading guilty to a crime he did not commit—nor in explaining how the murder actually happened—instead summons Chick to recover and illuminate the hard evidence that will prove his innocence: the distinctive bullet wound in the corpse, which could not have been produced by Lucas's gun. Accompanied by an older white woman, Eunice Habersham, and a black boy about Chick's own age, Aleck Sander, the three set off in the night to recover the corpse and save Lucas from the lynch mob that is already gathering.

Finally, after a confusing and complex set of events—involving Gavin Stevens, Sheriff Hope Hampton, an empty casket, a missing corpse, a mysterious mule and rider, another murder, a one-armed man, stolen lumber, quicksand, and poor-white fratricide—the physical evidence of the bullet wound eventually comes to light and proves Lucas Beauchamp innocent. This forensic revelation has a stunning effect on the small, Jim Crow–era Southern community, proving Lucas's innocence instantly and unequivocally to the public at large, disabling the lynch mob, and generally restoring a positive version of segregated order. The novel has subsequently come to be understood as bearing an uncomfortably conservative message, particularly regarding the white South and its ownership of racial violence and inequality.[4] Though the novel's explicitly ideological passages tend to get the most critical attention, particularly in analyses of the novel as a response to national efforts toward dismantling Jim Crow segregation—from efforts to pass antilynching legislation to the integration of the armed forces in 1948—this essay privileges a few key elements of it as a detective story.[5] Plot pieces that at first appear to be simply generic conventions—for instance, the quest for forensic evidence—upon closer examination bear just as condensed significance regarding contemporaneous issues and questions surrounding how to render an American version of racial justice.

Rather than a single detective, the hero of the story is finally a group: Aleck Sander, Lucas Beauchamp, Charles Mallison, Sheriff Hampton, Miss Habersham, and even Gavin Stevens. Each brings his own perspective to bear on recovering and interpreting evidence that resolves the narrative and makes Beauchamp's innocence believable to the larger community. Lucas Beauchamp himself however must first wait in jail for the evidence to be gathered and synthesized by whites before he can demand to be set free: not before he can *be innocent*, as Gavin Stevens would have it, but before he can successfully *claim it* with his own voice. With this limiting of Beauchamp's agency—along with the glaring and discomfiting portrayal of lynch mob behavior as bearing some relation to locally rendered "justice"—the novel cannot simply be considered progressive. But it does attempt, almost despite itself, to demystify irrational attitudes in ways that suggest racial progress requires a radical and fundamental clearing of vision, an "uncluttering" and "demythologizing" of the evidentiary trail. In the world of the novel, hard evidence ultimately triumphs over irrationalism: a corpse with a Luger slug in it is impossible for Jefferson and Yoknapatawpha County to argue with, even in the inexhaustible voice of Gavin Stevens. With this, despite its recurring muddying of the assumptions surrounding "facts," the story finally trades on the seductive allure of forensic crime solving. On into the cultural production of the present day, such a trail of evidence conjures a way of being a *national individual* and the protections such American citizenship promises, claiming with "scientific" authority an empirical ground from which one could imagine enacting egalitarian ideals. Lucas demanding Vinson Gowrie's dead body speak for him first is the quintessential demand of the American creed: that of habeas corpus and due process of law, the individual's right to evidence.

In an early scene from the short 1936 film *You Can't Get Away with It*, J. Edgar Hoover sits at his desk at the new FBI headquarters and speaks directly to the camera with a friendly but deeply authoritative tone. Regarding the crime fighting agents of the new FBI, Hoover claims emphatically: "He must know that no clue, no matter how seemingly unimportant, can be overlooked. He must have constantly before him the fact that science is the bulwark of criminal investigation." Though most of the film concerns *criminal* pursuit and capture—specifically the famous criminal captures of the 1930s including Baby Face Nelson, Alvin Karpis, and John Dillinger—soon after Hoover's opening statement we see an official smoky glass door emblazoned with bold capital letters: *Identification Division*. Behind the door, white children are lining up and having their fingerprints recorded by an agent of the new FBI. The narrator's voice explains this surprising turn, from the federal acquisition of decidedly guilty criminal identity to the collecting of certainly innocent child identity, as further example of the protections afforded by national citizenship: "But don't think the G-men deal entirely with crime. . . . This is fingerprinting that's ordinary and routine in everyday life: people record their prints and their children's too, for protection. A thousand sets like these come in each day—no connection with criminal records."[6]

This film, produced by a partnership between the FBI and Universal Pictures, underscores a central concept in the ascendency of the new national law enforcement agency: that of the indelibly inscribed and scientifically interpreted forensic trail. According to Hoover, even if one could not see it oneself, each American citizen carried and left behind a radically individual identity (from fingerprints to teeth marks) and a semiotic trail of their actions (from tire marks to ballistic patterns) in the form of "forensic evidence." Before the creation of the FBI, the trail left by even a half-wit criminal was not easily traced: fingerprint records were not yet shared between local police departments, a situation that made the already unreliable technology of latent fingerprint recording practically useless. In the propagandistic stories disseminated by Hoover's FBI, with the interpretive skills of their "forensic science" the federal agents of the FBI could infallibly recognize and definitively establish individual American identities and unarguable truths about guilt and innocence.

By the 1940s this matrix of events, personalities, and crime science had produced a new and enduring version of national identity, a sense of federally detectable "forensic" individuality that had the potential to officially trump the local, familial, historical, even racial signs of identity. In other words, the citizen forensic trail as figured by J. Edgar Hoover brought with it a new way of understanding American identity that appeared to eliminate the significance of the regional but maintained both a rhetorical and real sense of what it means to be an unrepeatable human individual, through the interpretive authority of the federal gaze. To complicate matters however, Hoover's understanding of the distinction between "federal" and "regional" was not an entirely oppositional one; by intentionally making his new agents a homogenous, tightly controlled group of men, all white and mostly Southern, to the extent that the FBI's criminal tracking was creating a new kind of federal identity for individual citizens, it tended to be Southern white men doing it.[7] To complicate matters even further, this rapid rise of a "provable" American individual identity grounded in "hard" evidence coincided with the early dismantling of de jure racial segregation, dramatic events of the 1940s that set the stage for the subsequent civil rights movement of the 1950s and 1960s.[8]

For William Faulkner, the FBI's scientific crime solving was closer than the movie screen. As early as 1925 and off and on until his retirement in 1965, Faulkner's brother Murry ("Jack") Falkner (the only brother not to change the spelling of the family name) served as one of Hoover's original "G-men." Though stationed at various field offices throughout his career, in the spring and summer of 1934 Agent Murry Falkner was one of a select number of agents assigned to the trail of "Public Enemy #1" John Dillinger.[9] The nation's most widely publicized "manhunt" gave Hoover an ideal narrative by which to publicize the new traceability of the individual and the federal agency's power over state lines. Jurisdiction had hitherto been an impediment. Without a well-defined federal law enforcement body, and with only a limited number of officially federal crimes, as soon as a criminal suspect crossed state lines he was often out of reach of local authorities. Visually represented in such films as the one referenced above, the criminal trail was often depicted crisscrossing over maps of the continental United States, and an additional animated line represented federal agents on the chase, zipping over state lines that had been rendered powerless to stop them from getting their man. Such animated maps illustrated the chases and captures that led to the public and Congressional support for the establishment of the new federal law enforcement agency.[10] The FBI, in other words, had rendered an empirically grounded version of American individuality.

The most nagging question of *Intruder in the Dust* becomes clear early on: why does Lucas Beauchamp wait so long to tell his self-exonerating eyewitness account of the murder? Why does the forensic story—that is, the revelation of ballistic evidence hidden in Gowrie's corpse—need to precede Beauchamp's "voiced" testimony?[11] Upending the typical structure of the crime story, the recovery of physical evidence in *Intruder in the Dust* finally compels not the full confession of guilt from the suspect, but the full confession of his innocence. In this forensic structuring, Faulkner's 1948 crime-detection tale of race in America tells a story of how the recuperation and interpretation of concrete evidence can overpower even entrenched regional prejudice and affect the liberation of a black individual via popular *Southern* consent to *American* rule of law.

Charles "Chick" Mallison's recollection of a profoundly shaping experience of race consciousness emerges soon after the novel begins. It begins when a twelve-year-old Chick falls through a thin sheet of ice into a freezing creek and is rescued by Lucas Beachamp. Chick's first encounter with Lucas consists of Chick unknowingly hearing Lucas's disembodied voice—"it doesn't matter whose"—directing his rescue. When Chick is finally pulled from the icy water and sees the face to which the voice belongs, the real story of the novel begins: "—a face . . . inside a Negro's skin but that was all even to a boy of twelve shaking with cold and still panting with shock and exertion because what looked out of it had no pigment at all, not even the white man's lack of it."[12] This recognition of an essential racelessness behind Lucas's face begins a destabilization of the race ideology Chick had absorbed since birth: the ideology that "Negroes" were all alike and not fully realizable, or recognizable, as particular persons, and that individuality itself, and the political rights it affords, was only available to whites. In other words, Chick has a moment of human recognition, "uncluttered" by traditional interpretive tools of his time and place.

With this scene, *Intruder in the Dust* takes up a political project in which racial ideology is undermined for a white moral agent by revising the physical signs of racial identity—skin, voice, and face—into

something like the evidence of a fingerprint: in this lifesaving instant
for Chick, Lucas Beauchamp's face and voice reveal no more or less
than the singular presence of a particular individual, such that "what
looked out of it had no pigment at all, not even a white man's lack of it."
The scene evokes Ralph Ellison's contemporaneous description of the
"tragic irrational" world of Jim Crow that renders the black man invisible
"because whites tend to regard Negroes in the spirit of the old song 'All
Coons Look Alike to Me,' seldom looking past the abstraction 'Negro'
to the specific 'man.'"[13] This moment of deracinated recognition unlocks
the possibility for Chick to think outside the narrowly prescribed codes
of his own family and the traditions of his socioracial set.

    After pulling him from the frozen creek, Lucas takes Chick to the
Beauchamp home, where he feeds him and gives him a dry set of
clothes. Here, Chick's humanistic race awakening continues, coming to
him through a set of sensory signs of "blackness" that suddenly appear
defamiliarized:

> . . . nigger food too, accepted and then dismissed also because it was exactly
> what he had expected, it was what Negroes ate, obviously because it was what
> they liked, what they chose; not (at twelve: he would be a man grown before
> he experienced his first amazed dubiety at this) that out of their long chronicle
> this was all they had had a chance to learn to like . . . afterward, ten minutes
> later then for the next four years he would be trying to tell himself that it was
> the food which had thrown him off. But he would know better; his initial error,
> misjudgment had been there all the time, not even needing to be abetted by
> the smell of the house and the quilt in order to survive what had looked out
> (and not even at him: just looked out) from the man's face. (13–14)

After his life-saving moment of (one-sided) human recognition, once-
familiar smells, tastes, sights, and tactile sensation seem suddenly different, leading Chick to the radical experience of "pondering speculating
if perhaps that smell were really not the odor of a race nor even actually
of poverty but perhaps of a condition" (11). In these moments, Chick's
moral and analytical imagination dislocates from his regionalized sense
of self and interprets clues evinced by the Beauchamp home free from
the prescribed narratives of Southern race ideology. This clarity of vision
occurs first as he considers the Beauchamps's food, when he realizes
the possibility that "out of their long chronicle this was all they had had
a chance to learn to like" rather than simply "because it was what they
liked, what they chose" (13–14). This new clarified vision leads him to
interpret a different story from familiar signs; behind the empty mystique of Southern blackness, Chick finds the deeper truth of politically
and materially circumscribed identities and systemic inequality.

In each of these crucial scenes, Faulkner evokes a kind of *forensic hermeneutic* whereby the racialized body can reveal a racially transcendent, or "universal," human individual. In these two scenes, Chick's new understanding of common humanity *and* human difference is thereby anchored by the idea of a universal individual subject that one might see "looking out" from behind the misleading clutter of ideological assumptions. As Chick later discovers, "surviving what looked out" required living according to the moral imperatives necessitated by a recognition of individual selfhood as transcending racial identity and Southern regionalism, living according to something like a fidelity to an egalitarian ideal of human and individual rights. The force exerted on Chick by this new creed is so powerful that it determines his sense of guilt, debt, and willingness to sneak out of his house in the middle of the night four years later to dig up a decomposing body in hopes of saving the life of Lucas Beauchamp. If the novel works in part as a parable regarding the role whites may play in racial progress, the role demands not only the gathering, but first the proper *seeing* of unarguable equalizing evidence.

Four years later, sixteen-year-old Mallison responds to a silent plea he detects in the eyes of an imprisoned Lucas Beauchamp and returns to the jail after Gavin Stevens's initial one-sided conversation with his "client." Lucas then explains to Chick how he must get him free, not by helping him break out of jail or arguing for his innocence, but through a forensic recuperation of the real evidence of the crime. Chick must replace the false evidence of Lucas's guilt—his blackness and the white prejudices that can only imagine he must be guilty if he was standing over a dead body with a gun—with the real forensic evidence of his innocence: the bullet hole in Vinson Gowrie. In asking this remarkable task of Chick, Lucas never directly professes his own innocence, claiming simply that it "wasn't [his] gun." Lucas lets the forensic evidence do his talking for him by commanding Chick to dig up the body of Vinson Gowrie and have a pair of authoritative eyes examine the bullet hole that could not have been created by his gun (67).

Early in the novel, the narrator compares Beat Four—the home of the Gowries and the originating area of the lynch mob—to the famous Chicago gangsters of the 1920s, a time when criminals could be famous but not yet effectively tracked by a national law enforcement agency: "alone out of all the county it was known to the rest of the county by the number of its survey co-ordinate—Beat Four—as in the middle twenties people knew where Cicero Illinois was and who lived there and what they did who neither knew nor cared what state Chicago was in" (35). Taken with the significance of the German Luger, and the frequent comparisons of the time between Nazi Germany and the Jim Crow regime, this set of associations presents Beat Four not as a deeply imbedded sign of the intractable South, but a modern sign of the nation's, even world's, sicknesses. There is no Southern mystique to Beat Four, but in their unexamined fidelity to clannish, irrational tradition, they do, like the fascist menace, pose a specific threat to democratic society and individual liberties. The seemingly out of place reference to Chicago gangsters connotes J. Edgar Hoover's FBI and their "modern science" of crime solving. But that is not all: like the gun itself, the comparison has its own unexpected history.

An earlier version of a similar analogy appears in a disturbing 1931 letter from Faulkner to the Memphis *Commercial Appeal*. In this letter, Faulkner (who here signs "Falkner") provides a historically evasive "explanation" for the phenomena of lynching. In the course of the letter, which ends with the observation that lynch mobs "like our juries, they have a way of being right," Faulkner compares the crimes of Mississippi to the crimes of Chicago, responding to the assertion that "history gives no record of lynching prior to reconstruction days" Faulkner writes: "The slave-holders and slaves of the pre–Civil War time, out of whose relations lynchings did, or could, take place, were not representative of either people, any more than the Sicilian expatriates and shopping women in Chicago stores, out of whose accidental coinciding the murder of innocent bystanders (or fleers) occurs, are representative of European emigrants or American women and children, or of the General Cooks and the George Rogers Clarks who made Chicago possible."[14]

In this passage, we see that Chicago, familiar to Faulkner as an emblematic location of federal crime solving and criminal capture, figured in his rationalizing of Mississippi extralegal violence well before *Intruder in the Dust*. Elements of the letter that "explain" Southern lynching also appear in the novel, though in less explicit form. Taking Lucas's predicament as a sample case of the threat of Southern racial violence, the novel, like the 1931 letter, erroneously depicts the lynch mob as a local means of affecting extralegal justice that simply skips over the time-consuming process of collecting evidence and building a case. Lucas is found standing over Vinson Gowrie's corpse with a smoking gun: for the lynch mob, the mise-en-scène renders a closed case. But by evoking such a leading crime scene, Faulkner paints the lynch mob as not much different from a jury who does not get the benefit of forensic science—the mob's potential mistake is not in the desire to kill a black man as a means of social control and racial terror, but in not waiting long enough for the evidence to be recovered and interpreted properly.[15] Once it is, they quietly disband and "forget." It is a misleading portrait of lynch mob violence, to put it mildly.

Though there is no direct federal involvement in the collection and interpretation of the evidence that finally frees Lucas Beauchamp, it is neither a strictly provincial undertaking. Sheriff Hampton's correct interpretation of the key ballistic evidence turns on his access to both local and global knowledge when he recognizes the evidence of a German Luger wound and also knows who had the gun and how he got it: "Like the one Buddy McCallum brought home from France in 1919 and traded [to Crawford Gowrie] that summer for a pair of fox hounds" (175). The freeing, therefore, of Lucas Beauchamp requires an understanding of the evidence in an international *and* national context—as well as Southern and local. Despite being a backwoods poor white from a deeply clannish regional group, Crawford Gowrie had already been imprinted by various forms of federal citizenship by the time he committed the crime, from enlistment in the Army to imprisonment in Leavenworth (161). At the level of plot, the complex provenance of the murder weapon is notable in that Lucas's freedom depends precisely upon the make of this gun: a German Luger, wielded by an army deserter, but acquired in a trade at home in Mississippi. Crawford Gowrie then represents not only the supposedly intractable backwardness of Beat Four (and all the many areas like it throughout the South) but also a tangled network of national, international, and local contexts, and the pathology such entanglements can either produce or conceal. Fittingly, Crawford Gowrie is finally himself killed with the very same Luger, allegedly by his own hand. When Lucas sends Chick on his forensic mission he tells him only this:

> 'My pistol is a fawty-one Colt,' Lucas said. Which it would be; the only thing he hadn't actually known was the caliber—that weapon workable and efficient and well cared for yet as archaic peculiar and unique as the gold toothpick, which had probably (without doubt) been old Carothers McCaslin's pride half century ago.
> 'All right,' he said. 'Then what?'
> 'He wasn't shot with no fawty-one Colt.'
> 'What was he shot with?'
> But Lucas didn't answer that . . . . Nor had he expected Lucas to and he knew that Lucas would never answer that, say any more, any further to any white man, and he knew why, and he knew why Lucas waited to tell him, a child, about the pistol when he would have told neither his uncle nor the sheriff who would have been the one to open the grave and look at the body. (68)

The evidence of Lucas Beauchamp's gun, when properly read, refers to more than his innocence: it signifies his racially mixed genealogy and something of his individual identity as well. The novel repeatedly engages a thematic logic regarding how a white subject may interpret the signs of black individual identity, or how human specificity can be recognized.[16]

In his initial processing of Beauchamp's startling command, Chick recalls a memory of a missing ring recovered through the power of conjure. The memory serves as a guiding fable for Chick as he tries to understand why he must be the one to perform this dangerous moral duty, recalling the words of Ephraim that will also echo those of Eunice Habersham: "Young folks and womens, they aint cluttered. They can listen. But a middle-year man like your paw and your uncle, they cant listen. They aint got time. They're too busy with facks. In fact, you mought bear this in yo mind; someday you mought need it. If you ever needs to get anything done outside the common run, don't waste yo time on the menfolks; get the womens and children to working at it" (70). The intentional misspelling of "facks," followed almost immediately by the correctly spelled "fact," suggests that a specific kind of evidence and interlocutor will be needed for Lucas's exoneration, that conventional "facts" of the white (adult) male status quo will not suffice. An imaginative vision that could seek out and recognize such oppositional evidence must be attuned to the unexpected, "uncluttered" enough to see clues for the objective truth they signify. By placing Chick in such a critical role, the novel makes the white "middle-year" Gavin Stevens not only incapable of helping Lucas Beauchamp, but also representative of a "kind" that are inescapably incapable of it, no matter their good intentions. Unlike Chick Mallison, such men cannot detect the signs of a "specific man" behind the face of "blackness"—unless they are shown the hard evidence. In the end, Gavin admits as much to Chick's father: "It took an old woman and two children for that, to believe truth for no other reason than that it was truth. . . . When did you really begin to believe him? When you opened the coffin, wasn't it?" (124)

Every significant character has their own version of what constitutes "truth," and various characters throughout the story espouse upon "facks" vs. "facts," "facts" vs. "circumstance," "probability" vs. "universal truth," and "simple truth" distinguished from its lesser cousin "fact." When Chick explains to Miss Habersham the seemingly impossible task ahead of them, she responds by explaining to Chick why Lucas withheld his story of the crime event in question from his putative lawyer Gavin Stevens "because what Miss Habersham paraphrased was simple truth, not even fact and so there was not needed a great deal of diversification and originality to express it because truth was universal, it had to be universal to be truth; all they had to do was just to pause, just to stop, just to wait: 'Lucas knew it would take a child—or an old woman like me: someone not concerned with probability, with evidence. Men like your

uncle and Mr Hampton have had to be men too long, busy too long.——
Yes?' She said. 'Bring him in to town where someone who knows can
look at the bullet hole'" (88). Though Habersham implies that what they
are digging up is not white men's version of "evidence," in this passage
Faulkner aligns the interpretation of forensic evidence directly with an
ideal of "universal" meaning through the formal coordination of Chick's
thoughts regarding truth with Miss Habersham's practical assessment
of the exonerating corpse they must recover. Though forensic evidence
is crucial to Lucas's exoneration, it takes the right kind of detective to
follow the trail in the first place.

Just before Chick, Miss Habersham, and Aleck Sander leave for
their grave-robbing mission, Chick recalls the words again, but adds a
more juridical framework: *"If you got something outside the common
run that's got to be done and cant wait, don't waste your time on the
menfolks; they works on what your uncle calls the rules and the cases.
Get the women's and the children at it; they works on the circumstances"*
(110–11). In his mind, Chick has transliterated the memory and added
an import of legal significance, thinking of the implications of the folk
wisdom now in terms of legal ratiocination: "rules," "cases," and "circumstances." Chick here is not finding a lost ring, but is serving as the
story's agent of progress on his way to affecting a very modern version
of race-blind justice, informed implicitly by the ideals of what Swedish
sociologist Gunnar Myrdal called, less than four years prior, "the American Creed": the belief that every citizen deserves equal access to and
protection by the law, including due process, and the general freedoms
presumed by conferment of individual human rights.[17] Chick, in this
revised role of detective, exemplifies Myrdal's widely influential description of "the Negro problem" as one that will be eventually solved, more
or less, through a combined effect of rational persuasion, indisputable
evidence, and national faith. Even before Myrdal, W. E. B. Du Bois
describes a qualified faith in the scientific in *Dusk of Dawn* (1940): "The
present attitude and action of the whole world is not based solely upon
rational, deliberate intent. It is a matter of conditioned reflexes; of long
followed habits, customs, and folkways; of subconscious trains of reasoning and unconscious nervous reflexes. To attack and better all this calls
for more than appeal and argument. It needs carefully planned and scientific propaganda."[18] The paring of "propaganda" with "scientific" here
suggests that the slanted "facts" produced in the sphere of Jim Crow can
only be fought with hard evidence, strategically deployed.

By the 1940s, the biological science of race and racial difference had
lost irrecoverable authoritative ground.[19] The science of race, however,
did not disappear entirely, becoming instead *social*, a turn indicated by

a cluster of key studies coincident with the writing and publication of *Intruder in the Dust*: E. Franklin Frazier's *The Negro Family in American Life* in 1939; St. Clair Drake and Horace Cayton's *Black Metropolis* in 1945; and Oliver Cromwell Cox's *Caste, Class, and Race* in 1948. But the most influential "scientific" study of America's racial landscape was Swedish sociologist Gunnar Myrdal's 1944 *An American Dilemma: The Negro Problem and Modern Democracy*. In this work, Myrdal concluded that the dissonance produced by coupling an inherently egalitarian belief system with the obvious irrationality of racial prejudice created for average white Americans a deeply unpleasant inner conflict. In Myrdal's optimistic diagnosis for the future of race in America, based upon over 1,300 pages of sociological evidence, Americans do not long abide inconsistencies between belief and action, and that this dissonance will not stand the test of time.[20] After the publication of Myrdal's widely influential study, for many progressive-minded black and white writers, rationalism and the "scientific" evidence attending it constituted their best hope for a future characterized by racial equality. Not all, however, were convinced by Myrdal's interpretations of the data.

Ralph Ellison begins his short (and unpublished) review of *An American Dilemma* by criticizing the "myth making" of sciences devoted to reconciling "the practical morality of American capitalism with the ideal morality of the American Creed."[21] With metaphors of removing the "clutter" from one's evidentiary vision that evoke the very advice that guides Chick Mallison, Ellison finally—after leveling a scathing critique of Myrdal's conclusions—offers some highly qualified praise: "If Myrdal has done nothing else, he has used his science to discredit all of the vicious non-scientific nonsense that has cluttered our sociological literature. He has, in short, shorn it of its mythology. . . . It will take a deeper science than Myrdal's, deep as that might be, to analyze what is happening among the masses of Negroes. Much of it is inarticulate, and Negro scholars have for the most part ignored it through clinging, as does Myrdal, to the sterile concept of 'race'" (339–40). In his complicated critique, Ellison weds American democracy with the uncontestable category of the human, calling on black Americans to take culture and use it to "help create a more human American" (340). Ellison concludes by suggesting the progressive conclusions that remain to be interpreted from Myrdal's sociological "facts": "Fortunately its facts are to an extent neutral. This is a cue for liberal intellectuals to get busy to see that *An American Dilemma* does not become an instrument of American tragedy" (340). The problem may remain one of "cluttered" interpretation, but the solution still potentially lies in the power of assimilating hard evidence.

For Oliver Cromwell Cox, Myrdal's true failure lies in an abandon-ment of scientific rigor and a recourse to mystified, nationalistic abstrac-tions when it comes to the interpretations of the evidence. Cox's strategy in evincing this critique is simply to reinterpret Myrdal's own evidence, noting summarily: "The reasoning which we are now following, it may be well to state, is not Myrdal's; we are merely culling those conclu-sions which the data seem to compel the author to make but which he ordinarily surrounds with some mysterious argument about caste."[22] Cox describes the demystified interpretation that should be read in the evidence of Myrdal's study: "The point which the author seems to have avoided is this: that both race prejudice and Negro standards are con-sistently calculated economic interests of the Southern oligarchy. Both prejudice and the Negro's status are dependent functions of the latter interests." (229) Such a historically and materially informed conclusion resembles Chick's own experience of enlightenment in Lucas Beau-champ's home, the sudden demystification of familiar "racial" signs that later compels the gathering of evidence toward Lucas's liberation and, symbolically, suggests what shape progress in the white South may take: a better reading of the evidence at hand.

Gavin Stevens's most prominent, confusing, and absurdly long-winded speech to his nephew Chick reveals a similar problem of rational analysis unconsciously relying upon the irrationalism of race. Though Stevens claims to recognize the *individual* integrity of Lucas Beau-champ, he stubbornly clings to faith in the mystified essentialism of *type*. This emerges most clearly in Stevens's reflexive conviction of Lucas's guilt, as well as his repeated and confusing equivalences of "Lucas" and "Sambo," particularly evident in this (in)famous passage: "That's why we must resist the North . . . three generations ago we lost a bloody war in our own back yards so that it remain intact: the postulate that Sambo is a human being living in a free country and hence must be free. That's what we are really defending: the privilege of setting him free ourselves: which we will have to do for the reason that nobody else can since going on a century ago now the North tried it and have been admitting for seventy five years now that they failed. So it will have to be us" (151). In this passage, the mystification of race, indicated by Stevens's insistence upon the typologizing logic of "Sambo," is paired with a nationalistic version of human freedom.

Lucas Beauchamp's final request for a receipt from Gavin Stevens, when taken as a record of exchange, carries a certain poetic resonance as the final element in the novel's evidentiary scheme. The moment, cut off abruptly on the last page before Stevens can respond, does more than symbolize white debt owed toward black suffering. It also suggests another version of the request Lucas previously made of Chick: to be provided with his evidence. The insistence indicates a recognition on Lucas's part that in a white supremacist society no voiced testimony of his own can "prove" the truth of an event after the fact. What he *can* do, however, is demand to be provided with evidence that can, in the ideal American society of social science, forensic science, and *Intruder in the Dust*, speak across the color line, can—under the right interpretive conditions—be heard above the "cluttering" din of race mystification. By understanding the receipt as Lucas Beauchamp's evidentiary right, Stevens's decision whether or not to comply—which we do not get to see—aligns this exchange with Chick Mallison's earlier forensic heroics and a parable of Southern progress that turns on the problems of interpretation, but maintains a certain empirical faith in the ultimate persuasive power of hard evidence.

NOTES

I thank the participants and attendees of the 36th Annual Faulkner and Yoknapatawpha Conference, particularly Sean McCann, for their thoughtful and generous responses to the earlier version of this paper.

1. Anne Joseph and Alison Winter, "Making the Match: Human Traces, Forensic Experts, and the Public Imagination," in *Cultural Babbage: Technology, Time and Invention*, ed. Francis Spuffort and Jenny Uglow (London: Faber & Faber, 1996), 193–214, 209–10, emphasis in original.

2. See for example Erik Dussere, "The Debts of History: Southern Honor, Affirmative Action, and Faulkner's *Intruder in the Dust*," *Faulkner Journal* 17:1 (2001): 37–57; Ticien Marie Sassoubre, "Avoiding Adjudication in William Faulkner's *Go Down, Moses* and *Intruder in the Dust*," *Criticism* 49:2 (Spring 2007): 183–214; Joe Karaganis, "Negotiating the National Voice in Faulkner's Late Work," in *A Gathering of Evidence: Essays on William Faulkner's "Intruder in the Dust,"* ed. Michael Gresset and Patrick Samway (Philadelphia: St. Joseph's University Press, 2004), 97–130.

3. See for example Edmund Wilson's initial review in the *New Yorker* collected in *Faulkner: A Collection of Critical Essays*, ed. Robert Penn Warren (Englewood Cliffs, N.J.: Prentice-Hall, 1966); also see Jay Watson, *Forensic Fictions: The Lawyer Figure in Faulkner* (Athens: University of Georgia Press, 1993); and Neil Schmitz, "Faulkner and the Post-Confederate," in *Faulkner in Cultural Context: Faulkner and Yoknapatawpha, 1995* (Jackson: University Press of Mississippi, 1995), 241–62.

4. See for example Keith Clark, "Lucas Beauchamp and the Limitations of Space," in *A Gathering of Evidence*, 18–32.

5. For a particularly compelling example of this historical criticism, see Sassoubre in *A Gathering of Evidence*.

6. From *You Can't Get Away with It* (1936) produced by FBI/Universal Pictures. FBI records, National Archives II. For a history of the FBI's early reliance on cultural production to cultivate popular support, see Richard Gid Powers, *G-Men: The FBI in Popular Culture* (Carbondale: Southern Illinois University Press, 1983).

7. Bryan Burroughs, *Public Enemies: America's Greatest Crime Wave and the Birth of the F.B.I., 1933–34* (New York: Penguin Press, 2004), 11.

8. For example, in 1941 the U.S. Supreme Court in *Smith v. Allwright* declared white only political primaries to be unconstitutional and in 1946 ruled in *Morgan v. Virginia* segregation in interstate bus travel unconstitutional. And in 1948 President Truman issued Executive Order 9981 directing the desegregation of the armed forces.

9. Joseph Blotner, *Faulkner: A Biography*, 2 vols. (New York: Random House, 1974), 1:969, passim.

10. For histories of the role played by the 1930s "War on Crime" in the creation of the FBI, see in particular Claire Potter, *War on Crime: Bandits, G-Men, and the Politics of Mass Culture* (New Brunswick: Rutgers University Press, 1998) and Burroughs, *Public Enemies*.

11. Citing Cleanth Brooks's criticism of this as key to the novel's "failure as a mystery," Joe Karaganis further describes the role Beauchamp's silence plays in the novel's plot: "Thus it isn't Lucas's innocence but, perversely, his silence that sets in motion the long deferral of information about the crime and its circumstances that constitutes, such as it is, the narrative arc of the novel," 115.

12. William Faulkner, *Intruder in the Dust* (1948; New York: Vintage Books, 1991), 7.

13. Ralph Ellison, "Working Notes for *Invisible Man*," in *The Collected Essays*, ed. John Callahan (New York: Modern Library, 2003), 344.

14. William Faulkner, from correspondence uncovered and discussed by Neil R. McMillen and Noel Polk in "Faulkner on Lynching," *Faulkner Journal* 8:1 (Fall 1992): 3–13, 4.

15. Cleanth Brooks also notes that anyone framed that way would have been accused of murder, "even in New York City, or Cleveland, or Detroit." Brooks, "The Community in Action," in *A Gathering of Evidence*, 3.

16. Noel Polk has alluded to this in distinguishing the historical Faulkner from the fictional Stevens: "Faulkner's concern was consistently with the *individual* Negro." Polk, "Man in the Middle: Faulkner and the Southern White Moderate," in *A Gathering of Evidence*, 167–88.

17. Myrdal discusses the "American Creed" throughout chapter 1 and introduces its relationship with the "Negro problem" in the introduction: "*The American Negro problem is a problem in the heart of the American. It is there that the interracial tension has its focus. It is there that the decisive struggle goes on. This is the central viewpoint of this treatise. Though our study includes economic, social, and political race relations, at bottom our problem is the moral dilemma of the American—the conflict between his moral valuations on various levels of consciousness and generality. The "American Dilemma," referred to in the title of this book, is the ever-raging conflict between, on the one hand, the valuations preserved on the general plane which we shall call the "American Creed," where the American thinks, talks, and acts under the influence of high national and Christian precepts, and, on the other hand, the valuations on specific planes of individual and group living, where personal and local interests; economic, social, and sexual jealousies; considerations of community prestige and conformity; group prejudice against particular persons or types of people; and all sorts of miscellaneous wants, impulses, and habits dominate his outlook*" (xlvii, emphasis in original). Gunnar Myrdal, *An American Dilemma: The Negro Problem and Modern Democracy* (New York: Harper & Brothers, 1944).

18. W. E. B. Du Bois, *Dusk of Dawn: An Essay toward an Autobiography of a Race Concept* (1940; New York: Harcourt Brace, 2009), 679. I thank Ken Warren for first drawing my attention to this passage.

19. See Elazar Barkan, *The Retreat of Scientific Racism: Changing Concepts of Race in Britain and the United States between the World Wars* (Cambridge: Cambridge University Press, 1992).

20. Gunnar Myrdal, *An American Dilemma*, xlvi.

21. Ralph Ellison, "*An American Dilemma*: A Review," in *Collected Essays*, 328–40, 330.

22. Oliver Cromwell Cox, *Race: A Study in Social Dynamics* (New York: Monthly Review Press, 2000), 223.

The Mysterious Case of the Cold War Imaginary: Faulkner's *Intruder in the Dust* and Paul Bowles's *The Sheltering Sky*

HOSAM ABOUL-ELA

Literary critics have often made the connection between detective fiction and the desire for social order. In such stories, regimes of policing are valorized as institutions that preserve and protect against threats of violence and anomie.[1] Recently, this observation has allowed us to see an intimate connection between the detective genre and colonialism. For example, the critic Yumna Siddiqi has written about what she calls "fictions of intrigue" as manifestations of anxieties that accompanied popular British attitudes toward their own imperial project in its later stages. By the late nineteenth and early twentieth century the British Empire had suffered but survived numerous assaults on its authority around the globe, including the Indian "Mutiny" of 1857, the Orabi revolt in Egypt in 1881, and the Mahdist uprising in Sudan in 1898, to name three of the most famous incidents of colonial subjects rising up against their British masters during the second half of the nineteenth century. Beyond this actual series of revolts, one can generalize that the British Empire had become bloated and overextended, and it strained to fulfill its promise to secure comfortable middle-class lifestyles for a large majority of Britons and to make Great Britain the greatest power in world history, the empire on which the sun would never set. For a large cross section of the British populace, by the turn of the century the question of Empire had begun to provoke anxiety instead of the old pride and confidence, and this shift was reflected in popular fiction. Whereas the stories and novels of imperialism authored by Rudyard Kipling and Rider Haggard had taken a celebratory position vis-à-vis the imperial project, a friend of these two men, one Arthur Conan Doyle, made wildly popular a relatively new genre of fiction in the atmosphere of the late century that systematically demonstrated the empire as a threat that Britain would have to contain through a regime of policing based on the scientific method and the belief in the power of reason and rational abilities. According to Siddiqi, these stories "rather than underscore the celebratory elements of imperial romance . . . point to anxieties about the nature and affects of imperialism."[2] Siddiqi's argument for the essential connection between the British detective story and imperialism includes empirical observations of particular details and recurring themes like "half-caste" Indians who are passing in England as locals, even as they wreak havoc with their affinities for magic and evil. But most generally, the connection between detective stories and empire that she establishes grows out of the genre's relentless faith in "Enlightenment rationality" (25) and its consistent deploying of this force against a version of the colonized, constructed as irrational, unenlightened, and dangerous.

In what follows, I consider the way William Faulkner's unorthodox appropriation of the detective genre in *Intruder in the Dust* (1948), coming as it does at a time when the United States itself emerges as a global power, indeed the possessor of its own distinct type of empire, appropriates and complicates the detective genre, with its ever-present implication in geopolitics. In reading this aspect of Faulkner's novel, I also compare Paul Bowles's novel *The Sheltering Sky* (1949), published the year after Faulkner's and to similar popular success. While not a detective story according to any conventional definition, *The Sheltering Sky* is also a literary novel that gestures toward the use of several popular genres to critique the emerging global nature of America's power, even as it embodies the limits of such critiques. For these two examples of American fiction at the beginning of the Cold War, the anxiety of empire, which manifested itself only in the late stages of British imperial history and in the work of British writers like Conan Doyle, is already present. One reason for this anxiety is the oppositional and antimainstream (if never fully antiimperialist) positions of Faulkner and Bowles, but another reason has to do with the very nature of American empire. As a kind of colonialism without colonies, United States imperialism has always denied its own existence, and its mere appearance has often been enough to inspire an anxiety expressed as self-criticism.[3] These two novels constitute early and important expressions of an American post–World War II anxiety about the global that remains with us—perhaps more powerfully than ever—today.

Although Joseph Blotner's biography of Faulkner reports that the author had initially thought of *Intruder* as a "mystery murder story" on the theme of black-white relations,[4] psychological and political themes had so infiltrated it by the time the text was delivered to the publisher that anyone looking into classical definitions of the detective genre would immediately want to point out all the exceptions that cause Faulkner's novel to fit the category so poorly. Tzvetzan Todorov explains the relationship between the literary writer and the popular detective genre pithily: "Detective fiction has its norms; to develop them is also to disappoint them: to 'improve upon' detective fiction is to write 'literature,' not detective fiction."[5] We should note here that *Intruder* was actually started by Faulkner at what might be considered a low point in his life, professionally and personally—but most of all financially. With almost all of his novels out of print, struggling with his major project of completing the antiwar novel *A Fable*, debts piling up, the prospect looming of possibly having to return to Hollywood to make money, and the string of successes that would change the direction of his career still on the horizon, the external motivation to write a piece of popular genre fiction would have been powerful. Yet, Faulkner's internal motivation was to eschew and even subvert the popular as he had in the past. Michael Grimwood writes about what he calls Faulkner's "struggle with vocation" and certainly one aspect of this struggle was a desire to produce finely crafted literature for his enjoyment without any concession to audience or "the market."[6] From his earliest works, Faulkner showed an awareness of and an interest in popular genres, yet this interest was always at war with his aesthetic ideology drawn out of the influence of high modernism in Europe. His experiences as a screenwriter in Hollywood heightened both his command of popular genre and his sharp ambivalence toward generic writing.

   Intruder in the Dust exemplifies Faulkner's ambivalence. Todorov conveniently lists eight characteristics that must inhere in any traditional piece of detective fiction for it to remain detective fiction.[7] Of the group, few apply to *Intruder*. Most flagrantly violated by Faulkner is the dictum that "there is no place for descriptions nor for psychological analyses" in detective fiction. Indeed, the psychological (in characteristic Faulknerian fashion) threatens to swallow the entire narrative from the first chapter, when the mystery of whodunit is temporarily sidelined for several pages of backstory that probes deep into the psychology of the boy who will become the detective. During this flashback, we learn of Chick Mallison's debt to the accused Lucas Beauchamp and of the role this debt plays in disturbing a rigid ordering of Chick's unconscious around the received notions of white supremacy. As a result of the flashback, we as readers are invited to consider the question of Chick's psyche and its growth, which we are led to read and interpret against the sociohistorical dynamic of race relations in Mississippi up through the 1940s. Thus, much of the criticism published about the book examines it as a kind of *Bildungsroman*, treating a transformative moment in the development of the young Chick Mallison.[8]

   If this emphasis on Chick's psychological journey is how the novel derails the classical mystery genre, a remaining question is why it is derailed and what this generic redirecting means. My earlier quotation from Todorov, combined with what we know about Faulkner's modernism-inflected sense of artistry, offers the beginning of an answer. Faulkner is an artist of the highest standing. No matter what his initial motivation for setting out to write a "mystery murder," ultimately his ingrained artistic impulses led him to begin to improve the genre, and in doing so, he ended up with something that was no longer genre fiction at all. But this is only the beginning of an answer. We can certainly say more about specifically why and how Faulkner appropriates the genre, without ever obliterating the role that "artistic genius" might have played in the result that we examine.

My argument regarding the Faulkner novel is that much of what's unique and radical about the form of it is the result not only of artistic genius, but also of what could be understood in the broadest terms as "geopolitics."[9] Specifically, Faulkner's position as a Southerner infused his work with insights into the processes of imperialism—particularly economic imperialism. Furthermore, these insights manifest themselves not only in the things that happen in the Faulkner novel, in their content, but also in their form. As a result, I have argued that we have long missed certain connections in what Faulkner does with writers of the postcolonial world and that this blindness has come about because of an overemphasis on understanding Faulkner as a modernist writer in the tradition of Yeats, Proust, Joyce, and Woolf when we speak of the form of his novels. In my opinion, understanding the full ramifications of Faulkner's form and its resonance among postcolonial writers requires us to balance the traditional modernist understanding of the Faulknerian form with one that thinks of him as a *Southern* writer in the sense of the term "Southern" invoked by the great historian C. Vann Woodward in his often-quoted pronouncement that "The South had undergone an experience that it could share with no other part of America—though it is shared by nearly all the peoples of Europe and Asia—the experience of military defeat, occupation, and reconstruction."[10]

In this global and geopolitical contextualization of Faulkner, his particular generic agenda in *Intruder* resonates more comfortably than in rigid structuralist definitions of the mystery genre. For example, Siddiqi's emphasis on anxieties, order, and social control speaks profoundly to the novel's basic concerns. More specifically than the theme of relations between blacks and whites that Faulkner mentions to his publisher, the novel raises the specter of lynching, which had become a scourge on both sides of the Mason-Dixon line, and which had very recently been the topic of federal legislation.[11] At the level of the nation-state, the lynching epidemic threatened a breakdown in the social order and subversion of state authority. To contrast this force with literary detection as *Intruder* does is to make reason and Enlightenment the opposite of vigilantism.

Furthermore, the novel describes vigilantism at times in specifically territorial terms. There are two territorial obsessions that recur in nearly all of Faulkner's work: the divide between North and South, and the divide between town and country. In general, the Faulkner novel makes these two spatiopolitical divisions reflections of each other.[12] *Intruder* starts with the divide between town and country, putting Chick in a position of vulnerability by beginning the action with his movement from his parents' comfortable home in Jefferson to the harshness of the countryside where he goes to shoot rabbits. Lest we miss the territorial connotations of the move, the narrator emphasizes the harshness of rural space: "It was cold that morning, the first winter cold-snap; the hedgerows were rimed and stiff with frost and the standing water in the roadside drainage ditches was skimmed with ice and even the edges of the running water in the Nine Mile branch glinted fragile and scintillant."[13] The threat against the authority of the state emanates from a specific piece of land, Beat Four, to which the power of law enforcement does not extend. Indeed, when Chick, Alek Sander, and Miss Habersham first arrive there in chapter 4, it is described as "the notorious, the fabulous" (92), and the position of the three as outsiders is emphasized: "it was never difficult for an outlander to do two things at once which Beat Four wouldn't like since Beat Four already in advance didn't like most things which people from town (and for that matter from most of the rest of the country) did" (93). In classical detective fiction, the city is often portrayed as a landscape full of the kind of threats, violence, and anarchy that the public needs to be contained by the rational powers of the detective. In *Intruder*, however, the displacing of this threat from an urban environment to the countryside invokes the contested question of land and control of land so central to the literature of occupation. This type of contest over the land, the question of who should control it and its resources, is at the center of the literature of colonialism in all its various discourses. (One classical example comes from Edward Said's widely cited *Culture and Imperialism*, which emphasizes the connection between geography, empire and culture throughout).[14]

Siddiqi points out that although the detective novel embodies a threat to state order, the detective is often not a state actor: neither Sherlock Holmes nor Philip Marlow nor Sam Spade are public sector employees. She states: "The detective and spy . . . work to uncover solutions to crimes or to expose subversive plots, though . . . they are often expressly not members of an official police" (Siddiqi 24). In this sense it is rationality, and not state power, that the genre presents as the opposite of the stateless, irrational anarchy so often represented as coming from individuals infiltrating the homeland from the colonies. In *Intruder*, this distinction is primary to the action. Neither Sheriff Hampton nor Gavin Stevens, acting as public defender, has much capacity to defend against the irrational mob. Rather the project of exhuming the truth and then shining the light of scientific discovery on the infection of mob rule is, and can only be, undertaken by those marginal to the centers of societal power: an elderly black man, a young dependent white boy, a young dependent black boy, and an elderly single woman—a "spinster," in the dated and sexist discourse of the time. Marginalization as a prerequisite for the pure scientific inquiry required for detection is referred to repeatedly in the novel, as when the African American Ephraim explains his philosophy for social reform: "'If you ever needs to get anything done outside the common run, don't waste yo time on the menfolks; get the womens and children to working at it'"(70).

Some of the details of the way Lucas Beauchamp is characterized are particularly interesting here. One group of critics has maligned Faulkner for this characterization, which they read as an embodiment of the author's political stance that African Americans should "go slow" in their quest for civil rights.[15] But it's important to also notice that Lucas is the only character in the novel who might wear the description "hard boiled," so often used for detective fiction of the time. So, in Chick's first glimpse of Lucas, he sees him as "not arrogant, not even scornful: just intractable and composed" (7), and through his first several appearances in the text, Lucas speaks almost exclusively in imperative verbs. If a figure like Humphrey Bogart's transition in the 1940s from gangster to detective-hero represents America's postwar desire for protagonists who are pragmatic, tough, intractable, and even a bit evil, *Intruder*'s characterization of Lucas as such a figure is particularly interesting for the way it reinforces the displacing of the detective figure to the societal margins.[16] A reader steeped in Faulkner's oeuvre may be blinded to how much tougher this Lucas is than the more enfeebled figure in *Go Down, Moses*, which appeared eight years earlier, if that earlier Lucas sticks in the reader's mind. But this toughness is noted, for example, by the Afro-Caribbean novelist and critic Wilson Harris in an essay about *Intruder*, which describes Lucas in his appearance in the flashback to Chick's accident as, "proud and pitiless as the white farmers on the land—who looms out of nowhere, it seems, and takes charge of the operation."[17] In contrast to Lucas and his marginalized allies, the mainstream social status of Gavin Stevens and others of his race-gender-generation are disqualified from such detection by their lack of mental and imaginative flexibility; in Ephraim's terms, the white men are "cluttered." Gavin Stevens clearly perceives himself as the inheritor of the tradition of European "Enlight-enment rationality," with his Harvard and Heidelberg degrees in tow, but the novel exposes his claim to knowledge and makes Lucas, Chick, and their helpers the possessors of detective acumen instead.

Here we see Faulkner's complicated relationship to colonial dis-courses. As described initially by Edouard Glissant in his book-length essay on Faulkner's art and his context, the Faulkner novel manages to maintain a double valence regarding questions of occupation and aes-thetics.[18] The Faulkner novel for Glissant is substantially an antioccupa-tion novel, a characteristic that stems from Faulkner's Southern milieu. But the Afro-Caribbean Glissant also acknowledges the history of the plantation and the traces that this history leaves on postplantation prop-ertied white Southern men, even those with the singular artistic genius of Faulkner. Similarly and brilliantly, Wilson Harris reads *Intruder*'s preoc-cupation with corpses as an inadvertent reference to the postplantation category of Voodoo, in order to express the pollution of the landscape that is Southern history and that operates as the unstated pretext of the novel's action. In the phenomenon of the marginalized instruments of detection, we see this very double valence of attitude toward the colonial regime. The empirical and rational are set against violence and disor-der in *Intruder*, just as in Conan Doyle, but by belaboring even further the necessity of a detective who comes from a marginal social position, Faulkner's novel subverts the entire structure of colonialism with its cen-tralized hierarchy of power. When Fredric Jameson talks about the ten-dency on the part of the detective to unveil crimes that indict an entire community, his immediate reference is the fiction of national allegory that proliferates in the cultures of the decolonizing nations of the "Third World," yet he might just as easily be referring to Chick, Aleck Sander, and Miss Habersham, whose work unmistakably indicts the community of Jefferson (including Gavin Stevens) in its rush to condemn Lucas as well as its thirst for vigilante justice.[19]

While colonialism of the classic Anglo-French type makes sense as a context for the work of Arthur Conan Doyle, the United States has its own distinctive relationship with the countries that came to be referred to as the Third World. Yet just as geopolitics undergirds British detective fiction of the late nineteenth century, we read evidence of a concern with global affairs in both the internal textual features of *Intruder in the Dust* and the external context of the novel. Much has been written about the rhetoric of Gavin Stevens in the novel, especially the long speeches to which he subjects Chick (and the reader), starting with the early morn-ing return of a group of town dwellers to the grave site that Chick and his two accomplices had dug up the night before. Early criticism of the novel, perhaps influenced by Edmund Wilson's misreading of it as a pro–state's rights political tract, tended to identify the bombastic rhetoric of Stevens with Faulkner, in spite of Faulkner's warnings against such an identification and the novel's subversion of Stevens as an authority figure. More recently, critics have established the incontrovertible distance between Stevens and Faulkner, but this correction leaves critics with the problem of how to understand the odd form Stevens's long monologues give the novel.[20] What has not been sufficiently attended to, however, is the way Gavin regularly returns to the geopolitical context of the question of American authority and the state. Furthermore, we know that Faulkner himself was becoming increasingly engaged with the global nature of American power around this time, and this is evident not only in the major biographies of him but also in recent scholarship by John T. Matthews and Harilaos Stecopolous on Faulkner's late period.[21]

Regarding the actual text of the novel, remember that Gavin begins the first of his long speeches by putting the twin problems of race and vigilantism not in a context of conflict between the North and South, but rather between the United States and Europe: "'the premise that man really wants peace and freedom—is the trouble with our relations with Europe right now, whose people not only dont know what peace is but—except for Anglo Saxons—actively distrust personal liberty; we are hoping without any real hope that our Atom bomb will be enough to defend an idea as obsolete as Noah's Ark'"(146–47). A few pages later, Gavin makes it explicitly clear that the ultimate threat to what he calls "homogeneity" and "national character" will come (in his view) not from the federal government, white vigilantism, or internal colonialism, but from forces outside the borders of the nation state, that is, from foreign powers (151). Beyond these specific references, we can understand Gavin's discourse of freedom as characteristic of a dominant Cold War rhetoric that John T. Matthews describes in his discussion of *The Mansion*. For Gavin, what he calls freedom is the goal of America in the world after the war, and the main threat to it globally is a counter discourse of equality emanating from those "non Anglo-Saxon" parts of Europe that he invokes. In addition to the fact of Faulkner's personal concern as a writer, thinker, and citizen with the geopolitical context of the Cold War, we can see a general concern with this context undergirding American letters at the time *Intruder* is published. This emphasis is logical enough given that the United States very suddenly had the mantle of strongest nation in the world thrust upon it at the end of the war and found itself having to compete for hegemony in various parts of the globe where its interests had been quite limited up until that point in time. Yet the connection between Cold War politics and literary culture has received relatively little attention among literary critics until quite recently.[22]

In order to give some idea of the Cold War milieu in American letters, I now shift my focus briefly to the example of the novel *The Sheltering Sky* by the American ex-patriot writer Paul Bowles, which was published ten months after *Intruder in the Dust*. Although there are obvious differences between these two American writers (of generation, regional background, and attitude toward travel and global settings), there are also striking similarities that bring them together as authors and invite comparison of their two novels of the late 1940s. Bowles had begun to establish a reputation as an eccentric composer in the 1930s, whose style was decidedly Francophile. At the same time, he had published a good amount of experimental poetry and become a protégé of Gertrude Stein and the companion of several lost generation writers in Paris. Prior to his first novel, Bowels had published a series of works of short fiction that had garnered some critical attention but also suggested that his career would be distinctly as a "writer's writer." Certainly, nothing he had written before *The Sheltering Sky* suggested that his first novel would become a bestseller and a book of the month club selection.

Given this background, several points of comparison between Bowles and Faulkner emerge. Both started out writing poetry. Both marginalized themselves prior to producing an art that often identified with the marginalized. Bowles was also a renegade from a mainstream, East Coast, orthodox conception of America, who stayed away from the centers of American literary and cultural power as much as possible. Like Faulkner, Bowles found himself in the late 1940s in an unlikely position. His pursuit of his art, which was always experimental and critical of mainstream, bourgeois American values, suddenly led him to author a novel that was widely successful in the American mainstream. If Faulkner's *Intruder* valorizes the role of those at society's margins in addressing the various postwar threats to American progress, Bowles also sets out to critique the American mainstream by writing a story portraying the lives and travels of American outsiders who have rejected the dominant values of the postwar American Goliath. So the novel begins with the narrator explaining that the three American travelers, whose journey in North Africa is the focus of the novel, "crossed the Atlantic for the first time since 1939, with a great deal of luggage and the intention of keeping as far as possible from the places which had been touched by the war."[23] Subsequently, the main characters develop a discourse that rejects what have come to be postwar American values in their statements about their trip, their connection to its setting, and even their relationships with each other. For example, Kit Moresby agrees with her husband, Port, immediately when he says of a dingy café where they find themselves at the beginning of the novel: "But I still a damned sight rather be here than back in the United States" (8). Later, Port thinks to himself that he feels "more closely identified with his great grandparents when . . . rolling along out . . . in the desert than he did sitting at home looking out over the reservoir in Central Park" (101), and still later, Kit insults their travel companion, Tunner, by calling him "a real American" (105).

The plot of *The Sheltering Sky* also offers up a set of trenchant critiques of the American scene in the years just after World War II. When Faulkner writes to his publisher that *Intruder in the Dust* is an old-fashioned mystery murder with American race relations as its theme, his suggestion of a theme has an interesting resonance with the Bowles novel even though the latter is set entirely in North Africa. About two thirds of the way through *The Sheltering Sky*, the main character, the American traveler Port Moresby, suddenly and surprisingly dies of typhoid fever, leaving his wife, Kit, alone and abandoned in a remote outpost in the Sahara. Equally surprising is her response to the situation. Rather than seeking the protection of local French legionnaires, waiting for their other American travel companion, Tunner, to come rescue her, or attempting to return to New York, Kit runs into the desert, joins a caravan of sub-Saharan traders, and allows herself for a time to become the willing sex slave of one of the traders named Belqassim.

Literary critics have long been aware of the way Bowles's novel appropriates the popular genre of the captivity narrative in this section in a manner highly comparable to the strategic use of murder mystery in *Intruder in the Dust*. American literature since its earliest stages has been fascinated with the phenomenon of captivity. In fact, this fascination has extended from the story of Mary Rowlandson's captivity among Indians in colonial times to media coverage of the taking of American hostages in Iran in 1979.[24] In the last section of *The Sheltering Sky*, Kit is held captive by a lusty native, but beyond this simple fact, the novel goes out of its way to pervert the traditional genre. The narrative makes clear that Kit is a willing participant in her own hostage taking. Furthermore, whereas Belqassim's sexuality would represent a primal threat in the traditional captivity story, here the narrative goes out of its way to highlight Kit's pleasure and anticipation in connection with their sexual liaison: "Since she lived now solely for those few fiery hours spent each day beside Belqassim, she could not bear to think of warning him to be less prodigal of his love with her" (278). It is in this aspect of the novel that Faulkner's theme of American race relations enters the picture. As Brian T. Edwards shows in a recent reading of Bowels's novel, this sequence can be understood as a critique of the Jim Crow regime that had split the nation. The novel dramatizes the act of sex across racial lines (an act outlawed not only in the Southern states, but in many other parts of the U.S. at the time) as part of Kit's comprehensive rejection of American normativity.[25] In this sense, the sequence in *The Sheltering Sky* simultaneously furthers the novel's theme of American characters rejecting mainstream American values at the same time that it ties the international setting into *Intruder's* theme of black-white relations inside the United States.

The question of detection in Bowles's fiction also has a specific character that both participates in the Faulknerian ethos of detection that has been my focus and furthers the discussion. Bowles uses the notion of the detective story as a metaphor to describe all of his fiction. In a letter to his publisher, for example, written the year after the publication of *The Sheltering Sky* and referring to his first story collection, *The Delicate Prey*, Bowles complains: "No one seems to have realized that practically all the tales are a variety of detective story. Not the usual variety, I admit, but still, detective stories in which the reader is the detective; the mystery is the motivation for the character's behavior, and the clues are given in the form of reactions on the part of the characters to details of situation and surroundings."[26] If the same metaphor can be applied to his novel *The Sheltering Sky*, it should also be noted that the novel directly incorporates a "murder mystery" into a short section of the novel at the beginning of part 2. An incorporated short story involves a French officer, Lt. d'Armagnac, who, in solving the case of a young mother who has killed her child, undercuts his own standing within the local community. In this passage, Bowles uses the genre to present a depiction of French colonialism's decrepitude in the immediate aftermath of World War II. Because of his clumsy handling of the case and the bad luck of the accused's accidental death while in his custody, d'Armagnac not only poisons his relationship with the locals whom he must govern (becoming himself literally poisoned by them in the process), he also raises in the eyes of his commanding officer in Algiers: "the question of his fitness to deal with the 'native psychology'"(146). Here again, detection in the colonial context goes hand in hand with the need to maintain order, and with the specter of decolonization looming, French powers of detection are depicted as flawed. But d'Armagnac's narrative also allows the novel to compare and contrast French and American styles in relating to North Africans. In the subsequent chapter, d'Armagnac meets Port Morseby, whose travels have brought him to the French officer's region. Another mystery, the loss of Port's passport, unfolds and is solved on the spot by d'Armagnac in the course of a brief first meeting between the two men. The scene serves to expose the American character's incompetence as a detective and, by extension, the lack of preparedness of the United States to replace the French as foreign power in the region.

As is the case with Faulkner, Bowles adapts the genre's traditional characteristics freely—even oppositely—in his fiction in general. Rationality, for example, is almost never valorized by Bowles. Rather, his characters are at their best when they display an awareness of their own intuition and sense of adventure and a willingness to pursue the magical and irrational that Bowles feels has been bleached out of mainstream American culture. Also, the Bowles novel removes the issues surrounding detection from their domestic setting of Conan Doyle's London or Chandler's Los Angeles. In the Bowles novel, the power and privilege of the First World vis-à-vis the Third World is placed in the foreground, whereas for Conan Doyle, the colonial dynamic remains a persistent subtext. This internationalization of setting by Bowles lends his work to comparison with the other great literary genre of intrigue discussed by Siddiqi: the spy novel. In spy novels the question of the need to contain violence, disorder, and chaos is played out in a global, transnational setting, which portrays the stakes as national security itself. Bowles juxtaposes the American hyperfixation with order and suppression with what he sees as the intuitive and magical, more authentic Third World space in his spy novel *Let It Come Down*. This second novel recapitulates many themes of *The Sheltering Sky*, particularly the theme of the unfulfilled young American trying to escape the soul-crushing conformity of American society.

Finally, what I would like to suggest about this comparison between two popular literary novels of America in the late 1940s is that together they make a statement about the United States and its literary culture in the earliest years of the Cold War. Both writers are critics of the American mainstream who are concerned with the global ramifications of the direction they see American culture going. Surely this is part of what we should understand from the action of each text. Equally significant, however, is what remains absent from these critiques. *Intruder* presents an intricate context made up of fierce contestations between country and city, Northern U.S. and Southern U.S., and even (through Gavin Stevens's discourse) Europe and America. In this context, the challenge is to create some sense of nation that can include the diverse cross section of identities represented by the novel's various characters. The novel does not show any obvious awareness of the movement toward decolonization in the Third World as another element of the geopolitical milieu in which Lucas's story plays out, even though the possibility of the internationalizing of the American civil rights movement that would become a hotly debated topic in the 1950s and 1960s had already been raised as an issue—specifically around the question of what to do about lynching, which a group of influential American civil rights leaders had argued should be brought before a United Nations tribunal as a campaign of genocide.[27] But the relative absence of questions of decolonization is perhaps more striking in Bowles's novel, which takes place in Algeria in the years immediately before its uprising against French colonial rule as its setting. Only after his success with *The Sheltering Sky* and his follow-up novel *Let It Come Down* did Bowles finally write a novel, *The Spider's House*, which acknowledged—highly critically—the growing tide of nationalism in the part of the world where he had chosen to make his home. Moroccan writer Mohamed Choukri, who had collaborated with Bowles on the latter's translation of his roman à clef, *For Bread Alone*, later pithily critiqued Bowles's relationship to his country of residence in a passage dealing with *The Spider's House* from Choukri's Arabic memoir of Bowles's life in Tangiers: "Paul Bowles loves Morocco, but he doesn't love Moroccans."[28]

The comparison of *Intruder in the Dust* and *The Sheltering Sky* suggests that the engagement of the American writer with American Empire at this early stage of U.S. Cold War hegemony showed little or no awareness of movements of decolonization and third world nationalism—and when such movements were acknowledged as in Bowles's third novel, there was little sympathy for them. An emphasis on the Soviet threat meant that the entire discussion around America in the world took place with only minimal acknowledgment that the United States was becoming the primary hegemon in most of the former colonies of France and Great Britain. In this relative ignorance, we find one of the unique characteristics of the new American brand of Empire, for the United States has always operated as an imperial power under a cloak of deniability that the British and French would have never seen any need for. The American Empire, in contrast, is one that feels compelled not to acknowledge itself. The questions of anxiety and the need to control an external threat that undergird the detective genre are, however, definitively global concerns for Americans and have been since before *Intruder in the Dust* was published.

In their widely cited explication of imperial power in the contemporary world published only a year before the attacks of 11 September 2001, Michael Hardt and Antonio Negri take as their point of departure the transformation in the post–Cold War era of all wars into what they call "police actions."[29] One can think of the two wars in Iraq and the ongoing conflict in Afghanistan as prime examples, given that they were not provoked by states' attacking the United States or declaring war against it, but rather by criminal acts of terroristic attack. In closing, let me suggest that the American deniability of our own implication in imperialism along with the absence of any space for Third World nationalist or other narratives of self-determination in our own internal critiques of imperialism have both played a large role in the situation in which we now find ourselves. That situation is ably embodied by Faulkner's title. Scholars have demonstrated that his title began with the prepositional phrase "in the dust" and only very late did he choose "intruder" from a number of unsatisfying alternatives. The novel does not explicitly clarify for its reader who the primary referent of the first term is; rather we are left various alternatives: Lucas, Chick, Vinson Gowrie, or Jake Montgomery. The various possibilities leave the term open. Fifty plus years later, the term takes on a new referent as the U.S.'s imperial venture has become its own intruder in Middle Eastern dust.

NOTES

I am indebted to Karen Fang, Chris Hudson, and John T. Matthews for insightful comments on a draft of this essay.

1. D. A. Miller's *The Novel and the Police* (Berkeley: University of California Press, 1988), which uses Michel Foucault's analysis of regimes of surveillance and control in post-Enlightenment western societies to examine the way social order was valorized in the emerging culture of British popular fiction of the nineteenth century, has been particularly influential in this regard.

2. Yumna Siddiqi, *Anxieties of Empire and the Fiction of Intrigue* (New York: Columbia University Press, 2008), 17. Henceforth cited parenthetically within the text.

3. Donald Pease critiques the way the doctrine of "American exceptionalism" has created a national discourse that has accommodated the denial of the U.S.'s implication in colonialism in spite of its historical verifiability. See Pease, "U.S. Imperialism: Global Dominance without Colonies," in Sangeeta Ray and Henry Schwarz, eds., *A Companion to Postcolonial Studies* (London: Blackwell, 2000). 203–20.

4. See Joseph Blotner, *Faulkner: A Biography* (New York: Random House, 1994), 490.

5. See Tzvetan Todorov, *The Poetics of Prose*, trans. Richard Howard (Ithaca, N.Y.: Cornell University Press), 43.

6. See Michael Grimwood, *Heart in Conflict: Faulkner's Struggle with Vocation* (Athens: University of Georgia Press, 1987). Grimwood avoids talking about the issue in terms of markets, although Faulkner's longstanding financial struggles were inevitably influential in his writing habits.

7. Todorov, 49.

8. See Theresa M. Towner, *Faulkner on the Color Line: The Later Novels* (Jackson: University Press of Mississippi, 2000), 54–57, and Lorrie Watkins Fulton, "Intruder in the Past," *Southern Literary Journal* 38.2 (2006): 64–73.

9. My line of thinking is part of a larger trend that has been promoted more generally in Faulkner studies by Deborah Cohn, Edouard Glissant, George Handley, Vera Kutzinski, Barbara Ladd, John T. Matthews, Jon Smith, and Annette Trefzer, among others. My argument regarding Faulknerian form and postcolonial historiography appears in chapters 3 and 4 of *Other South: Faulkner, Coloniality, and the Mariátegui Tradition* (Pittsburgh: University of Pittsburgh Press, 2007). As an example of the general trend in Faulkner studies, see Smith and Cohn's *Look Away! The U.S. South and New World Studies* (Durham: Duke University Press, 2004).

10. See C. Vann Woodward, *The Burden of Southern History* (Baton Rouge: Louisiana State University Press, 1960), 190.

11. The Democratic Party had split at its 1948 convention between a majority that supported a platform of civil rights and antilynching legislation and "Dixiecrats," led by Strom Thurmond, who opposed these points in the party's platform. See Noel Polk, "Man in the Middle: Faulkner and the Southern White Moderate," in *Faulkner and Race: Faulkner and Yoknapatawpha, 1986,* ed. Doreen Fowler and Ann J. Abadie (Jackson: University Press of Mississippi, 1987), 130–32 and passim, for a discussion of the novel's relationship to the 1948 Democratic convention and the history of attempts at legislating protection against lynching and greater civil rights for African Americans.

12. I would further assert, following Susan Willis's still innovative, if now decades old, use of dependency theory to read "The Bear," that these spatial divides often stand in for a global division between "First World" and "Third World." See Susan Willis, "Aesthetics of the Rural Slum: Contradictions and Dependency in 'The Bear,'" *Social Text* 1:3 (1979): 82–103.

13. William Faulkner, *Intruder in the Dust* (New York: Vintage, 1991), 4. Henceforth cited parenthetically within the text.

14. See Edward Said, *Culture and Imperialism* (New York: Knopf, 1993), 3–15 and passim.

15. Michael Millgate, for instance, calls Lucas "too proud to plead for himself"; *William Faulkner* (New York: Grove, 1961), 94. See also Thadious Davis, *Faulkner's "Negro": Art and the Southern Context* (Baton Rouge: LSU Press, 1983), 5, and Neil Schmitz, "Faulkner and the Post-Confederate," in *Faulkner in Cultural Context* (Jackson: University Press of Mississippi, 1995), 241–62.

16. "I aint got friends," Lucas announces to Gavin and Chick later (63).

17. Wilson Harris, "Reflections on *Intruder in the Dust*," in *The Womb of Space: The Cross-Cultural Imagination* (Westport, Conn.: Greenwood Press, 1983), 6. Actor Juano Hernandez, who plays Lucas in the 1949 film version of the novel, offers through his performance yet another reading of him as tough and fearless.

18. Edouard Glissant, *Faulkner, Mississippi*, trans. Barbara Lewis and Thomas C. Spear (Chicago: University of Chicago Press, 1999).

19. See Fredric Jameson, *The Geopolitical Aesthetic* (Bloomington: Indiana University Press, 1992), 37.

20. One effect of the monologues is to complicate the generic gesture toward detective fiction. Arguably, the long rants of Stevens expose the detective genre's actual implication in questions of state order. See Polk, "Man in the Middle," for a convincing treatment of the proper way to understand Stevens's rhetoric and its place in the novel. Also helpful on this issue are Towner, *Faulkner on the Color Line*, and Masami Sugimori, "Signifying, Ordering, and Containing the Chaos: Whiteness, Ideology, and Language in *Intruder in the Dust*," *Faulkner Journal* 22:1–2 (2007): 54–73.

21. John T. Matthews, "Many Mansions: Faulkner's Cold War Conflicts," in *Global Faulkner*, ed. Annette Trefzer and Ann J. Abadie (Jackson: University Press of Mississippi, 2009), 3–23; Harilaos Stecopolous, *Reconstructing the World: Southern Fictions and U.S. Imperialisms, 1898–1976* (Ithaca: Cornell University Press, 2008).

22. In addition to Pease, see Christina Klein's *Cold War Orientalism: Asia in the Middlebrow Imagination, 1945–61* (Berkeley: University of California Press, 2003).

23. Paul Bowles, *The Sheltering Sky* (1949; New York: Harper Collins, 2000), 6. Henceforth cited parenthetically.

24. Rowlandson recounted her captivity in 1682 in her wildly popular *A Narrative of the Captivity and Restoration of Mrs. Mary Rowlandson* (1682; Charleston, S.C.:

Bibliobazaar, 2006). On the fascination with captivity as a trope in the coverage of the hostages crisis in Iran in 1979–1980, see Melani McAlister, *Epic Encounters: Culture, Media, and U.S. Interests in the Middle East since 1945* (Berkeley: University of California Press, 2005), 199–216.

25. See Brian Edwards, *Morocco Bound: Disorienting America's Maghreb, from Casablanca to the Marrakech Express* (Durham: Duke University Press, 2005), 114. Edwards makes the connection between Kit's coupling with Belqassim and the domestic U.S. Jim Crow regime but maintains that Bowles's text insists on an "extranational" meaning of the encounter.

26. See Paul Bowles, *In Touch: The Letters of Paul Bowles*, ed. Jeffrey Miller (New York: Farrar, Strauss and Giroux, 1993), 226. In reading this passage aloud for the film director Jennifer Baichwal as part of a scene in her documentary *Let It Come Down: The Life of Paul Bowles*, which was released in 1998, a year before his death, Bowles extends the metaphor to the entirety of his fictional oeuvre.

27. This debate culminated in the petition authored by the Civil Rights Congress, presented to the United Nations, and published as a book under the title *We Charge Genocide* (New York: Civil Rights Congress, 1951).

28. See Mohamed Choukri, *Paul Bowles and the Solitude of Tangiers* (Cologne: Manshurat al-Jamal, 1996), 12 (my translation).

29. See Michael Hardt and Antonio Negri, *Empire* (Cambridge: Harvard University Press, 2001), 12.

Critical Intruders: Unraveling Race and Mystery in *Intruder in the Dust*

ESTHER SÁNCHEZ-PARDO

William Faulkner opens *Intruder in the Dust* (1948)[1] by immediately undermining the certainty of the white racial knowledge that has just landed Lucas Beauchamp, his black protagonist, in jail: "It was just noon that Saturday morning when the sheriff reached the jail with Lucas Beauchamp though the whole town (the whole country too for that matter) had known since the night before that Lucas had killed a white man" (3). As we soon discover, the sheriff, the town, and the country are in fact all wrong: what they think they "know" about Lucas's apparent act of murder (he is accused of having shot the white Vinson Gowrie in the back) turns out to be completely erroneous. In this deceptively simple opening sentence, Faulkner is asking us to examine, and indeed reject, the white southern legal system's presumption of black male criminality.

The problem of false knowledge—and particularly the unreliability of received white narratives—becomes a central motif in a text that is in part a detective novel in which Chick Mallison will have to uncover the mystery of who killed Vinson Gowrie but that is also a coming-of-age narrative in which Chick will attempt to uncover the "mystery" of Lucas Beauchamp himself. "[Chick] knew Lucas Beauchamp too," the narrator tells us, "as well that is as any white person knew him" (3–4). The mystery at the heart of this "detective" novel is not necessarily who killed Vinson Gowrie—Faulkner reveals that the true culprit is Crawford Gowrie, Vinson's brother and business rival, at the midpoint of the novel—but rather what precisely is going on in the mind of this black man whose individual subjectivity resists being categorized, contained, and understood by whites.

Where conventional crime fiction emphasizes conformity, social disruption as aberration, and a reinscription of order through resolution, *Intruder in the Dust* decenters those conventions in favor of a nonhegemonic point of view, an idea that sees social disruption as symptomatic of racial and political oppression, and a problematic inscription of order—or a sense that no order should be expected. The genre is clearly altered and, more importantly, perceptions of justice are altered as well. *Intruder in the Dust* is thus part of that Faulknerian universe that refuses Manichean dichotomies of good/evil, margin/center, criminal/crime-solver in favor of the understanding that "traditional" narratives and a "conventional" sense of social justice are bound to an arbitrary dominant order. That order, in one way or another, influences and affects all that come under its gaze; however the complex reflection that results from this specific novel offers us the means by which we can shield ourselves from that powerful gaze and from the privileged vantage point we get, we may imagine another form of justice.

In his book *Faulkner, Mississippi* (1996), Caribbean writer Edouard Glissant notes that *Intruder* "tells of a moment in the education (the initiation) of a young white male, the decisive player in the story," but then asserts that the novel "is also a picture-perfect portrait of a Negro's opacity, an opacity that, until the end and despite the explanations and a return to everyday life, never swerves from its course."[2] Faulkner's emphasis on Lucas's inscrutability, what Glissant calls his opacity, certainly suggests the possibility that Lucas's subversive self-possession, his refusal to be "read" by whites, can operate as a form of resistance to a justice system that contains no outlet through which he can be allowed to speak for himself.[3] In his view, *Intruder* is a "much more important book than is generally believed" (176).

In Glissant's formulation, Faulkner's Mississippi is a new space, parallel to Faulkner's Yoknapatawpha, forged between the writerly and readerly imaginations. Glissant theorizes a singular geography for Faulkner's South and his own based upon their shared historical past. He emphatically asserts a singular awareness and foundation for heterogeneity between and within the Caribbean and American South. In this way, he gestures to a new "South America," a zone Faulkner was aware of but, because of its dominant culture, feared. In my view, Glissant acknowledges Faulkner's latent racism and admits that he does not always know if Faulkner's black characters demonstrate that he is "respecting the opacity of the Other" (65). In any event, the reader's change of historical or geographical context alone does not explain Faulkner's radically new meanings. The ambivalence and undecidability of Faulkner's universe may well be the result of Faulkner's own contradictory ideas, and it does not seem to pose a problem for Glissant. In his efforts to claim and reassess the importance of Faulkner for a larger Caribbean and Southern hemispheric tradition, he refuses to grant the writer a certain predictability simply based on where and how he lived. In his work, Glissant traces the parallelisms in the histories of the Americas that, in his view, Faulkner incorporated into his fictional universe.

In *Intruder in the Dust* the relationship between Chick and Lucas is a relationship not only between two individuals on opposite sides of the

Jim Crow color line, but also between two characters who compete for space in a complex narrative. We can see the kind of conflict that this relationship generated in Faulkner's own conception of the novel as he described it in various letters and papers in the 1940s. In a June 1940 letter to Robert Haas, his editor at Random House (nearly eight years before he could actually begin writing the novel in earnest), Faulkner wrote that he had in the work "a mystery story, original in that the solver is a negro, himself in jail for the murder and is about to be lynched, solves murder in self defense."[4] Eight years later in a February 1948 letter to his literary agent, Harold Ober, Faulkner's language indicates a subtle shift in his conception of who—either Lucas or Chick, black struggle or white ethics of action—should hold the dominant position in the narrative: he describes his nearly completed manuscript as "a mystery murder though the theme is more [the] relationship between Negro and white, specifically or rather the premise being that the white people in the south, before the North or the govt. or anyone else, owe and must pay a responsibility to the Negro. But it's a story . . . a Negro in jail accused of murder and waiting for the white folks to drag him out and pour gasoline over him and set him on fire, is the detective, solves the crime because he goddamn has to keep from being lynched, by asking people to go somewhere and look at something and then come back and tell him what they found."[5] And finally, in an April 1948 letter to Haas after having completed a 321-page manuscript, Faulkner summarized the gist of the still untitled work as "a pretty good study of a sixteen-year-old boy who overnight became a man."[6] The tension in these descriptions between black agency (with Lucas as "the detective" who "solves the crime") and white control ("white people in the South, before the North or the govt. or anyone else"; "boy who overnight became a man") suggests something of the difficulties that Faulkner came up against during *Intruder*'s composition and also signals that, at least in his own mind, the novel was above all a coming-of-age story focused on a white boy who becomes an ethical Southern citizen.

And yet this almost linear trajectory (moving from a black man's actual struggle to a white boy's moral journey) is at odds with Faulkner's final published description of the novel in a discussion with a group of students at the University of Virginia in 1957. Returning the focus of the text decisively back to Lucas, Faulkner reveals that his initial idea for the novel was "a man in jail just about to be hung" who "would have to be his own detective" and who "couldn't get anybody to help him." He then adds that "the next thought was, the man for that would be a Negro. Then the character of Lucas—Lucas Beauchamp came along. And the book came out of that. It was the notion of a man in jail who couldn't hire a detective. . . . But once I thought of Beauchamp, then he took charge of the story and the story was a good deal different from the idea that—of the detective story that I had started with."[7] Faulkner's interest in the individual agency of the incarcerated black character—Lucas's struggle to free himself from unjust confinement, his ability to "t[ake] charge of the story"—suggests his own desire to write a novel that could articulate the process of black liberation carried out by blacks themselves, even if he remained in some sense unable to conceive of such a project without representing the intervention of whites. Because Gavin Stevens is so unwilling to listen to Lucas's story, Faulkner suggests, the responsibility shifts decisively over to Lucas himself to figure out how he might best go about planning his exoneration. The first stage of this process entails Lucas's effort to question Gavin's receptiveness to helping him dig up the Gowrie corpse, without giving him a far too explicit command of what he wants him to do. *Intruder in the Dust* is concerned with the freedom of Lucas Beauchamp, but more generally it attempts to suggest a solution to the problem of civil rights for African Americans. Many critics have commented on the fact that the novel seems to break into two parts which are not totally unified: Gavin Stevens's political speeches and the narrative account of Lucas Beauchamp's near lynching.[8]

Intruder's plot is quite simple and characteristic of the detective genre. Vinson Gowrie, a white man, and significantly a Beat Four white man, is murdered, and Lucas Beauchamp, an arrogant old black man, is discovered standing over the body holding a gun that has recently been fired. Lucas is put into jail by Sheriff Hope Hampton, and all of Jefferson waits expectantly for Monday (even poor whites like the Gowries do not lynch a black man on Sunday) when they feel Lucas will be lynched according to local custom by a mob led by Vinson Gowrie's father, brothers, friends, and relatives.[9] At first everyone assumes that Lucas is as guilty as the circumstances seem to indicate. Gavin Stevens agrees to defend Lucas, but wants him to plead guilty to manslaughter so as to avoid a death penalty. Lucas, wise in the ways of the world, knows that his only hope lies with women and children whose minds "aint cluttered" (70) and who sense certain things intuitively. Men like Gavin are "too busy with facks," according to Lucas (70). Consequently Lucas asks Chick Mallison to go out to the graveyard, dig up Vinson's body, and check the bullet hole. Lucas's gun is a Colt .45, and Vinson was killed, it turns out, with a German Lugar, the same type of gun Crawford Gowrie, Vinson's brother, brought home with him from World War II. Chick, Aleck Sander, and old Miss Habersham set out for the graveyard, and the question is whether or not they can dig up the body and get it back to Jefferson in time to prove Lucas innocent and save him. When they finally do dig up the grave they find not Vinson Gowrie, but Jake Montgomery, a lumber dealer from a nearby town. Although this is not exactly what they expected, it is enough to set the seemingly more rational types such as Gavin and the sheriff in motion. Eventually, Vinson's body is found buried in quicksand near the cemetery, and the sheriff sees that he was indeed killed with Crawford Gowrie's German Lugar. Crawford is thrown into jail where he commits suicide with a gun that is mysteriously smuggled to him. Lucas is released, thanks to the efforts of the three innocents who trusted their intuition rather than "the facks."

Truth simply will not stay buried, Faulkner seems to be saying, as he skillfully manipulates the conventions of mystery fiction laying bare the rationale behind Vinson Gowrie's murder. As Edouard Glissant remarks, what is most at stake in the novel "is not a matter of knowing what happened, because everyone knows that Lucas Beauchamp knows, but rather of finding out why he does not want to tell. How can he consider himself a silent and omnipotent protagonist when he risks an imminent, ignominious death?" (45). The sly wit that prompts Lucas to exercise restraint and keep his "cards" concealed emerges again a moment after, when Gavin, struggling to contain his anger, asks Lucas: "Has it ever occurred to you that if you just said 'mister' to white people and said it like you meant it, you might not be sitting here [in jail] now?" (60) Lucas's reply—"So, I'm to commence now. I can start off by saying mister to the folks that drags me out of here and builds a fire under me" (60)—is a clever reply that signifies his own awareness that no amount of politeness would stop the racial resentment he inspires among the town's angry whites, and that such behavioral codes are directly intended to keep blacks regulated and confined.

In the novel, Lucas's calculated decision to turn to Chick and not Gavin represents his own critical recognition of the necessary levers that he must pull if he is to attain his freedom. Even under such desperate conditions, Lucas "had in the end known better than to try to tell [Chick's] uncle or any other white man" about the grave-digging job (77). He knows that "[Chick] alone of all the white people [he] would have a chance to speak to between now and the moment when he might be dragged out of the cell and down the steps at the end of a rope, would hear the mute unhoping urgency of [his] eyes" (67). Faulkner's language here signals to us Lucas's pride as well as his recognition of the "urgency" of his situation. As Theresa Towner has observed, Faulkner "attempts something more difficult than . . . map[ping] the contours of Lucas's racial self: he is trying in *Intruder* to imagine the scope of effort it would take for a 'black' man in the late 1940s to create an audience of 'white' believers who will act upon his 'word.'" [10]

After the publication of the novel, early critics such as Irving Howe and Edmund Wilson[11] discussed *Intruder in the Dust* in the context of the civil rights movement, and they argued that as a realistic solution to the civil rights issue, the novel is simply too sentimental to be convincing. If blacks must depend on women and children to stand up against the forces that oppose racial equality, equality may never come. Faulkner's narrative minimizes and oversimplifies the difficulties involved in gaining freedom for black people for whom Lucas in his cell serves as symbolic representative. *Intruder* contains too many unusual and atypical characters[12] for it to be considered a description or illustration of how blacks will eventually gain their freedom.

That Lucas seeks help from Chick, who, as a teenage white boy, has not yet been fully indoctrinated by the social mores and legal regulations epitomized by his uncle, signals his understandable refusal to put any trust in a white-controlled legal system predicated on false racial knowledge. In this way, Lucas exhibits his own particular form of agency; he "directs" his liberation from the confines of his jail cell, enlists the right people in his cause, and gives Chick detailed instructions about the location of the body and the evidence that he expects that Chick will find there.

The jail in which Lucas is incarcerated is constantly and uncomfortably present throughout the novel, simultaneously representing the injustice being done to Lucas and his race and the hope for a future in which the institutions of civilization will work as they were intended to work. It is difficult for the reader to rid herself of the haunting image of Lucas isolated and alone in his cell, because Faulkner includes a rich description and discussion of the jail itself. He emphasizes the fact that the jail along with the courthouse is located at the geographical center of the community of Jefferson. This central location is symbolically appropriate, for these two institutions are the backbone of civilization in Yoknapatawpha County and in any other county: "[Chick] remembered how his uncle had said once that not courthouses nor even churches but jails were the true record of a county's, a community's history, since not only the cryptic forgotten initials and words and even phrases cries of defiance and indictment scratched into the walls but the very bricks and stones themselves held, not in solution but in suspension, intact and biding and potent and indestructible, the agonies and shames and griefs with which hearts long since unmarked and unremembered dust had strained and perhaps burst" (49). For Faulkner the jail is a repository of southern, and more specifically, Jefferson history. It is a link to the relatively pure and innocent times when Major DeSpain and Sam Fathers hunted Old Ben in the Big Woods, a link to the free and rural

South that Faulkner loved. And yet at the same time this jail is a survivor of the Civil War; it was standing and in use during the period described in *Go Down, Moses*, when white men still had black slaves. It was standing when "good" white men such as Uncle Buck and Buddy McCaslin locked up their blacks at night in the big house but left the back door open so that they could go wherever they wished, just as long as they were back the next morning in time to walk out the front door and into the fields. And in *Intruder in the Dust* the jail is still standing, chronicling this episode in the lives of Lucas Beauchamp and Chick Mallison, and thereby updating the historical treatment of black-white relationships that Faulkner had attempted in *Go Down, Moses* (1942).

In *Intruder* Lucas Beauchamp makes it to the town jail instead of being lynched by the mob gathering in the square because he is associated with the old planter culture of his white grandfather, and both Sheriff Hope Hampton and Gavin Stephens protect him and try to preserve the integrity of their community. As it is well known, *Go Down, Moses* (1942) functions as the urtext to *Intruder*. It spans more than a century in the history of the McCaslin family and deals with a range of crucial subjects in the Faulknerian universe. It is precisely in "The Old People," a story about Isaac McCaslin's childhood, where we also find the history of Sam Fathers—part Native American and part African American, the son of Chickasaw chief Ikkemotubbe, the chief who sold the land to the white people and also sold his son and wife into slavery. Sam left the Jefferson area for the big forest after the death of Jobaker, his Choctaw friend. At present, Sam tends the hunting camp of Major DeSpain and McCaslin Edmonds. In "The Old People" Sam teaches Isaac McCaslin how to hunt. When Isaac grows up, he should be able to join the hunting expeditions with Major DeSpain, General Compson, and his older cousin McCaslin Edmonds. Isaac's first lessons in hunting lead him to experience two epiphanic moments: his anointment in the blood of the first buck he kills (Sam Fathers ritualistically anoints him with the deer's blood), and his vision of the giant spirit buck. His acceptance of the tradition passed down to him by Sam, and understood by the "old people" whom the title of the story refers to, represents how the values of the hunt are absorbed by young Isaac, and he is granted a different kind of patrimony free from the violence and corruption associated with the inheritance of property,[13] a patrimony of moral tradition whereby values are handed down from one generation to another.

In *Intruder in the Dust*, in the paragraph following the one included above, Faulkner actually takes us inside the jail, where we see for ourselves the fear in the faces of the black inmates: "even the room behind it was dark, though it was not yet eight o'clock and he could see, imagine them not huddled perhaps but certainly all together, within elbow's touch whether they were actually or not and certainly quiet, not laughing tonight nor talking either, sitting in the dark and watching the top of the stairs because this would not be the first time when to mobs of white men not only all black cats were gray but they didn't always bother to count them either" (50–51). This sort of scene eventually causes the crucial change that occurs in Chick Mallison's perception of the South. In this passage it is unclear whether Chick actually sees or imagines the blacks huddled together watching the top of the stairs, waiting for the sounds of the mob. Later in the novel when he enters the jail with his uncle and also when he returns alone to bring Lucas some tobacco, this ambiguity does not exist. Chick sees the fear of the blacks and he knows that they have good reason to be afraid. This knowledge disturbs him as it would any liberal, sensitive, sixteen-year-old boy. He is torn between loyalty to his community and loyalty to his own emerging conscience.

The jail and what he observes in and around it has a tremendous physical and psychic impact on Chick. It helps to jolt him out of childhood and into manhood: it hastens and intensifies his initiation into the unpleasant reality of racial violence and prejudice in his homeland. Faulkner's rich descriptions of the jail also help to focus attention on the injustice being done to Lucas so that we do not forget about him, even while we leave him to follow Chick, Aleck Sander, and Miss Habersham out of Jefferson into Beat Four to dig up Vinson Gowrie's grave. The jail is at the center of Jefferson—the four roads coming from East, West, North, and South all converge at the Square—and it is appropriate that this social drama pitting the forces of justice and reason against the forces of injustice and irrational prejudice is enacted in and around the town jail with representatives from all sections of Yoknapatawpha County in attendance.

Along this line, Lucas Beauchamp is not the only prisoner in *Intruder in the Dust*. While attempting to help Lucas recover his physical freedom, Chick Mallison attempts to break free of the limitations of the community in which he lives. While helping Lucas avoid a lynch mob Chick strives to regain his moral freedom, a freedom that he lost to Lucas when he was twelve years old, four years before the events described in the main plot of *Intruder in the Dust* take place. As he does in so many of his novels, Faulkner juxtaposes a literal prisoner (Lucas) with a prisoner of another sort, in this instance, a prisoner of conscience (Chick) who attempts to free himself from the restrictive prejudices of the people of Jefferson, on one hand, and from his moral bondage to Lucas, on the other.[14]

One should also be aware that at an early stage the relationship between these two characters is still not exactly what we might call amicable; indeed, Faulkner makes it clear that their rapport remains something of a competition: Lucas is too proud to enlist Chick's help strictly as a favor, so he insists on paying Chick to dig up the grave, just as he stubbornly insists on "pay[ing] [his] own way" when he asks for Gavin's legal services (63). And Chick, for his part, notices "the bleared old man's eyes watching him, inscrutable and secret," and thinks to himself, "He's not only beat me, he never for one second had any doubt of it" (71). In "Change the Joke and Slip the Yoke" (1958), Ralph Ellison argues that "For all the racial and caste differences between them, Lucas holds the ascendancy in his mature dignity over the youthful Mallison and refuses to lower himself in the comic duel of status forced on him by the white boy whose life he has saved."[15] And yet what the jail-cell encounter with Lucas most instills in Chick is not anger or resentment but rather a newfound sense of urgency about his efforts on this man's behalf, a realization that what is at stake is not merely his own moral journey but rather the need to prevent "the death by shameful violence of a man who would die not because he was a murderer but because his skin was black" (70–71).

In arguing that Faulkner posits Lucas as a figure of racial resistance in the novel and that he uses Lucas's relationship with Chick as a kind of model for grappling with the larger problem of the black male's imperiled status in a white controlled southern legal system, I am consciously taking issue with one classic criticism of *Intruder*: namely, that its central character, Lucas, remains entirely too isolated from any semblance to an authentic black community to serve as a viable figure of black rebellion in pre–civil rights South. Faulkner's characterization of Lucas as a supremely *singular* hero relies too heavily on a kind of abstract humanist individualism that would likely have meant very little to what would become a decisively *collective* black struggle against racism, segregation, and state-sponsored racial inequality. Even if Lucas represents, as many critics concede, the most self-possessed black character in Faulkner's entire body of work, he nevertheless remains in *Intruder* "solitary kinless and intractable" (23).[16] Thus, Frederick Karl faults Faulkner for attempting "to graft onto Lucas, a Negro, what he believed generally about man's independence of spirit and ability to endure."[17] And Keith Clark, noting that the wife, daughter, and son-in-law who surround Lucas in *Go Down, Moses* are all but absent from *Intruder*, wonders why Faulkner "felt it necessary to estrange his black hero from family and community" and concludes that "the book's outcome—a stoic black man saves himself from lynching by reflecting the corrosive violence used to oppress blacks—celebrates self-marginalization and individuality as means of surviving racism, even at the expense of wife, daughter, and community."[18]

While my discussion here is not intended to deny the very real tension between liberal "individualism" and the practical realities of collective black political struggle in the late 1940s, I would nevertheless argue that Clark's critique overlooks the extent to which Faulkner's representation of Lucas's struggle to be heard can itself act as a conscious critical agent against the limiting definitions imposed on black male subjects by the justice system. To ask Lucas himself, within the text, to lead or enact a collective black rebellion against the social order of the entire town would be a rather plainly literalist opposition and would betray a rather reductive understanding of the ways in which a black literary character can act as an agent of social critique and racial resistance. Lucas's primary power in *Intruder* comes not necessarily from his ability to intervene directly in actual social struggles but rather from the way in which his presence as a character in the novel intrudes critically into the coherence of the white-run social structures that seek to define him. Thus while it is commonly assumed that Chick is the novel's titular "intruder" (for his digging up of Vinson Gowrie's grave), I would argue that Lucas himself may also be seen as an intruder for the way in which he, as Glissant puts it, "disturbs the order of things" (89).[19] In my view, Faulkner does not necessarily need to offer a fully "interior" portrayal of Lucas's subjectivity in order to engage in a critique of the legal system and its perversion. For Faulkner's representation of Lucas as indomitable and unwilling to compromise makes the implicit case that for a white author to try to represent black subjectivity from within would be to risk falling into the very trap for which the novel critiques Gavin, namely, falsely defining a black man's interior according to one's own impressions and a priori assumptions. In this sense, *Intruder* makes the case for racial unknowability as a form of tacit respect.

While it is unlikely that Faulkner is attempting to critique Lucas's forced estrangement from the black community of Jefferson, the novel does grapple implicitly with the problem of what social significance or meaning can accrue around African American "individuality" at this historical moment. As Chick's black boyhood friend Aleck Sander wittily remarks when Chick asks him to help him dig up the Gowrie grave, "It's the one like Lucas makes trouble for everybody" (84). In this sense, Faulkner's description of the town's African Americans "acting exactly as Negroes and whites both would have expected Negroes to act at such a time; they were still there, they had not fled, you just didn't see them . . . just keeping out of sight and out of the way" (94–95) draws our attention toward the law and the social tensions that repress an entire population into fearful submission and stoic acceptance of their invisibility.

Lucas's individualism may represent only a symbolic threat to the white community, but it represents an even deeper problem for the black community because the social and political costs of his individualism are highest for his fellow African Americans; although estranged from them, his actions still reflect back on them in the eyes of the white world. Thus Faulkner's representation of the inaction of the town's black population in the wake of Lucas's arrest suggests a critique not of black apathy per se but rather of the extent to which the force of white racial terror has drained much of the agency and resistance out of the black community and has undermined, as a result, that community's willingness to tolerate the very idea of black individualism. In this way, Faulkner's individualist characterization of Lucas becomes not an evasion of black political realities but rather an interrogation of the near impossibility of a viable black individualism in pre–civil rights America. Faulkner seems to suggest that black individualism is dangerous not only because of the reaction that it is likely to elicit from whites (arrest, lynching), but also because of the disapproval that it might engender within a black community accustomed to harsh reprisals from whites who only see—and only wish to see—in them a single conforming mass.

The idea that Lucas's political power lies largely in his role as a critical model within *Intruder* emerges particularly strikingly in the novel's semicomic conclusion, in which Lucas, having been exonerated by the physical evidence produced by Chick's grave digging, visits Gavin's office to pay him—as he originally promised he would—for the legal services that Gavin has (not) rendered. Lucas's very insistence on paying a man who has done little if anything to warrant such remuneration is itself a form of critique against Gavin's inaction, his tendency to pontificate and theorize while Chick (and to some extent Miss Habersham) have been the true actors in Lucas's liberation.

At the end of *Intruder in the Dust*, Chick, like Lucas, is finally free, yet he is free with typically Faulknerian limitations. His debt to Lucas has been paid, and Lucas acknowledges this when he pays Gavin Stevens two dollars (in coins) for Gavin's and Chick's services. Lucas is certainly aware that money can never repay what Chick has done for him and his gesture should be interpreted as a proud man's acknowledgement of this fact. Chick is also free of those attitudes that he passively accepted as a boy of twelve. He now sees blacks as people rather than as nonhuman stereotypes. He no longer feels threatened as he once did by Lucas's refusal to "act like a nigger." And yet for all his newfound freedom he is not totally free; like Gavin Stevens, he is not free of his responsibility to other human beings, and he will never be free of this responsibility. And although he has rid himself of his feelings of personal guilt in regard to Lucas, he realizes that as part of Jefferson he shares in the communal guilt incurred by the town. The best he can do is to follow the advice of his uncle and "never stop" resisting those immoral forces that would continue to keep Lucas and his race in bondage.

Faulkner's anxious attempts to reconcile Lucas's claims for freedom with his own belief in Southern independence should not blind us to the fact that *Intruder in the Dust* embodies a much more hopeful view of society than the novels of the twenties and early thirties. His use of the jail and the fates of Lucas and Chick make this clear. Seventeen years earlier in *Sanctuary* (1930), when Lee Godwin is accused of a murder he did not commit, only Horace Benbow steps forward to defend him. [20] The Jefferson community sits idly by and allows an innocent man to be lynched; the community allows injustice to win over the forces of justice and decency, and as a result Horace himself succumbs to despair and gives up his efforts to escape the trap of his loveless marriage. As we know, shortly after Goodwin is pronounced guilty of murder and rape, an angry mob takes him from the jail and burns him alive. Unlike Lucas Beauchamp, Goodwin has no one to protect him from the mob. By 1948 Faulkner's bitter judgment of society had somewhat mellowed; by then he apparently felt that there was a small but courageous minority who were willing to act in a morally responsible manner to see to it that justice was done. By contrast, in *Sanctuary*, described by Cleanth Brooks as the bitterest of all Faulkner's novels, we find no hopeful alternatives.[21] The forces of evil ultimately triumph. The main characters in this novel are prisoners, trapped in an overwhelming web of evil from which escape seems impossible. Faulkner gives us careful descriptions of the men society puts in jail, considers the reasons why they are there, and ultimately comes to some negative conclusions about the system of justice and society's ability to deal with the problem of evil.

In *Intruder in the Dust* the social balance of power has shifted and the forces of justice and decency win over prejudice and injustice. Chick Mallison, because other responsible members of the community eventually come forward to assist him, is successful in his efforts to prove Lucas innocent. It is true that the inhabitants of Beat Four such as the Gowries and their neighbors are still present in Jefferson and represent a real threat to the social order, but by 1948 Faulkner felt that the tide was changing and that more progressive elements in the South were beginning to prevail. Chick does not stand alone, as Horace Benbow in *Sanctuary*, and even Mr. Gowrie, turns out to be an essentially decent, albeit rough, character, a father distraught with grief over the death of a son he loved, yet still willing to listen to reason and to accept Lucas's innocence when the evidence is put before him. Lucas is released from jail by contrast to Lee Godwin who is lynched, and Chick is finally freed from his burden of guilt, by contrast to Horace Benbow, a beaten man who remains a prisoner in his own home at the end of *Sanctuary*. In short, *Sanctuary* describes a world in which prisoners remain prisoners and in which injustice prevails. In *Sanctuary* we do see one murderer dealt with justly, but this man is black, and as Faulkner was painfully aware, blacks always seem to receive their "share" of justice and perhaps a bit more.[22] Lee Goodwin is morally and literally innocent of raping Temple Drake and of killing Tommy, and yet he is found guilty and lynched. And Popeye, although guilty of many other crimes, is not guilty of the murder for which he is executed. Just as importantly, those characters who seem most morally culpable, Narcissa Benbow, Temple Drake and her father, and Eustace Graham, go free and retain their standing as respectable members of the community. At one point in this bitter novel, Horace muses that "Perhaps it is upon the instant that we realise, admit, that there is a logical pattern to evil, that we die" (124). The most hopeful pronouncement that can be made in the face of the vision Faulkner presents us with in *Sanctuary* is that, although evil seems pervasive, there appears to be no discernible pattern to it. This is small consolation, but in *Sanctuary* it is all we have. *Intruder in the Dust* views society more benevolently. Innocent victims find effective and successful champions to defend them and are released from jail; young boys, such as Chick Mallison, are supported by the best people in the community of Jefferson; and most importantly, justice seems a very real possibility rather than an impossible dream.

That Faulkner ends the novel (literally its final line) by juxtaposing Gavin's tautological double question "Now what? What are you waiting for now?" with Lucas's blunt one-word reply, "My receipt" (241), suggests a final way in which Lucas's silent self-possession can act as a source of political power precisely because it undermines, by its sheer contrast with, the tedious, painfully long-winded speech of Gavin. In this light, the extent to which Faulkner seems to ignore Lucas during the novel's middle section (much of which is dominated by Gavin's "liberal" pronouncements on the need for Southern resistance to Northern meddling), suggests an ironic critique of Gavin's empty rhetoric. As Teresa Towner has argued, rather than silencing Lucas, the novel, and particularly this closing scene, "charge us readers to acknowledge Lucas as the book's most powerful, if careful, speaker of himself" (33). Faulkner's recognition that the liberal subject is thoroughly contained by the invisible structures of social control echoes D. A. Miller's shrewd argument that a "community's policing apparatus is inscribed not just 'in' but 'as' the ordinary practices of the world."[23] In *Intruder in the Dust*, racism operates as an ordinary world practice. However, while Miller envisions an all inclusive disciplinary power in canonical texts, Faulkner reserves the marginal social position as a space of agency. In this way, Lucas Beauchamp's reply mitigates Miller's overarching totalization and provides an instance of how, as in the narratives of crime noir fiction, the quest for justice must be personalized as society is depicted as too corrupt to render justice. In *Intruder in the Dust*, the quest functions as the means by which the corrupt society is juxtaposed not just against the one incorruptible man who operates alone, but rather against the joint efforts of Chick and Lucas, the transgressive interracial couple by means of which Faulkner positions his protagonists as members of a larger collectivity to which they feel a responsibility. By means of this strategic positioning, Faulkner persuasively demonstrates how in the 1940s this subversive racial combination successfully functions in mystery fiction, a genre that has historically been so ideologically bound to the existing social order.

NOTES

1. William Faulkner, *Intruder in the Dust* (New York: Vintage, 1948).

2. Edouard Glissant, *Faulkner, Mississippi*, trans. Barbara B. Lewis and Thomas C. Spear (Chicago: University of Chicago Press, 2000), 45.

3. "Lucas's silences do not decisively deepen the mystery," Glissant says, "rather they emphasize his personal implacable opposition to all attempts at explanation, assistance, comprehension, and reconciliation" (89).

4. William Faulkner, *Selected Letters of William Faulkner*, ed. James Blotner (New York: Random House, 1977), 128.

5. Ibid., 262.

6. Ibid., 266.

7. William Faulkner, *Faulkner in the University*, ed. Frederick L. Gwynn and Joseph L. Blotner (Charlottesville: University Press of Virginia, 1995), 141–42.

8. Irving Howe is among the first critics who feel that imagination and ideology, which were fused in the earlier works, are not fused in *Intruder in the Dust*. See Irving Howe, *William Faulkner: A Critical Study* (New York: Random House, 1962). Joel Williamson has argued that *Intruder* was a racially progressive text in its day, though it has frequently been read along the lines of statements made later in Faulkner's life as a reactionary text. The changing perceptions of Faulkner's own positions, and the common equation of Gavin Stevens's views with those of the Southern writer, have made things even more complicated (Joel Williamson, *William Faulkner and Southern History* [New York: Oxford University Press, 1993], 270, 310). Contemporary reviewers shared Williamson's position. See, for example, Elizabeth Hardwick, "Faulkner and the South Today"; and Andrew Lytle, "Regeneration for the Man," both in *Faulkner: A Collection of Critical Essays*, ed. Robert Penn Warren (Engelwood Cliffs, N.J.: Prentice Hall, 1966).

9. In response to the news of the murder of Vinson Gowrie and the arrest of Lucas, the black population remains out of sight while the white population streams into the town square in order to be there for the lynching. Faulkner makes it clear that the white community looks forward to Lucas's death with particular relish, because, as we know

from *Go Down, Moses*, Lucas has never shown the deference or dependence whites expect.

10. Theresa M. Towner, *Faulkner on the Color Line* (Jackson: University Press of Mississippi, 2000), 32.

11. See Irving Howe (1962) and Edmund Wilson, "William Faulkner's Reply to the Civil Rights Program," *New Yorker*, 23 October 1948, 120–28.

12. Chick Mallison, upon whom Lucas's life depends, is far more sensitive to moral issues than most teenagers tend to be. Along the same lines, Elizabeth Kerr pointed out that the jailers, the warden, and the sheriffs in Yoknapatawpha county are superior to the men who "have made Mississippi prisons notorious" (Elizabeth Kerr, *Yoknapatawpha: Faulkner's "Little Postage Stamp of Native Soil"* [New York: Fordham University Press, 1969], 205).

13. Thadious M. Davis has suggested that *Go Down, Moses* might serve as both "Faulkner's accommodation to and contestation of cultural rituals and ideologies that ultimately as a white racial southern male subject he cannot dissemble" (Thadious M. Davis, *Games of Property: Law, Race, Gender and Faulkner's "Go Down, Moses"* [Durham: Duke University Press, 2003], 197).

14. In the novel, we are told that four years ago, while a twelve-year-old Chick was hunting with two companions, he fell through the ice into a creek and was taken home by Lucas, to dry out and have some food. Lucas refused all offers of payment leaving Chick with an unpaid obligation on his conscience. Four years later, when Lucas is accused of murder, Chick goes to his assistance and helps to prove his innocence.

15. Ralph Ellison, "Change the Joke and Slip the Yoke," *Partisan Review* 15 (Spring 1958): 212–22; repr. in Ellison's *Shadow and Act* (New York: Random House, 1964), 50.

16. Critics have frequently observed Lucas's exceptional status in the text. See, for example, Blyden Jackson, "Faulkner's Negroes Twain," in *Faulkner and Race: Faulkner and Yoknapatawpha*, ed. Doreen Fowler and Ann J. Abadie (Jackson: University Press of Mississippi, 1987), and Richard H. King, "Lucas Beauchamp and William Faulkner: Blood Brothers," in *Critical Essays on William Faulkner: The McCaslin Family*, ed. Arthur F. Kinney (Boston: G. K. Hall, 1990).

17. Frederick R. Karl, *William Faulkner. American Writer* (New York: Weidenfeld & Nicolson, 1989), 771.

18. Keith Clark, "Man on the Margin: Lucas Beauchamp and the Limitations of Space," *Faulkner Journal* 6.1 (1990): 75.

19. Glissant's argument is worth quoting at length, "Lucas Beauchamp stands apart. . . . although fathered by a White man (one of the McCaslins), he represents the essential Black. His hard-and-fast silences serve to deepen the mystery of what has happened. But the reader never believes that he is guilty, that he will be condemned, or that he is at risk of being lynched. The suspense is not there. Lucas is not a victim; he is the Intruder who disrupts the order of things. Lucas's silences do not conclusively deepen the mystery; rather, they emphasize his implacable personal opposition to all attempts at explanation, assistance, comprehension, and reconciliation" (89).

20. William Faulkner, *Sanctuary* (1931; New York: Vintage, 1958).

21. Cleanth Brooks, *William Faulkner: The Yoknapatawpha Country* (New Haven: Yale University Press, 1963), 127.

22. Faulkner gives us several brief descriptions of a minor character, a black murderer who is hung for murdering his wife. This man adds to the list of prisoners in the novel and at the same time adds complexity to Faulkner's theme. Here is a case in which the justice system does work. A man murders his wife and pays the price for his act. Setting aside moral objections to capital punishment (not an issue in the novel), this is the way

in which our justice system is supposed to work; this is the way in which Horace Benbow would like to see it work. When people do something wrong, they should be tried, and if convicted, punished in an appropriate manner.

23. D. A. Miller, *The Novel and the Police* (Berkeley: University of California Press, 1988), 48.

Reimagining the Femme Fatale: *Requiem for a Nun* and the Lessons of Film Noir

SUSAN V. DONALDSON

When *Requiem for a Nun* was published in 1951, a year after William Faulkner had been awarded the Nobel Prize for 1949, critics and readers were hard-pressed to make sense of this curious half-novel, half-detective film screenplay that Faulkner himself described as "an interesting experiment in form."[1] The book was structured, for one thing, by three acts of dialogue prefaced by historical prose sections recounting the founding and building of key Mississippi legal institutions—a courthouse, the state capitol, and a jail. For another, the storyline of the dialogue focused on the murder of an infant girl by a seemingly devoted black nurse maid in an effort to hold together the family of her white employers. But it was the "casting," as it were, of the nursemaid and her white employer that added a distinct whiff of sensationalism. For these two characters Faulkner turned to a couple of his more disturbing and scandalous texts—the 1931 novel *Sanctuary* and the short story "That Evening Sun"—from which he retrieved the "fallen" coed debutante Temple Drake, now a society matron, and Nancy Mannigoe, a laundress for the Compson family and sometime prostitute.

In his New York *Post* review Maxwell Geismar denounced the book as "cold, empty, slick" and its plot as "far-fetched," but Malcolm Cowley, fresh from his efforts to domesticate Faulkner in the pages of *The Portable Faulkner*, enthusiastically proclaimed Nancy a noble heroine worthy of Greek drama and the book itself a great success as well as a telling demonstration of "a reformed Faulkner, conscious of his public duties, who has become the spokesman for the human spirit."[2] Robert Penn Warren, for his part, held something of a middle ground by uneasily declaring the story to be one of sacrifice and redemption but conceding that Nancy Mannigoe's murder of Temple Drake Stevens's baby seemed "shocking and implausible." Perhaps even more to the point, Warren complained that Nancy's murder had been presented "bare and alone without the benefit of Faulkner's voice to delineate motive and bemuse us into acceptance." Readers might have been able to accept Dilsey Gibson of *The Sound and the Fury* in such a role, he added plaintively, "for we know Dilsey and Dilsey's world massively and hypnotically." But Nancy, he suggested, remains from start to finish unknowable and for all intents and purposes illegible—and the same might be said, he added, of Temple Drake, whose "stagey" story seemed to defy the requirements of suspended disbelief.[3]

It is that last insight—of the virtual illegibility of Nancy Mannigoe and Temple Drake and their defiance of any and all efforts to under-stand and categorize them—that anticipates the resistance of a good many contemporary critics to categorizations of the book as a story of affirmation, sacrifice, redemption, and Christian belief. A special word of thanks is certainly due to Noel Polk for his 1981 take-no-prisoners study of *Requiem for a Nun*, which rightly points out that Nancy's murder of Temple's infant daughter is arguably the most shocking and violent act in all of Faulkner's work and offers precious little support for any final pos-sibilities of redemption or fully restored order. Thanks are due as well to critics like Diane Roberts, Theresa Towner, Doreen Fowler, Kelly Lynch Reames, and most recently John T. Matthews for pointing out the suffocating sense of imprisonment that marks the stories of Nancy Mannigoe and Temple Drake and their singular resistance to the best efforts of that ubiquitous lawyer Gavin Stevens to solve the secrets that bind them to each other and to the crime itself.[4]

In that resistance Temple and Nancy resemble nothing so much as those strangely ambiguous and alluring women distracting private detec-tives, policemen, investigators, lawyers, and audiences alike in hard-boiled thrillers, problem pictures, and horror films of the 1940s and 1950s that later came to be known as film noir. Temple and Nancy prove to be just as disturbing, illegible, and eventually disruptive as a good many of these femmes fatales—like the highly ambiguous sisters Vivian and Carmen Sternwood, played by Lauren Bacall and Martha Vickers, respectively, in the 1946 Howard Hawks classic *The Big Sleep*—and with good reason since Faulkner himself was listed as chief screenwriter on a project that represented probably the apex of his longtime collaboration with Hawks.[5] Despite his constant complaints in the 1940s about his bondage to Hollywood, Faulkner was able to draw liberally in *Requiem for a Nun* from the imagery, vocabulary, and storylines of film noir long before that term, invented by a French film critic enamored of postwar American movies, was widely used by American filmmakers, critics, and writers.[6] In doing so Faulkner managed to produce in this curious and disturbing work his own version of film noir that articulated his evolving and often highly equivocal feelings about women and their relation to his art and perhaps more to the point an emerging critique of the racial and sexual fantasies undergirding the culture of segregation and something like a sad half-admission of his own complicity in those fantasies and the violence required to perpetuate them.[7]

It is, to be sure, a hesitant and stumbling critique, obscured in part by the dominating voices of white men in the first historical preface recounting the establishment of Jefferson's courthouse—and by implication of course the establishment of white patriarchal law. But also contributing to that obscurity are the cacophonous arguments in the dramatic dialogues over what secrets have remained hidden, whose stories have been rightfully told, and who has the right to tell them. The chief participants in those arguments are Gavin Stevens, Nancy Mannigoe's defense attorney; his nephew's wife, Temple Drake Stevens; the state governor, a largely symbolic figure, we are told in the stage directions; and to a certain extent toward the end, Nancy herself, whose cryptic pronouncements throughout seemed directed at confounding legal proceedings, legal authority, and the white men who dictate them. Ostensibly seeking to save Nancy on the eve of her execution, Stevens is arguably at his most irritating in this work. After dragging Temple to the governor's office, he insists that she rehearse the sad history of her rape and exploitation recounted in *Sanctuary*, confess the secrets of the sinful sisterhood she seemingly shares with Nancy, and own up to her own sexual sins and complicity in the murder of her own child. Before he finishes, he very nearly succeeds in turning Temple's story into that of her husband, Gowan, who seemingly prides himself on "redeeming" Temple from her status as fallen woman through marriage, condescending doses of forgiveness, and constant demands for gratitude. Temple in turn complains that the lawyer's constant interruptions of and interference with the narrative she tries to tell of her past and of her bonds with Nancy have created two Temples and two stories begging for clemency. Nancy's contribution in contrast is seemingly all too brief: She simply leaves Temple with the single, cryptic word, "Believe"—but not before her own story of abuse, loss, and violence are briefly rendered visible to Temple, who suddenly "sees" something of Nancy's own pain and suffering—the loss of an unborn baby to violence—just as she abruptly recalls earlier white blindness to everything about black prisoners in the county jail but their hands reserved for labor designated by whites.[8] It is no wonder, then, that so many critics and readers have been left in confusion about just whose story is being told here—and just what nun, saintly or otherwise, is being mourned in the title.

Part of that confusion no doubt has a good deal to do with the work's highly complicated origins, which date back to 1933, when Faulkner briefly mentioned in a letter to his publisher that his newest work, about a black woman, had a good title–*Requiem for a Nun*. "It will be a little on the esoteric side," he added, "like *As I Lay Dying*."[9] We know from Noel Polk's study and from Faulkner's letters that two unfinished rough drafts, one of them portraying a black man and woman meeting with Gavin Stevens, date back to this period. Nearly two decades later Faulkner was still describing the work as a black woman's story, with details reminiscent of the Compson laundress and part-time prostitute Nancy Mannigoe in the 1931 story "That Evening Sun," but by then the work in progress had become deeply entangled with his relationships with two women, one of whom he was ardently pursuing as a protégé-collaborator and as a potential lover. In 1950 he sketched an outline of the play in letters to the aspiring young writer Joan Williams, partly as an offer of mentorship and partly as a ruse to lure her into a romantic relationship. "I tell you again," he wrote in March 1950, "the play is yours too," and he added, "I would not have thought of writing one if I hadn't known you." Years before, though, the actress Ruth Ford, who had known Faulkner since the early 1930s, had asked him to write a play for her while they were both working at Warner Brothers. When it became apparent that Joan Williams would not respond wholeheartedly to the offer of collaboration on this particular project or to a sexual relationship, Faulkner seemingly shifted his attention to Ruth Ford. By the end of 1951 he was unequivocally declaring "that this play is for Ruth, the part, character-part, is hers, until she herself refuses it."[10]

The question of just for whom the novel-play was indeed written reminds us of those gift books Faulkner as an apprentice writer produced for the women he was wooing in the nineteen-twenties and his experimentation with the recurring motif of nympholepsy, a term pillaged from Conrad Aiken, that Faulkner had inherited from Romantic poetry and from James Branch Cabell's racy 1919 novel *Jurgen*, all evoking enticing nymphs pursued by frustrated mortal males. Cleanth Brooks's term for this motif—the erotic sublime—still seems appropriate for describing imagery that combined Faulkner's erotic longings with his poetic evocations of transcendent moments defined by their radical alterity and unattainability.[11] Though Faulkner as an apprentice writer might have joked about using his poetry as a tool for seduction, one detects in those gift books and even his earliest venture into drama, the 1920 symbolist play *The Marionettes*, a distinct preference for idealized women whose value was determined by the simple fact of always being out of reach. Yet, as Joan Williams herself recalled in her 1980 reminiscence of her complicated relationship with Faulkner, her mentor and ardent suitor genuinely wanted to "save" her from middle-class conventions and open her to the liberating possibilities of art.[12] In a manner of speaking he was, she declared, quoting from his letters to her, "Pygmalion, not creating a cold and beautiful statue in order to fall in love with it, but taking his love and creating a poet out of her. He refused to believe he could take a young woman into his life, and spirit, and not have her make something new under the sun whether she willed it or not."[13] Throughout much of his life Faulkner would remain torn between those idealized representations of women inherited from Romanticism and French symbolism and half-formulated, half-repressed longings for women who seemingly had escaped convention altogether—as he certainly wanted Joan Williams to do on some level.

Nowhere was that equivocation displayed to greater effect than in *The Sound and the Fury*, in which Caddy Compson serves as the absent center of the four narrative sections that seek to capture and contain her but never quite succeed in doing so. She provides the inspiration and the instigation for each of the narrative sections told by her brothers Benjy, Quentin, and Jason, but she herself remains forever out of reach, far beyond their efforts to command and control her. Like that crucial passage in Quentin's section, where Caddy is envisioned at her wedding running *"right out of the mirror, out of the banked scent"* that Quentin associates with her sexuality, Caddy flees all efforts to impose narratives of white Southern womanhood upon her from early childhood on. Her refusal to abide by that narrative—"she never was a queen or a fairy," we learn in Quentin's section, "she was always a king or a giant or a general"—is a source of special anguish to Quentin himself, who sees her sexual adventurousness and independence as a form of insubordination and as a damning reflection upon himself and their family sense of honor. Above all, he sees her willingness to explore her sexuality against all the rules of white Southern moral codes as a violation of whiteness—and his own masculine prerogative. *"Why wont you bring him to the house, Caddy?"* he remembers interrogating his sister. *"Why must you do like nigger women do in the pasture the ditches the dark woods hot hidden furious in the dark woods."* But to his father he can only ask, "Why couldn't it have been me and not her who is unvirgin." From first to last Caddy threatens his authority and his role as the eldest male Compson offspring simply by refusing to follow the rules stipulated by narratives of white womanhood; and in this respect she anticipates the disruptive and ambiguous presence of femmes fatales in those hard-boiled detective movies charged with anxiety over violated boundaries between femininity and masculinity and between blackness and whiteness.[14]

The Compson brothers never succeed in catching hold of their errant sister, who repeatedly glides away into twilight, misty rain, and the overpowering scent of honeysuckle, all potent reminders of the dissolving hierarchies of gender, sexuality, race, and class that finally drive Quentin

Compson to death by drowning. But in *Sanctuary*, Faulkner's 1931 experiment with the hard-boiled detective novel, we learn the consequences of catching up with the genre's version of femmes fatales when the idealistic attorney Horace Benbow finally runs to ground in a Memphis brothel the missing coed Temple Drake, the murder witness whom he needs to prove his client Lee Goodwin innocent and who recites at length the story of the brutal rape she suffers at the hands of the gangster Popeye. We as readers hear the details leading up to the rape—including her desperate fantasies to transform herself into a middle-aged schoolteacher or an old man as last lines of defense against assault—but Temple herself abruptly cuts off her account. It is not until Horace Benbow returns home that we discover how devastating the effects of Temple's story are upon him. Running to the bathroom to be sick, Benbow finds himself sliding into Temple's story, feeling and experiencing what Temple did as all the boundaries he knows and values between masculinity and femininity, assailant and victim, whiteness and blackness, blur and merge. It is as powerful a preview as one could hope to find of the disordering impact of femmes fatales upon masculine authority in many of those dark films and thrillers of the 1940s and 1950s. A good many commentators on film noir and femmes fatales, in fact, have argued that antecedents can be traced back to the hard-boiled crime fiction published in *Detective Story Magazine* and *Black Mask* in the 1910s and 1920s, fiction that echoes throughout the pages of *Sanctuary*.[15]

It was in the 1940s, though, during Faulkner's longest stints in Hollywood, that those mysterious and destructive women who often led male representatives of law and authority astray began to make a pronounced impact on the silver screen—and on French critics who got their first look at Hollywood movies bottled up by World War II with the 1946 release in France of five startling pictures—*The Maltese Falcon*; *Murder, My Sweet*; *Double Indemnity*; *Laura*; and *The Woman in the Window*. The critic responsible for coining the term *film noir* was Nino Frank, who was trying to describe what he saw as major changes in Hollywood films during the war, and he was struck in particular by the connections of these films to the crime fiction published in French translations as "*Série noire*," among them novels by Dashiell Hammett, Raymond Chandler, and James M. Cain. These were films, according to Frank and critics to follow, that seemed to be distinguished by a stylized chiaroscuro lighting, a deeply pessimistic view of postwar American society, psychological readings of characters, and a general obsession with sexuality, criminal or otherwise. The term *film noir* itself, as Frank Krutnik argues in his entertaining 1991 study *In a Lonely Street*, is "a post-constructed category," not one that audiences or Hollywood would have recognized in the 1940s, and while film critics continue to disagree over whether or not film noir can be called a genre, a mood, a style, or a perspective, there does now seem to be a consensus that the term can be applied to crime thrillers, problem pictures, gangster films, melodramas, and even westerns. But it was the "tough" thrillers, descended from those hard-boiled crime stories published in the teens and twenties, that seemed to draw all the attention and to articulate a deep unease about the profound social, economic, and demographic changes that had transformed American society during the war. The typical thriller, Krutnik argues, follows the trajectory of a male hero, who is either investigating or about to commit a crime, and the challenges and threats to male authority and male identity he meets along the way.[16]

Those challenges and threats, Jans B. Wager suggests in his equally entertaining study *Dangerous Dames*, were usually the result of feminine wiles, duplicity, and sexuality. More often than not, the femmes fatales who crossed the paths of those investigators or potential criminals quite simply refused to play roles of support and comfort assigned to them by society, and so ubiquitous were these threatening feminine presences in thrillers and detective films that noir women as they later came to be called simply seemed interchangeable with disorder.[17] From the perspective of Mary Ann Doane in her classic study *Femmes Fatales*, those dark and sinister ladies who haunt these films are frightening precisely because they carry the threat of being not just disorderly but unreadable as well, especially to the male investigators who seek to learn their secrets. Hearkening back to nineteenth-century works by Charles Baudelaire, Theophile Gautier, and Dante Gabriel Rossetti, the femme fatale, Doane declares, represents "a potential epistemological trauma" precisely because "she never really is what she seems to be." The threat she offers is one, Doane adds, that "is not entirely legible, predictable, or manageable."[18]

We see, I think, something of that threatening quality in the startling glimpse Faulkner offers us of Caddy Compson during World War II in the appendix he wrote for Malcolm Cowley's *The Portable Faulkner*. She appears just briefly—in a glossy magazine photograph with a Riviera background that shows her paired with a German staff-general—and she is described in the appendix in language evocative of a femme noire, "ageless and beautiful, cold serene and damned." The power that she commands, even in a photograph, is briefly acknowledged by her brother Jason, who seems to take courage from the fact that his sister is now finally contained within the confines of a photograph. But even the photograph seems to foment the possibility of disorder. The timid librarian who discovered it takes it to Memphis in the hope that Dilsey too will recognize Caddy as someone worth saving, but her efforts are greeted first by Dilsey's refusal and then by the huge crowds of seemingly homeless women in train and bus stations, lobbies, restrooms, and hotels who are following soldiers and sailors "enroute either to leave or to death."[19]

It was those large crowds of women on the move during the war that represented the real threat to order and authority evoked by Caddy and the dark ladies of film noir, and it is highly significant that Faulkner lets his most compelling female character make her last appearance in his work alongside the massive demographic shifts and upheavals marking the lives of American women during World War II. Over six million women entered the labor force in response to the war's labor demands, an increase of more than 50 percent, according to historian William Chafe.[20] They joined labor unions, toiled on road maintenance crews, and kept the assembly lines of war industries going.[21] By 1944, Jacqueline Jones reports in her prize-winning history of black women and work, "three out of ten white women and four out of ten black women worked."[22] At the end of the war the American work force included nearly 20 million women.[23]

It was during this period of massive change that Faulkner put in one of his longest stints toiling for Warner Bros., on and off between the summer of 1942 and the fall of 1945. He worked largely as a reviser of scripts and tried to pursue a few projects of his own, like adapting F. Scott Fitzgerald's "The Curious Case of Benjamin Button," but his most significant work was produced in collaboration with his favorite director, Howard Hawks, first with the 1944 film *To Have and Have Not*, based on the 1937 Hemingway novel and modeled in part on *Casablanca*, and then with *The Big Sleep*, based on the 1939 Raymond Chandler novel. Faulkner worked on the screenplay with writers Leigh Brackett and Jules Furthman during the second half of 1944, and the final version of the screenplay was polished off by Furthman to meet the requirements of the Hays Code censoring office.[24]

Released in 1946, *The Big Sleep* eventually came to be hailed as one of the classics of "tough" detective films as well as an endless source of legends about its making and its two stars, Humphrey Bogart and Lauren Bacall, who had been successfully paired in *To Have and Have Not* and who appear in the opening credits of *The Big Sleep*, appropriately enough, as shadowy outlines meditatively smoking cigarettes. Hawks had directed his scriptwriters to keep the plot moving at a fast pace, and the result was a highly complicated storyline of deceit, blackmail, and multiple murders that occasionally baffled even its director, who reportedly had to ask first Faulkner and then Chandler himself how one of the murder victims fit into the plot—and just who killed him.[25] For our purposes, though, what is most memorable about *The Big Sleep* is the prominence given to women in the public sphere, who seem to be everywhere detective Philip Marlowe turns, from shop clerks and taxi-cab drivers who give him knowing and suggestive glances to the slightly sinister daughters of his employer who inhabit the same twilight region that Marlowe himself does between middle-class respectability and a looming underworld of gambling, petty criminals, Lotharios, and runa-way wives. All the women Marlowe meets seem to possess secrets and to elude his best efforts to read them, and no one more so than the film's two chief femmes fatales, Vivian and Carmen Underwood, the daugh-ters of the wheelchair-bound General Sternwood, who describes them as possessing "the same corrupt blood." Linked with gambling, blackmail, sexual adventurousness, and a mounting body count, both daughters, played by Lauren Bacall and Martha Vickers, underscore the limita-tions and failings of their wheelchair-bound father, and it is no accident that this faltering patriarch receives Marlowe in his hothouse filled with orchids and by implication the "rot of corruption" associated with female sexuality. Though Bogart's Marlowe is paired off with Bacall's Vivian in the end, he finds her nearly as baffling and unsettling as the even more reckless Carmen, who early on reveals her sexual aggressiveness and her susceptibility to drugs, gambling, and blackmail. Vivian even briefly confesses to a murder to protect her sister Carmen, but only when Car-men is unmasked as the real culprit does Vivian herself emerge from the same sinister shadows and stand distinctly apart from the sister she tries to protect—now on her way to a sanitarium to be "cured."

Or is Vivian so distinct after all? One of the most striking aspects of this film, along with other movies associated with film noir and shady ladies, is the pronounced tendency to conflate female sexuality with blackness in a manner reminiscent of European colonialist discourse and Freud's own association of femininity with "the dark continent." By the early nineteenth century, as Sander L. Gilman has ably argued, the female Hottentot had become for Europeans "the exemplary represen-tation of . . . hyperbolic sexuality," and photography, poetry, and essays produced under the banner of empire and colonialism tended if any-thing to equate the European conquest of the African continent with the conquest of African women.[26] In U.S. culture before and after slavery, the figure of the Jezebel, hypersexualized, manipulative, and destructive, contended for dominance of black female stereotypes with the figure of the mammy—and continued to exert a compelling hold on the American popular imagination in films from D. W. Griffith's *Birth of a Nation* to Douglas Sirk's 1959 version of *Imitation of Life*.[27]

In the American South, though, the figure of the Jezebel tended to be paired as the defining underside, as it were, of the white lady, whose outline was first etched out by the ideology of slavery and then by the culture of white supremacy and segregation. As a good many commentators including Deborah White, Jacquelyn Dowd Hall, Hazel Carby, Diane Roberts, and Grace Elizabeth Hale among others have argued, black women's bodies, sexual availability, and sheer physical labor made possible the cult of the pure, ornamental, fragile white lady, who was after all, charged with the perpetuation of white patriarchy through reproduction, a responsibility that required the assurance of white female chastity to maintain white male authority. White women stood on the pedestal provided by black women's bodies, which served as reservoirs for all the sexuality drained from those pristine images of female whiteness. Proslavery theorists insisted that this logic of dichotomy was reinforced by the peculiar institution, and it was in the name of maintaining that dichotomy—and of protecting white Southern womanhood—that legalized segregation was established and every form of racial violence against African Americans was defended in the opening years of the twentieth century.[28]

Those boundaries between white and black womanhood, though, seemed to waver and blur in the movies of the 1940s, which often cast white women in shadows, blurred the boundaries between ladies and "fallen" women, and sometimes even paired white and black women in Horatio Alger stories of success. These were films made at a time when both white and black women were pursuing work opportunities in unprecedented numbers, when the traditional boundaries between white and black cultural definitions of womanhood seemed more and more blurred amid those changes, and when African Americans in particular were becoming increasingly restive with a racial status quo at radical odds with the democratic aims of the war effort against Nazism and fascism. Some 500,000 black Southerners left the region between 1942 and 1945 to find war industry jobs, many of them black women lured out of domestic service by high-paying factory jobs. Protests at discriminatory practices in hiring and unions were mounted by the NAACP, the Urban League, and the Negro Youth Council for Victory and Democracy, and racial tensions over the disparity in treatment between American black soldiers and Nazi prisoners of war led in part to the establishment of the Congress of Racial Equality. Nervous whites responded in part by trading rumors of "Eleanor Clubs," secretive groups named in honor of the outspoken Eleanor Roosevelt that supposedly enabled black women to extract the highest possible wage from desperate white employers. And by 1943 race riots had broken out in Harlem, Detroit, and twenty-five other cities across the country.[29]

Few of these events, though, found visibility in Hollywood films. In his study of film noir contexts, James Naremore specifically notes that even the most daring examples of film noir from the 1940s and early 1950s "made no overt attempt to critique . . . segregated society" or to present a genuinely black point of view.[30] But what those films did do—and here Kelly Oliver and Benigno Trigo have a compelling argument to offer in their aptly titled *Noir Anxiety*—was to highlight the increasingly ambiguous boundaries between men and women, whites and blacks, and any and all ethnic origins at a time when the country was undergoing considerable social and economic upheaval.[31] These were increasingly ambiguous boundaries, Oliver and Trigo argue, that evoked at the time nothing so much as abjection from the perspective of Julia Kristeva, the expulsion of all that seems to lie, as Kristeva observes in *Powers of Horror*—"beyond the scope of the possible, the tolerable, the thinkable" and thus all that "disturbs identity, system, order," that "does not respect borders, positions, rules," the "in-between, the ambiguous, the composite."[32] In a word, what those strange thrillers, detective films, and women's pictures did was destabilize the "whiteness" of those simultaneously white-dark ladies whose sexuality, insubordination, and illegibility threatened the very status of patriarchal authority. Moreover, a good many of these films—often women's pictures like *Mildred Pierce*, on which Faulkner actually worked briefly—brought new attention to the "unrecorded stories" of black women who served as maids for those ambiguous and sometimes undefinable white women, as Paula Rabinowitz argues in her wonderful study of film noir's treatment of white and black women *Black & White & Noir*.[33] To be sure, those pictures, like *The Great Lie* (1941), *Since You Went Away* (1944), *The Reckless Moment* (1949), and the two versions of *Imitation of Life* (1934, 1959), invariably cast black women as maids and servants in ways that did indeed hearken back to the pairing of white Southern lady and devoted mammy finding its most popular representation in *Gone with the Wind*. But even that stereotyping served as a something very like recognition and even a forecast of what was to come, "a template," Rabinowitz suggest, "for sketching an alternative to either Betty Crocker or Aunt Jemima."[34] At the very least, as Mary Ann Doane argues, these relationships underscored how crucial the black servant's labor was to the white woman employer's story and by doing so highlighted the interdependence—and potential reversibility—of the maid's ground to the employer's figure, the story in the shadows to the narrative given the spotlight.[35]

It was, I think, even those tentative attempts in film noir to bring that interdependence to visibility, along with those largely "unrecorded" stories of black woman, that drew Faulkner at a time when he was not just simultaneously pursuing and mentoring Joan Williams but also casting about—and with increasing desperation—for a vocabulary to address black restiveness, women's new ambitions, and his mounting sense of the wrongs wrought not just by segregation but by the cultural narratives of white and black womanhood that had long served as the legitimizing underpinnings of American apartheid. And what he found, first of all, were movies made by directors with leftwing sympathies, often adapted from leftist authors, that vividly depicted the sweeping demographic, social, and economic changes marking American society in the war years and immediately thereafter.[36] But he also found new uses for detective and crime fiction, for it was in the nineteen thirties that African American writers like Richard Wright, Chester Himes, and Ann Petry made use of crime stories to evoke the mounting tide of black frustration and anger at a racial system that justified second-class treatment and citizenship for African Americans in the U.S. military fighting against fascism.[37] We know from his correspondence that Faulkner read both *Native Son* and *Black Boy*, and it is very likely that he read Ann Petry's 1946 novel *The Street* as well since it was widely hailed at the time, in part as the first novel by an African American woman to sell a million copies. It was also frequently paired with *Native Son* as an example of black protest fiction during the war years and immediately thereafter.[38]

It is notable as well, though, that Faulkner was in an increasingly retrospective mood by the end of the forties and that the fiction he produced in the last fifteen years of his life "enter[ed] the library," as Karl Zender so aptly put it, by taking a long reflective look back at what he had produced over the years and where he had seemingly fallen short.[39] *Requiem for a Nun* fairly echoes with earlier stories and novels—and not just Temple's story in *Sanctuary*. There are other references to *Sanctuary*, like that condemned black prisoner slated for execution whose singing every night before his death hypnotizes the impromptu audiences by the jail. But there are also far more overt references to earlier works, as in Temple's long speech in the second act, when she ponders the inability of whites to see anything of black prisoners but the hands that can undertake every possible task of menial labor. In this speech she recounts Ryder's story in "Pantaloon in Black," the black man whose blinding grief for his lost wife drives him to violence and self-annihilation just to stop thinking and feeling and whose story is told twice in *Go Down, Moses*, once by an omniscient narrator who reveals that grief in full and once by the sheriff's deputy, who sees nothing of that grief and less of his humanity.

Most striking of all are the references to "That Evening Sun," the story in which Nancy as part-time nursemaid to the Compson children resorts to every possible measure to protect herself from the murderous intent of her ex-lover, only to find herself in the end abandoned by the

Compsons, who ultimately cannot bring themselves to see or rectify her plight—except, perhaps, for the young Quentin, who at least acknowledges the very real danger of her situation and the inevitability of her death by asking his father who will now do their laundry. Early on in that story, though, before Nancy for all intents and purposes is dismissed by the Compsons, she erupts into very public view when she confronts a white man for payment of sexual service. "When you going to pay me, white man?" she demands, until he knocks and kicks her into the gutter—and so vivid and unsettling is this brief eruption that it signals something like violence to come in *Requiem for a Nun*, where Nancy Mannigoe serves as a dark doppelganger to Temple Drake Stevens's supposedly redeemed white lady and where her act of murder, trial, and impending execution underscore both the threat she represents to white law and authority and the violence required to exert that authority.[40]

Certainly Nancy's first appearance in the play's first act is so dramatic and disturbing–where she answers the Judge's sentence of death by saying simply, "Yes, Lord"—that the courtroom spectators collectively gasp in shock and the stage directions suggest that the setting itself has been disrupted: "the judge bangs his gavel, the bailiff springs up, the curtain starts hurriedly and jerkily down as if the judges, the officers, the court itself were jerking frantically at it to hide this disgraceful business."[41] That last curious detail—the curtain itself threatening to come down upon the stage to hide the "disgraceful business"—sets in motion Gavin Stevens's drive to know just what Nancy's motive was in murdering Temple's child and what links her as murderer to the mother of her victim, a murderer who is referred over and over again by Temple, as though to persuade even herself, as a "nigger dope-fiend whore."[42] But the curtain itself threatening to come down offers a clue as well to that curious tension between the three acts of the play and the seemingly anomalous historical prefaces, which evoke nothing so much as the opposition between the story binding Nancy and Temple together and the legal institutions—the courthouse, the state capitol, and the jail–undergirding the brutally imposed, intransigent system of segregation.

Those prefaces, on the face of things, seem to have nothing at all to do with the story of Temple Drake Stevens and Nancy Mannigoe. The historical narrative they tell together, though, suggests something like an enfolding curtain of restrictions, taboos, laws, silences, and barely repressed violence that threaten to hide from view the story that lies behind Nancy's crime—and the connection between Nancy and Temple. That history is an increasingly melancholy and claustrophobic one, recounting the establishment of legal authority and institutions in Mississippi, "born," we are told in the last act, "a hundred and twenty-five years ago out of a handful of bandits captured by a drunken militia squad, and a bitter ironical incorruptible wilderness mail-rider, and a monster wrought-iron padlock."[43] These are images introduced in the vein of Old Southwest Humor and gradually darken preface by preface to a somber meditation on a legal system defined by violence implicit and explicit— first by dispossession of the Indians and then of the slaves who helped build the symbols of those institutions. A few lingering pioneers would regret the passing of the wild old days with the emergence of the town and its symbols of authority, but the disappearance of the wilderness would be forever linked with the elusive and ever-accelerating goal of progress "because," the narrator notes shortly, "this was a white man's land; that was its fate, or not even fate but its destiny in the roster of the earth."[44] Consolidating that destiny—and seemingly closing down alternative fates—was the mounting number of slave owners and slaves entering the community and the emergence of accelerating racism evidenced by those whites "who never owned a slave and never would since each had and would imbibe with his mother's milk a personal violent antipathy not at all to slavery but to black skins."[45] The first historical preface ends, significantly enough, with the building of the courthouse, accompanied by the construction not just of two churches but "what would be known through all North Mississippi and East Tennessee as *the* Academy, *the* Female Institute"—a not too subtle reference to the emerging ideals and narratives of white womanhood that would be closely allied with the enforcement of laws in the Courthouse and with the intertwined goals of progress and white supremacy.[46]

Walter Benjamin, I think, would readily recognize the link between law and violence that is implicitly traced in this first preface. In his 1921 essay "Critique of Violence"—which commentator Mathew Abbott refers to as his "critique of the disavowed violence of law"—Benjamin argues that the violent origins of law can be most starkly discerned in death sentences imposed on convicted criminals: "For if violence, violence crowned by fate, is the origin of law, then it may be readily supposed that where the highest violence, that over life and death, occurs in the legal system, the origins of law jut manifestly and fearsomely into existence."[47] By Benjamin's lights, violence is intimately intertwined with law and justice, for violence is inevitably required in the making of law—violence that is always mystified and rendered invisible in order to maintain the authority of law and its monopoly over violence. Any violence outside that authority is perceived as an immediate threat to the authority of law precisely because law, as Abbott points out, is grounded in its own foundational violence and thus is invested in resorting to violence to preserve its own legal authority. Or as Benjamin himself asserts, "law sees violence in the hands of individuals as a danger under-mining the legal system," which is itself invested in violence required for preserving law.[48]

Hence the line to be traced between violence associated with law-making and violence associated with law-preserving is often thin indeed—and it is the thinness of that boundary between two kinds of violence and between the law and violence itself that is probed as well by Faulkner in the historical prefaces tracing the emergence of law in frontier Mississippi through the reign of Jim Crow and in the dramatic scenes where Nancy Mannigoe awaits execution for the murder of her white charge. Almost as though he were echoing Benjamin, Faulkner evokes the dexterity of law in mystifying its origins by way of the elusive appearances and disappearances of the fifteen-pound monster padlock that is first brought into frontier Mississippi by Alexander Holston, assigned to the mailbag rider between the tiny settlement and Nash-ville, relegated to duty as a lock for the newly established jail to house the notorious Harpe gang, irretrievably lost with the Harpes' escape, temporarily charged to accounts of the dispossessed Chickasaws leaving for Oklahoma, and finally transmogrified into a fifteen-dollar reimburse-ment to its original owner. This rapid series of transformations suggest the speed with which the violent origins of Mississippi law—born in the incarceration of legendary outlaws and nurtured through the dis-possession of Indians and slaves—are quietly rendered invisible until Nancy Mannigoe's murder of Temple Drake Stevens's baby exposes the underlying violence of the narratives of womanhood and race that have imprisoned both Temple and her.

For the historical arc that seemingly begins with the elusive and ever-changing padlock and that culminates with Nancy Mannigoe's judgment before the bar of Mississippi law does not follow the conventional pat-tern of frontier settlement by starting with the jail, moving on to the courthouse, and then finishing with the state capitol. Instead the pref-aces describe and expand upon the settings that take us from Nancy's sentencing, to Gavin and Temple's meeting with the governor in his offices, and finally to Gavin and Temple's encounter with Nancy at the jail where she awaits execution. Moving from the courthouse to the state capitol to the jail, this narrative arc replicates to an uncanny degree the rise and entrenchment of a panoptic legal system devised to establish, guard, and consolidate white supremacy, first under the aegis of slavery and then under the system of segregation. The prefaces take us back to a heterogeneous frontier mingling Indians, the notorious Harpe gang, early settlers, slaves, tall tales of jail escapes, and comic attempts to establish some visible legal authority through that enormous padlock

that is all too easily swiped. This is a world, though, that is fast disappearing as Indians sign over their lands and silently glide from sight and as
town buildings are thrown up almost as abruptly as Thomas Sutpen tore
his plantation from the earth in *Absalom, Absalom!* In the second act we
move suddenly to Jackson, where Temple and Gavin have gone to appeal
to the governor, and there we find only the faintest reminders of "the old
brave innocent tumultuous eupepetic tomorrowless days" amid statistics
bristling with economic growth, transport, and every imaginable modern
convenience.[49] This was the site of war, reconstruction, and carpetbag-
gers, the narrator tells us, until the "State as a whole had dispossessed
them too," where black colleges were quickly founded to educate freed
people, and where, most significantly of all, "the state's greatest convention" drew up the 1890 constitution establishing segregation between
white and black as state law.[50]

It is in the third preface—focusing on the jail with a curious epigraph
that reads "(Nor Even Yet Quite Relinquish—)"—that this melancholy
history of segregation comes to a culmination of sorts, and it does so
after expanding its narrative purview from the first to the second preface, only to shrink to the confines of the jail, described in terms that
eerily anticipate Michel Foucault's description of the modern panoptic
regime of discipline and punishment—and Robyn Wiegman's discussion
of economies of visibility under segregation.[51] It is in the jail's multiple
layers of walls, the narrator asserts, that the full history of the community
is most fully captured, both recorded and unrecorded. The jail itself is
repeatedly described as looking out over its community, back in history
and up through the years to come, and in doing so surveys the coming
of cotton, war, destruction, rebuilding, commemoration of the Confederacy by those "unreconciled" and "unvanquished" women, and finally
modernization in the form of cars, radios, electricity, running water, and
window screens to accommodate summer sleep. But these technological
advances, the preface emphasizes, are for the benefit of whites only as
black men and women undertake the labor of the community, endure
the inequitable and racialized allocations of economic rewards under
segregation, and finally desert the now mechanized cotton fields. Left
strangely bereft are the whites who now man the machinery and who no
longer bail black servants and handymen out of jail because those black
subordinates have already left for parts north.

Yet this is the order—a community in which modernization has
become interchangeable with segregation, for which "progress" signifies
both the racially restricted distribution of consumer goods and the disappearance of those whose subordination defines whiteness—to which
Gavin Stevens seeks to reconcile Temple Drake Stevens. Like nothing so

much as a garrulous detective in a detective film—and a rather parodic one at that—Gavin is distracted from the crime at hand, Nancy's murder, by his own femme fatale whose secrets seem even more enticing than the crime itself—and that figure seems to vacillate between Nancy herself and Temple. In the second act Gavin and Temple meet with the governor to seek clemency for Nancy—but he undertakes this project not by making a plea of insanity but by badgering Temple into confessing her own culpability in the murder of her infant. By Gavin's lights, what that confession should consist of is Temple's never-ending recounting of her rape, her incarceration by Popeye, and her brief affair with Popeye's rival Red—as well as a new chapter in the saga, which includes blackmail, an affair with yet another gangster, her plans to run away with him, and the murder to which Nancy resorts to hold Temple's family together.

This is, in fact, the story that Temple tells—and with considerable anguish. But it is not quite what Gavin really wants—which is for Temple to repudiate her own sins and in particular the strange, symbiotic secret bond she feels with the woman she constantly refers to as "a nigger dope-fiend whore." Temple has apparently hired Nancy with the ostensible purpose of rescuing her, but what Nancy has done is rescue Temple—and in ways that remind us of those curious pairings of light and dark femmes fatales and white employer and black maid that characterize so many examples of film noir, including *The Big Sleep*. A black maid like Nancy—seemingly a foil to whiteness—appears on the face of things to signify Temple's restoration to the narrative of white womanhood, and we are reminded of just how emphatically black characters, like mammies and Jezebels, have been used to bolster white femininity in narratives of white womanhood.

The problem, though, is that Nancy, like a good many dark twins and black women characters in film noir, problematizes Temple's whiteness precisely because both women do feel that sense of secret sisterhood to which Temple so freely admits, albeit after considerable nagging by Gavin. Nancy may indeed evoke all that Temple must repudiate and expel in order to be rehabilitated in the sense that Julia Kristeva would readily recognize as abjection, representing the ambiguous boundaries between black and white womanhood, but what Nancy really manages to accomplish, even within the confines of the jail, is to serve as a potent reminder of just how dependent Temple's white womanhood is on the violence imposed upon black womanhood. This is the lesson, I think, that Temple finally learns, one inherited in a manner of speaking from the lessons of film noir, and it is one that finally renders Nancy fully visible to Temple in a way that the former never is to Stevens, who, toward the end, even manages to speculate that Nancy might well continue her humble services in the afterlife as a domestic to angels who retain even in heaven the superior status of whites.

In the third act Temple actually seems to see Nancy—as she sees those worn hands of black laborers in the jail—and what she learns as well is how closely linked black and white are despite the strictures of Jim Crow. In the second act Temple quite frankly tells the governor that Nancy served as "nurse: guide: mentor, catalyst, glue, whatever you want to call it, holding the whole lot of them together," in a manner that is reminiscent of no one so much as Dilsey Gibson in *The Sound and the Fury*.[52] But in that last act Temple goes even further and suddenly brings up the unborn child that Nancy had lost to the brutality of a former lover—a loss that parallels Temple's own loss and renders even more ambiguous the racial boundaries supposedly separating them. It is that sudden glimpse of who and what Nancy is—apart from the taboos and enforced blindness of Jim Crow and decidedly not shared by Gavin Stevens—that provides Temple herself with a brief moment of illumination. To that moment Nancy herself assigns the single word "Believe."[53] She offers no explanation of just what to believe in, and certainly no mention is made of traditional Christian belief as critics in the past have tried to argue, but that single word by itself seems to underscore something like an existential leap of faith—not in transcendence nor in orthodox religion—but in the reality of and substance of a fellow subjectivity apart from violently imposed definitions of race or class or even gender. That single word can be taken as a fissuring of old narratives of womanhood, white and black, an exposure of the violence required in the making of those narratives, and an anticipation of new stories to come.

They are, it appears, probably not stories to be written by Nancy and Temple themselves, who have both by the play's ending been restored in a manner of speaking to the orderly expectations of society after the fashion of a good many femmes fatales in the movies—or at least in *The Big Sleep*. Nancy is scheduled to hang, and Temple leaves the jail feeling doomed and responding to the call of her husband Gowan, who has been offstage for much of the play and who remains out of sight even to the very end. Nor does Temple's soul seemed to have been saved in the end as Temple herself speculates at the end of act 2. Both of them seem destined to follow out the trajectories designated for them by a rigidly segregated society—but with one important difference. Together they seem to have unsettled the authority of the detective-lawyer who investigates them both and feels duty bound to restore them to their separate categories of whiteness and blackness. But if the play itself reveals anything it is that Temple and Nancy recognize on some level the intertwined nature of whiteness and blackness and the literal and figurative violence that has gone into the making of narratives about black sexuality and white purity.

The last word, though, is not left to Temple calling to her absent husband, whose authority from start to last remains highly problematic, but to a seemingly minor character associated with the panoptic jail in the third act's historical preface. Overseeing the establishment and entrenchment of segregation, the jail nonetheless seems to bear within its walls unrecorded, unofficial histories as well, and one of them is that of the jail turnkey's daughter, who leaves her signature—Cecilia Farmer—on a window pane marked by a diamond ring. Through that simple act of signing her name, Cecilia seems to evoke the possibility of writing her own story apart from the strictures of a racially defined society—or even apart from the demands and desires of readers and writers. That lone signature might well touch the imagination of a stranger, an outlander as termed by the preface's narrator, who may indeed try to envision a story for Cecilia beginning as a bride and ending with the grave. But somehow by virtue of that signature, signaling her presence and her voice, Cecilia manages to extricate herself from the dream images of "demon-nun and angel-witch; empress, siren, Erinys: Mistinguette too"—images that haunt Temple and Nancy and too many other women created by Faulkner.[54] The last sight we have of Cecilia, besides that signature and its assertion of self, is on a mule behind her newly chosen Confederate veteran husband, riding out of town, out of the gorgeous web of Faulknerian prose that might well have engulfed her, out of the preface, and out of *Requiem for a Nun* altogether.

Behind her she leaves a swirl of glittering words now suddenly bereft of a potential muse, and therein, I think, lies a gloss of sorts upon the book's title itself. When asked to identify the nun of the title, Faulkner would refer quite simply to Nancy.[55] But if one takes into account the far reach of this curious experiment of Faulkner's—its searching scrutiny of the narratives bolstering segregation and its self-referential survey of a long and highly prolific literary career—it might well be more accurate to describe the book as a requiem for Faulkner's lost women as both poetic inspirations and as racialized fantasies. Faulkner would never quite relinquish that crucial figure, as we know from his portraits of Eula Varner Snopes and Linda Snopes Kohl in *The Town* and *The Mansion*, but after *Requiem for a Nun* he was never quite able to see her the same way. Like the femmes fatales in the movies, she had proven herself to be just a little too dangerous for Yoknapatawpha's inhabitants—and perhaps even for Faulkner himself.

NOTES

1. William Faulkner to Robert K. Haas [22 May 1950], in *Selected Letters of William Faulkner*, ed. Joseph Blotner (New York: Random-Vintage, 1977), 305.

2. Maxwell Geismar, "Faulkner's New Novel Will Win No Prizes," New York *Post*, 23 Sept. 1951, 12-M, rpt. in *William Faulkner: The Contemporary Reviews*, ed. M. Thomas Inge (New York: Cambridge University Press, 1995), 332; Malcolm Cowley, "In Which Mr. Faulkner Translates Past into Present," *New York Herald Tribune Books*, 30 September 1951, 1, 14, rpt. in Inge, 341.

3. Robert Penn Warren, "The Redemption of Temple Drake," *New York Times Book Review*, 30 Sept. 1951, 1, 31, rpt. in Inge, 345.

4. See in general Noel Polk, *Faulkner's "Requiem for a Nun": A Critical Study* (Bloomington: Indiana University Press, 1981); Theresa M. Towner, *Faulkner on the Color Line: The Later Novels* (Jackson: University Press of Mississippi, 2000); Diane Roberts, *Faulkner and Southern Womanhood* (Athens: University of Georgia Press, 1994), 218–23; Doreen Fowler, "Reading for the 'Other Side': *Beloved* and *Requiem for a Nun*," in *Unflinching Gaze: Morrison and Faulkner Re-Envisioned*, ed. Carol A. Kolmerten, Stephen M. Ross, and Judith Bryant Wittenberg (Jackson: University Press of Mississippi, 1997), 139–51; Kelly Lynch Reames, "'All That Matters Is That I Wrote the Letters': Discourse, Discipline, and Difference in *Requiem for a Nun*," in *William Faulkner: Six Decades of Criticism* (East Lansing: Michigan State University Press, 2002), 127–52; and John T. Matthews, *William Faulkner: Seeing through the South* (Malden, Mass.: Wiley-Blackwell, 2009), 237–47.

5. *The Big Sleep*, DVD, directed by Howard Hawks, 1946, Burbank, Calif.: Warner Home Video, 2006.

6. John Tuska, *Dark Cinema: American* Film Noir *in Cultural Perspective*. Contributions to the Study of Popular Culture No. 9 (Westport, Conn.: Greenwood Press, 1984), 136.

7. John Carlos Rowe argues that *Absalom, Absalom!* foregrounds, as no other work by Faulkner does, the writer's self-aware complicity in the regional narratives fostering the sexual and racial fantasies "on which slavery and Southern racism relied" ("Faulkner and the Southern Arts of Mystification in *Absalom, Absalom!*," in *A Companion to William Faulkner*, ed. Richard C. Moreland (Malden, Mass.: Blackwell, 2007), 445.

8. William Faulkner, *Requiem for a Nun* (1951), in *Novels 1942–1954* (New York: Library of America, 1994), 663.

9. William Faulkner to Harrison Smith, something October [1933], in *Selected Letters*, 75.

10. William Faulkner to Lemuel Ayers, 29 December 1951, in *Selected Letters*, 323. Lisa Hickman points out in her 2006 book on the romance with Joan Williams that in 1951 Faulkner was writing fervent letters to no fewer than four women—Meta Carpenter Rebner, Joan Williams, Ruth Ford, and Else Jonnson (*William Faulkner and Joan Williams: The Romance of Two Writers* [Jefferson, N.C.: McFarland & Co., 2006], 99. William Faulkner Collection, Small Special Collections Library, University of Virginia.

11. Cleanth Brooks, *William Faulkner: Toward Yoknapatawpha and Beyond* (New Haven: Yale University Press, 1978), 45. Judith L. Sensibar sees his marriage with Estelle Oldham Faulkner as a something like a continuation of the motif of nympholepsy—as well as a decades-long artistic collaboration—in her monumental biography *Faulkner and Love: The Women Who Shaped His Art* (New Haven: Yale University Press, 2009), 237–500. See also my discussion in "Faulkner's Versions of Pastoral, Gothic, and the Sublime," in *A Companion to William Faulkner*, ed. Richard C. Moreland (Malden, Mass.: Blackwell Publishing, 2007), 359–73.

12. Joan Williams, "Afterword: Twenty Will Not Come Again," in *The Wintering* (1971; Baton Rouge: Louisiana State University Press, 1980), 373.

13. Ibid. Williams is quoting from Faulkner's letter to her dated 7 January 1950, William Faulkner Collection, Small Special Collections Library, University of Virginia.

14. William Faulkner, *The Sound and the Fury: The Corrected Text* (1929; New York: Vintage International, 1984), 77, 173–92, 78.

15. Frank Krutnik, *In a Lonely Street: Film Noir, Genre, Masculinity* (New York: Routledge, 1991), 35. Walter Wenska makes an excellent case for the free use Faulkner made of gangster fiction from the 1920s in "'There's a man with a gun over there': Faulkner's Hijackings of Masculine Popular Culture," *Faulkner Journal* 15:1&2 (1999–2000): 35–60.

16. Krutnik, 15, x, 24–25.

17. Jans B. Wager, *Dangerous Dames: Women and Representation in the Weimar Street Film and Film Noir* (Athens: Ohio University Press, 1999), 78, 80, 79.

18. Mary Anne Doane, *Femmes Fatales: Feminism, Film Theory, Psychoanalysis* (New York: Routledge, 1991), 1.

19. William Faulkner, "1699–1945: The Compsons," in *The Portable Faulkner*, ed. Malcolm Cowley (New York: Viking Press, 1946), 746, 749.

20. William Chafe, *The American Woman: Her Changing Social, Economic, and Political Roles, 1920–1970* (New York: Oxford University Press, 1972), 135.

21. William Chafe, *The Unfinished Journey: America since World War II*, 6th ed. (New York: Oxford University Press, 2007), 9–10.

22. Jacqueline Jones, *Labor of Love, Labor of Sorrow: Black Women, Work, and the Family, from Slavery to the Present* (New York: Random House-Vintage, 1985), 234.

23. Krutnik, 57.

24. Gene D. Phillips, *Fiction, Film, and Faulkner: The Art of Adaptation* (Knoxville: University of Tennessee Press, 1988), 32-34, 42-45, 48-49.

25. Ibid., 48.

26. See Doane's discussion in her chapter "Dark Continents: Epistemologies of Racial and Sexual Difference in Psychoanalysis and the Cinema," 209–48 and especially 212–13. See also Sander L. Gilman's classic essay "Black Bodies, White Bodies: Toward an Iconography of Female Sexuality in Late Nineteenth-Century Art, Medicine, and Literature," *Critical Inquiry* 12 (1985): 204–42.

27. See, for example, Deborah Gray White's classic discussion of these two stereotypes of black women in *Ar'n't I a Woman? Female Slaves in the Plantation South*, rev. ed. (1985; New York: W. W. Norton, 1998). Doane explores how these stereotypes—and the interwining of black and white female stereotypes—play out in films of the 1940s and 1950s (232–33 and 239).

28. See in general White's discussion as well as Grace Elizabeth Hale, *Making Whiteness: The Culture of Segregation in the South, 1890–1940* (New York: Pantheon Books, 1998), 85–119; Jacquelyn Dowd Hall, "'The Mind That Burns in Each Body': Women, Rape, and Racial Violence," in *Powers of Desire: The Politics of Sexuality*, ed. Ann Snitow, Christine Stansell, and Sharon Thompson (New York: Monthly Review Press, 1983), 328–49, and *Revolt against Chivalry: Jessie Daniel Ames and the Women's Campaign against Lynching* (New York: Columbia University Press, 1993); Hazel Carby, *Reconstructing Womanhood: The Afro-American Woman Novelist* (New York: Oxford University Press, 1987); and Diane Roberts, *The Myth of Aunt Jemima: Representations of Race and Region* (New York: Routledge, 1994), 153–92. 92. See as well *The Ideology of Slavery: Proslavery Thought in the Antebellum South, 1830-1860*, ed. Drew Gilpin Faust (Baton Rouge: Louisiana State University Press, 1981); Elizabeth Fox-Genovese's classic study *Within the Plantation Household: Black and White Women of the Old*

South (Chapel Hill: University of North Carolina Press, 1988); and Joel Williamson, *The Crucible of Race: Black-White Relations in the American South since Emancipation* (New York: Oxford University Press, 1984), 1–43.

29. Jones, 236, 237, 233, 237.

30. James Naremore, *More than Night: Film Noir in Its Contexts*, rev. ed. (Berkeley: University of California Press, 2008), 237.

31. Kelly Oliver and Benigno Trigo, *Noir Anxiety* (Minneaolis: University of Minnesota Press, 2003), xxx.

32. Julia Kristeva, *Powers of Horror: An Essay on Abjection*, trans. Leon S. Roudiez (New York: Columbia University Press, 1982), 1, 4. Oliver and Trigo discuss their application of Kristeva's theory of abjection in their introduction, xiii–xxxv.

33. Joseph Blotner, *Faulkner: A Biography*, one-vol. ed. (New York: Random House, 1984), 461. Paula Rabinowitz notes that one of film noir's contribution was bringing attention, however dimly, to those "unrecorded stories" of black women (*Black & White & Noir: America's Pulp Modernism* [New York: Columbia University Press, 2002], 81).

34. Ibid. See Also Rabinowitz's discussion, 79–81.

35. Doane, 232–33, 239.

36. Rabinowitz, 80.

37. Rabinowitz notes that film noir and related crime fiction in the 1940s, especially work by Ann Petry and Gwendolyn Brooks, focused on "the new kinds of social relations forged during the Depression and World War II" (ibid., 63).

38. Faulkner even sent Richard Wright a letter expressing his appreciation for both *Black Boy* and *Native Son*. See William Faulkner to Richard Wright [probably 11 September 1945], in *Selected Letters of William Faulkner*, ed. Joseph Blotner (New York: Random House-Vintage, 1977), 201. He was particularly explicit about the necessity of changing the American racial status quo in his letters to his stepson, Malcolm Franklin, during World War II. See William Faulkner to Malcolm Franklin [postmarked 6 Dec. 1942] and William Faulkner to Malcolm Franklin [postmarked 9 July 1943], in *William Faulkner's Letters to Malcolm Franklin* (Irving, Texas: Society for the Study of Traditional Culture, 1976), n.p. William Faulkner Collection, Small Special Collections Library, University of Virginia.

39. Karl Zender, *The Crossing of the Ways: Faulkner, the South, and the Modern World* (New Brunswick, N.J.: Rutgers University Press, 1989), 107.

40. William Faulkner, "That Evening Sun," in *Collected Stories* (New York: Random, 1950), 291. When Temple retells the incident in *Requiem for a Nun*, she quotes Nancy as demanding, "Where's my two dollars, white man?" (*Requiem for a Nun* (1951), in *Novels 1942–1954* [New York: Library of America, 1994], 554).

41. Faulkner, *Requiem for a Nun*, 507.

42. Ibid., 553.

43. Ibid., 641.

44. Ibid., 499.

45. Ibid., 501.

46. Ibid., 503.

47. Matthew Abbott, "The Creature before the Law: Notes on Walter Benjamin's Critique of Violence," *Colloquy: Text Theory Critique* 16 (2008): 84; Walter Benjamin, "Critique of Violence" (1921), in *Reflections: Essays, Aphorisms, Autobiographical Writings*, trans. Edmund Jephcott, ed. Peter Demetz (New York: Schocken Books, 2007), 286. I am indebted to Richard Godden for pointing out how relevant Benjamin's "Critique of Violence" is to the length and breadth of *Requiem for a Nun*.

48. Benjamin, 280. See also Abbott's analysis of the distinction between law-making violence and law-preserving violence, 82–83.

49. Faulkner, *Requiem for a Nun*, 543.

50. Ibid., 547.

51. See Michel Foucault, *Discipline and Punish: The Birth of the Prison* (New York: Vintage Books, 1995); and Robyn Wiegman, *American Anatomies: Theorizing Race and Gender* (Durham, N.C.: Duke University Press, 1995).

52. Faulkner, *Requiem for a Nun*, 579.

53. Ibid., 662.

54. Ibid., 648.

55. See for example *Faulkner in the University*, ed. Frederick L. Gwynn and Joseph L. Blotner (Charlottsville: University Press of Virginia, 1995), 196.

Open Spaces, Open Secrets:
Sanctuary's Mysterious "Something"

LISA HINRICHSEN

Faulkner's work frequently articulates trauma through the rhetorical performance of its displacement. Temple Drake's rape, the central moment of sexual violence at the core of *Sanctuary*, is not directly represented; rather, it is spoken about repeatedly, urgently reemerging in dislocated, disruptive images to haunt this hardboiled novel. In describing Temple's rape as a moment when "sound and silence . . . become inverted," Faulkner represents sexual violence as a blank "something" unnarratable and suspended between tenses: at the moment of her violation, Temple states "something *is* going to happen to me. . . . Something *is* happening to me!" . . . I told you it *was*!"[1] She forcefully screams these exclamations, but her words emerge "like hot silent bubbles into the bright silence around them" (102). Here, Temple literally "void[s] the words" (102) that describe the rape, concealing the violence of her violation while simultaneously underscoring its psychic impact. Her grammatical confusion ("is going to," "is," "was") signals both an inability to place the trauma inside a continuous history—to put the crime within time—and an inability to witness it at the moment it happens.[2]

Unable to psychically integrate injury, to correctly conjugate it into a coherent narrative, Temple Drake is left with only her body to dramatize the trauma through theatrical symptoms: manic and on alert, her body conveys a psyche dissolved and fragmented by fear. With her private ritual of looking at herself in her mirror, opening and closing her compact, as if checking to make sure she is still there, Temple attempts to resituate herself in her own body, in her very materiality that, violated, has become profoundly and numbly disconnected, made inanimate and thing-like: an "effigy on an ancient tomb" (71), a "papier-mâché Easter toy" (69).[3] Yet her body continually evades her attempts to control it, to quell its mania, to awaken its mysterious silences.

In dramatizing the story of a crime while simultaneously problematizing how and if it can be coherently told, Faulkner locates *Sanctuary*'s central formal and thematic inquiry in the tension between acting and knowing—between ontology and epistemology—that Tzvetan Todorov argues is fundamental to the classic detective story. In *The Poetics of Prose* (1971), Todorov argues that the classic detective tale has a dual structure whereby the reader encounters "not one but two stories: the story of the crime and the story of the investigation. In their purest form, these two stories have no point in common. . . . The first story, that of the crime, ends before the second begins. But what happens in the second? Not much. The characters of this second story, the story of the investigation, do not act, they learn."[4]

Yet in *Sanctuary* Faulkner both modernizes and subverts this classic form, emphasizing the difficulty of telling—and learning from—a coherent "story" of crime: first, by eliding direct narrative representation of Temple's rape, problematizing its ability to be a narratable "story," as I have already suggested; second, by undermining Horace Benbow's reliability as "detective" by revealing his lack of analytic impartiality (that is, his fantasies of violating his niece Little Belle, fantasies that Faulkner links to the type of paternal pathologies that circulate throughout the novel and culminate in Temple's rape); and third, by dramatizing Temple's inability to testify to Popeye's multiple crimes in the novel's climactic courtroom scene, which results in the conviction of Lee Goodwin, and his grotesque punishment by a vigilante mob who violently lynch and burn him.

Temple's motives for refusing to tell the truth in court are multifaceted and mysterious. They are also morally problematic, as critics have noted, since they appear to implicate Temple in the violence of which she has been a victim. The trial scene is thus a moment when the epistemological drive of classic crime fiction fails to create resolution, for the legal ruling in the case, which is ostensibly about murder, not rape, fails to provide justice for the violations Temple suffered, leaving her sexual trauma as an unspoken "something" that everyone knows but refuses to directly—and legally—acknowledge.[5] By representing and eliding the rape both at the moment of its occurrence and at the moments of its narration, Faulkner creates a structural link between events: the courtroom scene reiterates and replays the rape itself. Temple cannot function as an accurate, honest witness at the trial precisely because she could not bear witness during the rape's occurrence; instead, she struggles with the representational difficulty inherent to trauma, the way it forms, as trauma theorist Cathy Caruth writes, "a history without a place" that can only be articulated "as the transmission of a gap."[6] Significantly, Temple's mouth itself is aligned with this "something": Faulkner describes her bow-shaped mouth "like something both symbolical and cryptic cut carefully from purple paper and pasted there" (284), foreshadowing her difficulties in providing testimony, as her mouth itself is papered over and pasted closed.

Thus, Faulkner shifts the focus of detection in *Sanctuary* from "whodunit" to the failure of the "second story, the story of the investigation," namely, the coherent narrative supposed to give closure to the crime. Instead of closure we are led to more questions, for the trial is marked by the mystery of Temple's strange reticence to properly resolve the question of "who" by naming Popeye publicly, perjuring herself and wrongly accusing Lee Goodwin of the crime. This false testimony cannot be explained solely as a result of social pressure that demands she conceal her brief residence in the brothel, for the rape is acknowledged in the courtroom with the spectacle of the bloody corncob.[7] It may be that Temple's influential father counsels her before the trial to implicate Goodwin, so that the family name can be shielded from further smears. It may also be that Popeye's lingering psychological grasp upon Temple causes her to misguidedly point her finger at Goodwin in an attempt to displace blame. And perhaps the arbitrariness of her accusation is meant to indicate that responsibility rests with anyone and everyone, for the community itself, as I will show, is complicit in the swirl of drunkenness, violence, and fraught desire that surrounds her throughout the novel.

Temple's motivations, then, remain cryptic: we are given little in the way of contextual clues or hints of unconscious motives, and her verbal testimony largely consists of silence. Throughout the trial, Temple speaks in a "scarcely distinguishable voice" (285), delivering "parrot-like answers" (286), and either does not answer or reluctantly answers the questions put to her. "What is your name?" the District Attorney asks. "She did not answer. She moved her head slightly, as though he had obstructed her view, gazing at something in the back of the room" (284). Mysteriously, her vision is drawn to the back of the room, toward a "something" that seems to be the blankness of the wall itself. "At once the girl's gaze went to the back of the room and became fixed there. . . . A man [came] stalking up the aisle toward the Bench. . . . He walked steadily up the aisle in a slow expulsion of silence like a prolonged sigh, looking to neither side. He passed the witness stand without a glance at the witness, who still gazed at something in the back of the room. . . . She sat in her attitude of childish immobility, gazing like a drugged person above the faces, toward the rear of the room" (287–89). Here, we see Temple from the outside, as though we are members of the jury or audience, and can only speculate on her motives; by keeping Temple blank, empty, reduced to her "eyes blank and all pupil" (289), Faulkner suspends and mystifies both the question of what she sees, and why her gaze is "fixed," but his prose urgently underlines the importance of her gaze, pointing out three times in a few brief pages that her vision gravitates toward the back of the room. His prose specifies that she looks at "something," not "someone," eliminating the possibility that she is receiving cues from someone shaping her testimony, for she looks "above the faces," and in effect beyond the social space of the courtroom. Indeed, Faulkner emphasizes that those in the courtroom, like the man who comes "stalking up the aisle toward the Bench," pay Temple no mind, passing her "without a glance" (288). Furthermore, the magnetism that the "something" in the back of the courtroom exudes noticeably distracts Temple from the proceedings: the pull of this mysterious "something" is greater than that of the DA's persistent questions, and through her eyes we come to see his presence as an "obstruct[ion]" (284) interfering with her impulse to see. "Something" thus marks the presence of an inanimate absence, a figure of ellipsis in Faulkner's writing with no determinate content, left implicit and nonspecifiable, forming a gap in the narrative reminiscent of the "something" that happened to her in the corncrib.[8]

I want to concentrate on this mysterious "something" at the back of the courtroom, focusing on why Faulkner resists filling in this "something" with a clear referent. As I will ultimately show, Temple's fixation is deeply significant, representing at once the silence of her trauma, which cannot be brought into and acknowledged within the legal proceedings of the courtroom, as well as the gap in the symbolic order of Southern culture itself, which the trial exposes. By opening the gap between the story of the crime and the story of the investigation of the crime—manifested as the blank "something" Temple silently witnesses—Faulkner thus subverts the usual ideologically conservative function of crime narratives, creating a story that critiques rather than conserves the status quo. What we see in the text is a crisis of witnessing that calls into question the juridical limits of truth and witnessing; the trial scene, in its absurdity, argues against the conflation of ethics and law and the reduction of truth and justice to judgment.[9] Here, the crime is not mastered, but mystified. A profoundly psychoanalytic text, *Sanctuary* thus induces us to question the relationship between psychoanalysis, detection, law, and testimony.

As critics such as Ernest Mandel have argued, the genre of the crime story is fundamentally intertwined with the development of modern industrial society and "bourgeois society [that] in and of itself breeds crime, originates in crime, and leads to crime."[10] Faulkner illustrates how crime underlies the (bourgeois) public sphere, the "collective breath" (286) that fills the courtroom after Temple fails to speak and dictates what can and cannot be openly said, and exposes how the culture of a dominant white male masculinity depends upon the unspoken dynamics of shame, blame, and violence. In the trial scene at the climax of *Sanctuary*, the (mis-)identification of *a* criminal conceals the criminality of culture itself: in other words, the Southern legal system that deems Goodwin criminal does not—and cannot—recognize its own criminality (i.e., the racism, classism, and sexism of "justice"). As Charmaine Eddy persuasively argues, the courtroom scene "delineates the prohibitive function at its most extreme, where the policing of sexual violation does not proceed to the punishment and eradication of that violation."[11] Notably, a link between the initial rape and the courtroom scene occurs structurally in the way Faulkner represents and elides both moments: the testimonies of the chemist and the gynecologist are obscured from the text and never directly delivered (283–84). The courtroom scene, then, reiterates and replays an earlier moment of nonnarratability in the novel, namely the rape itself.

Indeed, *Sanctuary*'s emphasis on sexual trauma leads many readers to overlook the text's ongoing alignment of multiple, resonant traumas that form the deep structure of the text: the violations of Southern paternalism (as figured in the Drake family's control of Temple and in Horace's fantasies about Little Belle); the influx of urbanization and modernism (as figured in the Memphis scenes) that rapidly and radically refigured the South; and, as registered in Faulkner's preface to *Sanctuary*, the trauma of high art and culture debased by mass industrial forms. By withholding the rape from direct representation, Faulkner shifts our attention from the traumatic "event" to its generative social context, emphasizing how individual acts of violence are located in and entangled with historically and socially sedimented modes of denial, disavowal, and misrecognition that maintain a corrupted social order by refusing to acknowledge the ongoing crimes upon which it is founded. By connecting Temple's rape and her injured individual psyche to the ongoing violations of a Southern paternalism struggling to preserve its privileges in an old order already vanishing, Faulkner makes clear the consequences of maintaining modes of order that depend upon the deployment of silence and violence. By setting Temple's rape at the Old Frenchman Place, a site that the opening pages of *The Hamlet* tell us was "the original grant and site of a tremendous pre–Civil War plantation" (3), Faulkner points to a trail of violations that stem back to the time of slavery.[12] In making this reference to the slave economy and its sustaining plantation modes of paternalism, *Sanctuary* recovers the past to demonstrate its presence in the present, revealing the psychological workings of denial, disavowal, and misrecognition that grant a false stability to a contradictory social order anxious about its own continuance.

This entanglement of a set of sociohistorical traumas with Temple's sexual trauma suggests the characters' inability to bear witness not only

to the rape itself but also to their historical complicity with its occurrence and with the present violence that surrounds bringing the rape to
an incomplete "justice." Think here of Gowan's drunken irresponsibility
in leaving her alone at the Old Frenchman place; the Jefferson District
Attorney whose incendiary remarks, in prosecuting Goodwin, incite his
lynching; Popeye, the gangster who kidnaps and brutally rapes her with a
corncob; the father who conceals her in Europe without hope of psychi-
atric help at the end of the novel; in sum, the Southern patriarchy that
made Temple Drake.[13] Furthermore, this entanglement produces an
unnerving conflation between victim and victimizer: as a white woman
of leisure, Temple has been both produced from and violated by the
initial traumas of plantocratic paternalism, slavery, and land ownership.

Situated against this monopoly of gender and power, the function of
the trial seems to be less about justice than about how the institutions
of justice and law, in their most conservative forms, depend upon the
habitual, institutionalized replication of elite social investiture. The DA's
request for Temple to "speak out" comes with the reassurance that "no
one will hurt you," because she is surrounded by "fathers and husbands,"
and links social power explicitly to a patriarchy that the text sharply critiques (285).[14] As Horace's driver wryly states near the end of the novel,
"We got to protect our girls," because we "might need them ourselves"
(298). The threat of violence ensures that women will remain "our
girls," juvenile because vulnerable. The "our" signals ownership, nodding toward the remnants of antebellum planter culture in which white
ownership doubles as legal authority, and underlining and critiquing the
relationship between community based norms and the source and limit
of the law.

Notably, the trial's incendiary results are fueled not only by the spectacle of the stained corncob phallus strategically showcased at the start
of the trial by the DA, but also by his reiteration of the pervasive fantasy of sacred Southern womanhood. The DA invokes "the most sacred
affairs of that most sacred thing in life: womanhood—who says that this
is no longer a matter for the hangman, but for a bonfire of gasoline—"
(284). Here his charged phrases immediately gesture toward the possibility of vindication outside the space of the courtroom, reconciling illicit
desires with the law, and condoning an illegal vigilante justice driven by
the fantasy of the sacred purity of white Southern femininity and the
masculine violence needed to defend it.

It is against this world that Temple comes to stand and speak at the
trial. While her verbal testimony emerges in reluctant fits and starts, fragmented sentences and unfinished thoughts, the testimony her traumatized body delivers is striking: her mannerisms and her "fixed" gaze reveal
the imprint of the trauma she has suffered. While her silences interrupt

and rupture the articulations of the law, standing in opposition to the trial's effort to create a conscious, totalizing memory and narrative, they cannot be translated into legal consciousness and into legal idiom, for the law cannot recognize what cannot be verbally disclosed. Largely passive in the courtroom, Temple avoids responsibility by avoiding response. The DA's opening invocation to "Let these good men, these fathers and husbands, hear what you have to say and right your wrong for you" gives the pretense of a social and verbal openness, while hiding the fact that the trial does not "hear" nor heal her (285). Within the sensationalized space of the courtroom that he creates and orchestrates, Temple is never adequately able to articulate what it is she has to say.

Notably, when Temple realizes she has failed to speak the truth at the trial and has accused Lee Goodwin rather than Popeye, she tries to return, go back and correct herself: "Again the girl stopped. She began to cringe back, her body arching slowly, her arm tautening in the old man's grasp. . . . They moved toward the door. Here they stopped again; the girl could be seen shrunk against the wall just inside the door, her body arched again" (289–90). Yet she is immediately submerged within the strong male bodies that surround her and carry her away, visually erasing her presence and occluding her opportunity for agency: "She appeared to be clinging there, then the five bodies hid her again and again in a close body the group passed through the door and disappeared" (289–90). Through the phrase "a close body," Faulkner correlates intimacy with violence, nodding to the subjective pressures of familial and physical closeness on the shaping of Temple's testimony.[15]

As Faulkner subtly indicates in this crucial scene, this orchestration of patriarchal protection is punctuated with sublimated violence, from the arms that grasp and guide Temple forward against her will, to the men who stand "like soldiers" (289) near the exit of the courtroom. As she proceeds down the aisle with her father, Temple drops her "platinum bag" and her father, with "the toe of his small gleaming shoe" (289), kicks it into the corner of the courtroom, near the spittoon, positioning it like wasted refuse, an act that nods to the bodily waste and devaluation at the heart of the novel. Like the discarded purse, whose devalued platinum surface goes scudding along the filthy floor, Temple herself becomes a wasted fantasy object, an objectified "something" upon which the trial's interpretative machinery churns, judges, and fixates. Notably, the "good men, these fathers and husbands" that surround Temple fail to "right [her] wrong" (285), yet the trial still functions to put the crime to momentary social rest through its public orchestration of the social and linguistic rituals of "justice."

Faulkner thus situates the trial as a performance of what Anne-Lise François has termed the "open secret."[16] The "open secret," as François

defines it in her book of the same name, involves "the paradox of a disclosure that only opens the eyes of the seeing and closes the eyes of the
unseeing" (2), ultimately ushering in a "self-canceling revelation" (3).
Drawing on Eve Kosofsky Sedgwick's and Frank Kermode's work on
secrecy, François outlines how an open secret is "essentially preventative
or conservative mode of communication that reveals to insiders what
it simultaneously hides from outsiders or, more specifically, protects
them from what they do not wish to know, from what it is in their power
to ignore" (4).[17] In post-Marxist, psychoanalytically informed ideology
theory, the "open secret" becomes, in François's words, "a trope for the
implicit workings of ideology itself—for the way in which the ideological not only gains assent without show of force and polices imagination
without explicit censorship, but occupies the space of the blank page
from which it can produce a consensus that no actually written document could ever yield."[18]

The trial thus "closes the eyes of the unseeing"—the eyes of men like
Gowan who find the "prospect of facing Temple [to be] more than he
could bear" (85), and the social sphere that deems rape an unspeakable
and invisible crime—but opens the eyes of the seeing reader who knows
more than the judge, jury, and detective. What stands at the center of the
trial is therefore not only the unspoken sexual trauma but the blindness
it induces. In nodding toward and exposing judicial blindness, Faulkner
underlines how the court's verdict actually ratifies the inherent cultural
invisibility of culture's complicity with this violence, marking the relation
between patriarchy and violence.

A brief moment early in the text foregrounds the mechanism of hiding in the open that the trial will later dramatize. When Horace briefly
stops at Popeye's house at the conclusion of chapter 1, he observes
Goodwin walking into the kitchen to retrieve bootleg liquor: "In passing,
he looked at Popeye with a glance at once secret and alert, as though he
were ready to laugh at a joke, waiting for the time to laugh. He crossed
the kitchen with a shambling, bear-like gait, and still with that air of alert
and gleeful secrecy, though in plain sight of them, he removed a loose
board in the floor and took out a gallon jug" (10). Here, we see how
bootlegging hides in the open, with its secrecy made public and "alert":
even though "the law" is present and embodied in the form of Horace,
the bootlegging operation only bends in the most cursory of ways to the
law's rule. The flouting "air of alert and gleeful secrecy" that Goodwin's
face evinces stems from the knowledge that this violation will never be
called out by Horace: though the alcohol appears "in plain sight," Horace simply "quit[s] looking" (12).

Likewise, Faulkner's text highlights a number of moments in which
characters see but do not know. When Gowan awakens from his ongoing

drunken stupors, for example, Faulkner highlights a cognitive gap, noting that "Then he was *seeing again, without knowing* at once that he was awake" (35, emphasis added). Similar moments of cognitive and sensory breakdown flood the text at crucial moments and underscore the way the men in the text fail to recognize their own complicity with the violence that Temple has experienced. During the mob scene, Goodwin's lynching is rendered as a moment of sensory breakdown in Horace's mind, as a moment of blankness and aporia: "Horace ran among them; they were holding him, but he did not know it; they were talking, but he could not hear the voices" (296). Rendered in the language of silence and void, "Horace couldn't hear them. He couldn't hear the man who had got burned screaming. He couldn't hear the fire, though it still swirled upward unabated, as though it were living upon itself, and soundless: a voice of fury like in a dream, roaring silently out of a peaceful void" (296). Unable to "hear," and therefore unable to comprehend, Horace is willfully spared from a recognition of his complicity with the fire and the fury that fuels it; instead, the violence is rendered "dream[-like]" and transformed into "a peaceful void" via his sensory breakdown. Such scenes underline what will later happen in the trial: namely, the production of a spectacle reliant upon a breakdown in knowledge. The jury sees Temple without really reckoning with her.

The mystery of Temple's passivity in the courtroom, while a symptom of her traumatized condition and a demonstration of the hold her community has over her, can thus also be understood as her means of telling us "something" the community doesn't want to know; i.e., making the secret "open." Her gaze at the blank space at the back of the courtroom—which François deems "the space of the blank page"—underscores a knowingness regarding the confluence of censorship and consensus at the heart of the (white, masculine) legal system. Repeatedly, Faulkner emphasizes how the inhabitants of the courtroom compose a collective with seemingly no dissent, no alternative voice: the room forms a space where even belated newcomers to the trial immediately gather in "a clump," a phrase which foreshadows the mob violence yet to come (286). Throughout the courtroom scene, the spectators and jury alike react as a unitary public, a political "all": "The room sighed, a long hissing breath" (288). In the sound of the public's collective "long hissing breath," we can hear what François deems "a consensus that no actually written document could ever yield" (5).

Of course, every trial is contingent on the act of seeing; courtrooms are places of visual spectatorship, showmanship, and theatricality. The district attorney knows this when he holds up the bloody corncob, one of the many moments in the text where Faulkner plays with our voyeuristic complicity, allowing us as readers to peep at scandal and sexuality through proxy "Popeyes" while remaining apart from it. As numerous critics have noted, the opening language of the novel indicates its later reliance upon parameters of visuality and its obfuscation.[19] In the novel's opening scene, which takes place in the woods near the Old Frenchman's Place, Popeye is situated "beyond the screen," watching Horace in a prolonged visual standoff (3). The novel is punctuated with other moments structured around visual domination: at Miss Reba's whorehouse, for example, her maid Minnie peers through the keyhole of a bedroom door, while inside Popeye gapes and gawks at Temple and Red in bed "nekkid as two snakes" (258). Everything—even the moment when Temple shamefacedly defecates in the woods (91)—is subject to visual inspection, exposure, and control.

Yet, by pointing us to the mysterious "something" at the back of the courtroom, Temple's gaze gives us an alternative to this hegemonic consensus. In the manner in which her gaze induces us to look askance at the power dynamics of the courtroom scene, Temple guides us into what Slavoj Žižek terms an "ideological anamorphosis."[20] In his reading of Hans Holbein's 1533 painting *The Ambassadors*, a still life painting consisting of two men surrounded by objects tied to the age of exploration (globes, a sundial, a quadrant), Žižek highlights what he calls a "meaningless spot" prominently displayed in the foreground of the painting. Viewed from the side, this "spot" is in actuality a skewed skull, rendered in anamorphic perspective (a visual puzzle technique invented in the Early Renaissance). Žižek links this visual morphology to the work of ideological and political cohesion: "If we look at what appears from the frontal view as an extended, 'erected' meaningless spot, from the right perspective we notice the contours of a skull. The criticism of ideology must perform a somewhat homological operation: if we look at the element which holds together the ideological edifice, at this 'phallic', erected Guarantee of Meaning, from the right (or, more precisely—politically speaking—left) perspective, we are able to recognize in it the embodiment of a lack, of a chasm of non-sense gaping in the midst of ideological meaning."[21] As Žižek notes in his reading of *The Ambassadors*, anamorphosis underscores how the "meaningless stain" of the skull, "disclos[es] thus the true meaning of the picture—the nullity of all terrestrial goods, objects of art and knowledge that fill out the rest of the picture."[22] The "stain"—or the "something"—acquires a shape only when looked upon from a standpoint distorted and denatured by the subject's terrors and desires. Building upon the principles of Lacanian psychoanalysis, which rejects the idea that there is a neutral or objective perspective from which everything fundamental to the point of inquiry can be apprehended, Žižek utilizes the principles of anamorphosis to query how one perception or social phenomenon might make us blind to another. As *The Ambassadors* richly suggests, we fail to see (our) death head-on, instead rendering it a "meaningless stain" within the rich realism of the rest of the painting; when we are able to see it, the rest of the symbolic order is rendered askew.

An early moment of anamorphic distortion in *Sanctuary* can be found when Horace looks at the photograph of Little Belle and sees it shift as a result of the press of his own desire: "As of its own accord the photograph had shifted, slipping a little from its precarious balancing against the book. The image blurred into the highlight, like something familiar seen beneath disturbed though clear water; he looked at the familiar image with a kind of quiet horror and despair, at a face suddenly older in sin than he would ever be, a face more blurred than sweet, at eyes more secret than soft" (167). Like Temple, Little Belle looks at "something" as she uncannily gazes out of the photograph: she "looked in turn at something just beyond his shoulder, out of the dead cardboard" (166). Horace's vision is constantly defamiliarizing the familiar and seeing it morbidly awry. His gaze is acutely attuned to the horror of the placid everyday: he thinks of the faces on the train "washed lightly over as though with the paling ultimate stain of a holocaust, blinking at one another with dead eyes" (168) and thinks of a guillotine in relation to the "severe trim of hair across [a] man's vast, soft, white neck" (173).

Likewise, in the courtroom scene, Temple's gaze unsettles the smooth workings of the justice system, and of culture itself, by looking awry at the "meaningless stain" in the back of the courtroom, and her gaze transforms the void of the "something" into a discontinuity opened in reality, reconfiguring its lack as a source of surplus meaning. As Žižek writes, "The ground of the established, familiar signification opens up; we find ourselves in a realm of total ambiguity" and "nothing is what it seems to be, everything is to be interpreted" (91).[23] The "something" in the back of the courtroom significantly undercuts the symbolic order of the courtroom, which is to say the impotency of the phallic itself, and the (masculine) law by which it exercises its power. The "something" Temple sees is the surplus element in the social structure, the scrap that evades the grasp of symbolization. Temple—and by proxy, the reader—sees through the existing power structure, exposing its drive toward mastery and opening a space for social critique. The "something" thus comes to signify the insufficiency of paternal law and the arbitrariness of justice. Thus, through this elided "something," we become aware that the courtroom's discourse circulates around a rent, a gap in the order of being where discourse's capacity to "fill" this hole breaks down.[24]

Psychoanalysis teaches us that trauma is that which cannot be accurately seen; it is something that psychoanalytically and politically evades sight, even when it comes into contact with a trial's legal desire for visibility. But seeing—as the foundation of witnessing, and as cornerstone of both consciousness and memory—is, as critics such as Shoshana Felman persuasively note, "inherently, unwittingly political."[25] In examining the intersection of law and trauma, Felman cites French philosopher Louis Althusser's articulation of how seeing and not seeing are dependent upon the limits of a given frame of reference and, in turn, its corresponding ideological framework. Intrigued by what "defines and structures the invisible as its definite outside—*excluded* from the domain of visibility and *defined* as excluded by the existence and the structure of the problematic field itself," Althusser writes that "[t]he invisible is defined by the visible as *its* invisible, *its* prohibited sight. . . . To see this invisible . . . requires something quite different from a sharp or attentive eye, it takes an *educated eye*, a revised, renewed way of looking, itself produced by the effect of a 'change of terrain' reflected back upon the act of seeing."[26]

Temple's gaze directs and educates our eyes, educating our vision through exposing the antinomy—the split or gap between beliefs, between justice and law, speech and silence—and initiating us into the profound alienation of the traumatized subject. Through Temple's gaze, we are enabled to "see through" the trial and know that it is not about "justice," but about a social closure ultimately rendered outside the law in the form of vigilante justice. In gazing toward the gap in the back of the courtroom, Temple implicitly signals that she has seen through the façade of justice, the way its openness to truth is dominated by the desire for closure. The blankness of that space on the wall implicitly invites us to fill it in with all sorts of contents and fantasies, and to paper over its blankness.

Of course, within the parameters of the novel, closure comes not with the trial, but instead with a highly aestheticized scene set in Paris. Faulkner notably changes register—moving from the legal to the heightened language of the literary—in order to have us witness the failure of closure. Faulkner here highlights the lingering symptoms of trauma, again exposing the severance, the schism between justice and law, wrenching apart what was closed or covered over by the legal trial, reopening the case, and "dis-solving" its failure of accountability. The last image of Temple is in the Luxembourg Gardens with her father, where, as Faulkner writes, "from beneath her smart new hat she seemed to follow with her eyes the waves of music, to dissolve into the dying brasses, across the pool and the opposite semicircle of trees where at somber intervals the dead tranquil queens in stained marble mused, and on into the sky lying prone and vanquished in the embrace of the season of rain and death" (317). Faulkner leaves us in a world of impersonal, severe shapes and forms, symbolically charged and yet silent, a frozen world in which the only movement is Temple's eyes following "the waves of music," ready "to dissolve into the dying brasses." The uncertainty of her gaze—"she seemed to follow"—is set against the rigidity of her father's presence next to her, with "his hands crossed on the head of his *stick*, the *rigid bar* of his moustache beaded with moisture like frosted silver" (317, emphasis added). Here, Temple's father figures as both policeman and prison guard, a source of "rigid" authority, of a straitlaced social geometry that "bar[s]" change and stands in contrast to the more fluid "waves" that Temple seems to see. As his final gesture, Faulkner subtly signals the fluid motion of Temple's synesthetic gaze, which moves in a quest to "dis-solve" the brasses, the trial, and the logic of vision itself in her search for sanctuary.

NOTES

1. William Faulkner. *Sanctuary: The Corrected Text*, ed. Noel Polk (New York: Vintage, 1993), 102, italics added.

2. It is important to note here that Faulkner, like other modernist writers such as Joseph Conrad, often elides central traumatic events. In *Lord Jim*, Jim's jump is retold in multiple grammatical tenses and yet it is never seen or witnessed by the reader in the present tense. In *The Secret Agent* the exact moment in which Verloc is violently stabbed by Winnie is cinematically cut from an otherwise highly detailed narration. Yet the evasions of the rape that Faulkner presents in *Sanctuary* do more than replicate modernist techniques of stylistic experimentation: they nod toward crucial gaps in cultural visibility and recognition of violence. Furthermore, *Sanctuary* remains different from other Faulkner novels in which a central crime of sex or violence is deliberately withheld from the reader (*Absalom, Absalom!* and *As I Lay Dying*). In *Sanctuary* the traumatic moment is not chronologically antecedent to the main narrative but encased within it.

3. André Bleikasten notes that "identical gestures and postures repeat themselves through different characters and situations" and that "in displaced form, the repressed scene keeps returning again and again" (18, 19). Yet his observations on the compulsive repetitiveness of the text are not drawn out to their full and illuminating potential, for these repetitions function as textual gestures toward absent, encrypted stories—places of nonnarratability, numbness—in the text that ache for articulation. Bleikasten's close reading of the imagery in *Sanctuary* provides a good groundwork for examining how a consciousness of rape physically plays itself out through repeated gestures, although the conclusions he draws need to be reworked in favor of a more subtle and empathetic treatment of both Temple and Popeye. Bleikasten's remark that "there is no interior to be exteriorized" in *Sanctuary*, only "body signs" that are, "at best," indices "of disturbance or symptoms of disease; they are no longer the tangible manifestations of an inner or transcendental world" prompts a further disagreement, for I read the repeated physical gestures as symptoms that point to an "inner or transcendental world," manifesting this

world in the only way possible (18). Bleikasten concentrates on Temple's "transformation from victim to aggressor" and terms her a "raving nymphomaniac, fastened like a leech to her paralyzed prey," damning her despite his recognition that many of her behaviors are responses to overwhelming terror (25). See André Bleikasten, "Terror and Nausea: Bodies in *Sanctuary*," *Faulkner Journal* 1.1 (Fall 1985): 17–29.

4. Tzvetan Todorov, *The Poetics of Prose*, trans. Richard Howard (Ithaca: Cornell University Press, 1977), 44.

5. While the legal ruling in the case centers on the murder of Tommy, the trial itself emphasizes the spectacle of the corncob rape, drawing on the way it infuriates and inflames the audience and jurors alike. The DA's showcasing of the corncorb in the court-room can thus be seen as directly tied to the lynching, linking vigilante violence directly to the law itself.

6. See Cathy Caruth, ed. *Trauma: Explorations in Memory* (Baltimore: Johns Hopkins University Press, 1995), 156. See also Caruth's *Unclaimed Experience: Trauma, Narrative, History* (Baltimore: Johns Hopkins University Press, 1996).

7. Interestingly, the "bloody stains" on the corncob are not rendered as such in *Sanctuary*. Instead, the corncob "appeared to have been dipped in dark brownish paint" (283), hinting at a cultural, man-made origin for the injury. The corncob phallus, likewise, is an artificial substitute for the real thing, and Popeye's need for it underscores his des-perate impotency. As it figures in the courtroom scene, the stains on the corncob evince the strains of paternalism's collapse, denaturalizing the phallus and exposing its impotency.

8. Ellipses repeatedly function throughout the text to blur and elide the central events and narrative concerns. As John T. Matthews notes, "the elliptical nature of the [rape] is not eccentric . . . but paradigmatic; like a template, the figure of ellipsis pervades the rhe-torical, psychological, narrative, and thematic structures of *Sanctuary*" (246). See John T. Matthews, "The Elliptical Nature of *Sanctuary*," *Novel: A Forum on Fiction* 17.3 (Spring 1984): 246–65.

9. I see this confusion regarding knowing versus solving and ethics and law fore-grounded in chapter 1 of *Sanctuary* where Popeye, after engaging in a prolonged visual standoff with Horace Benbow, still expresses confusion about who exactly Horace is. Seeing him with a book, Popeye repeatedly and mistakenly calls him "Professor," fore-shadowing how Horace will later confuse "to solve" and "to know" (8–9). This error also underscores how Horace is unable to publically "profess" his guilty desires for Little Belle.

10. Ernest Mandel, *Delightful Murder: A Social History of the Crime Story* (Minneapolis: University of Minnesota Press, 1984), 135.

11. Charmaine Eddy, "The Policing and Proliferation of Desire: Gender and the Homosocial in Faulkner's *Sanctuary*," *Faulkner Journal* 14.2 (1999): 21–39, 34.

12. See William Faulkner, *The Hamlet*: The Corrected Text, ed. Noel Polk (New York: Vintage, 1991). Temple Drake's assault at the Old Frenchman Place is posed against the history of the site that we are given in the opening pages of *The Hamlet*: "It had been the original grant and site of a tremendous pre–Civil War plantation, the ruins of which—the gutted shell of an enormous house with its fallen stables and slave quarters and overgrown gardens and brick terraces and promenades—were still known as the Old Frenchman place" (3). Haunted by the legacy of slavery, the Old Frenchman Place becomes a reso-nant site at which present and past traumas intersect and overlap.

13. Faulkner clearly makes attempts at the end of *Sanctuary* to provide some poten-tially and partially humanizing background on Popeye's social and psychological develop-ment, although the delayed deliverance of this material until the near-end of the novel puts its purpose and potential effectiveness into question (see 304–10). I believe that we are to understand from this final glimpse into Popeye's personal and familial history that

he himself has experienced traumatic events, and that trauma tends to beget trauma: it becomes a cycle fated to repeat.

14. It is worth noting here, as John N. Duvall does in "Silencing Women in 'The Fire and the Hearth' and 'Tomorrow,'" that juries during this period were composed solely of men over the age of twenty-one. While justice was literally dependent on "fathers and husbands" in the South, I argue that in *Sanctuary* Faulkner stresses the limitation of this gendered ruling and the way in which it contributes to judicial blindness. Duvall's essay can be found in *College Literature* 16.1 (1989): 75–82.

15. As Matthews persuasively notes in "The Elliptical Nature of *Sanctuary*," this scene also "bristle[s] with sexual imagery" (257) and the pattern of the bodies walking down the aisle of the courtroom forms a "dreamy reverse wedding" that attempts to "undo a ravishment that has been broached originally by its own avengers" (258).

16. Anne-Lise François, *Open Secrets: The Literature of Uncounted Experience* (Stanford: Stanford University Press, 2008).

17. In particular, see Sedgwick's *The Epistemology of the Closet* (Berkeley: University of California Press, 1990) and Kermode's *The Genesis of Secrecy: On the Interpretation of Narrative* (Cambridge: Harvard University Press, 1980).

18. François, 5.

19. The role of visuality in the novel has been highlighted in criticism by Greg Forter, Jay Watson, Andrew J. Wilson, Ted Atkinson, and Peter Lurie, among others. Atkinson argues that the opening scene introduces Popeye "with a vivid use of imagery, creating a visual frame that evokes the discovery shot in film" (121). Forter sees the opening as offering a vision of a "species of narcissistic gazing, but one that precisely fails to recover an adequate image of self," ultimately offering a "specular scene that disturbs the objective function of vision" (390). He brilliantly notes that it is Popeye's spit that distorts the watery mirror into which Horace gazes, thus "link[ing] the disturbance of vision to a confrontation between sight and oral expulsion" (390). Jay Watson claims that vision plays a decisive and divisive role throughout the text: "Whereas the promise of speech is to unite individuals, to invite them together and by means of its immanence to provide a medium for interaction, *Sanctuary* makes it clear that watching holds them apart, establishes the space of their separation, reaffirms their impenetrable privacies, their inscrutable purposes" (49). See Greg Forter, "Faulkner, Trauma, and the Uses of Crime Fiction," in Richard Moreland, ed., *A Companion to William Faulkner* (Hoboken, N.J.: Blackwell Wiley, 2007), 373–94; Jay Watson, "The Failure of Forensic Storytelling in *Sanctuary*." *Faulkner Journal* 6.1 (Fall 1990): 47–66; Andrew J. Wilson, "The Corruption in Looking: William Faulkner's *Sanctuary* as Detective Novel," *Mississippi Quarterly* 47.3 (Summer 1994): 441–60; Ted Atkinson, *Faulkner and the Great Depression: Aesthetics, Ideology, and Cultural Politics* (Athens: University of Georgia Press, 2006); and Peter Lurie, *Vision's Immanence: Faulkner, Film, and the Popular Imagination* (Baltimore: Johns Hopkins University Press, 2004).

20. Slavoj Žižek, *The Sublime Object of Ideology* (London: Verso, 2001), 99.

21. Ibid., 99–100.

22. Slavoj Žižek, *Looking Awry: An Introduction to Jacques Lacan through Popular Culture* (Cambridge: MIT Press, 1991), 91.

23. Ibid., 91.

24. *Sanctuary* is a novel marked by an obsessive attentiveness to holes, gaps, and spots of blankness. The temporarily exposed hole in Red's forehead when the bullet falls out is an especially curious instance of this fixation: "When they raised the corpse the wreath came too, attached to him by a hidden end of wire driven into his cheek. He had worn a cap which, tumbling off, exposed a small blue hole in the center of his forehead.

It had been neatly plugged with wax and was painted, but the wax had been jarred out and lost. They couldn't find it, but by unfastening the snap in the peak, they could draw the cap down to his eyes" (248–49). Here, Faulkner draws our attention to the driving social urge to immediately "plug" the hole, to cover the gap from prying, observant eyes by "draw[ing] the cap down to his eyes." This moment of covering over is especially resonant when placed in relationship to the courtroom scene, where the social consensus is to not see and not acknowledge the holes in Temple's elliptical testimony. The ellipses in the testimony (and the text as a whole) function as moments of blankness that the reader desires to fill in—and thus necessarily distort. As Sabine Sielke notes, "Filling in the textual gaps, we supplement our own rape fantasies, so to speak, necessarily misconstruing the moment" (87). See Sabine Sielke, *Reading Rape: The Rhetoric of Sexual Violence in American Literature and Culture, 1790–1990* (Princeton, N.J.: Princeton University Press, 2002).

25. Shoshana Felman, *The Juridical Unconscious: Trials and Traumas in the Twentieth Century* (Cambridge: Harvard University Press, 2002), 82–83.

26. Louis Althusser, *Lire le Capital*, I (Paris: Maspero, 1968), 26–28. As cited and trans. Shoshana Felman in *The Juridical Unconscious*, 82–83 (italics as in the original).

Unvanquished Uncertainty

SARAH MAHURIN

In "Skirmish at Sartoris," the second-to-last chapter of *The Unvan-quished*, Bayard Sartoris's Aunt Louisa sends an anxious, unwieldy letter to Mrs. Compson, seeking her aid and—more crucially—her understanding, since "Mrs. Compson was a woman too, Aunt Louisa believed, a Southern woman too, and had suffered too, Aunt Louisa didn't doubt."[1] But the more Aunt Louisa writes, the more convoluted her missive becomes: Bayard, who reads it secondhand, concludes, "I couldn't make any sense out of that one too and I still dont know what Aunt Louisa was talking about and I didn't believe that Mrs. Compson knew either" (193–94). Many of the most memorable moments in *The Unvanquished* center around such misunderstandings, during which one character is uncertain—often comically so—of another character's meaning. Consider the following exchange between Granny Millard and some irate Yankee soldiers:

> "You won't find any locked doors," Granny said. "At least let me ask you—"
> "Don't you ask anything, grandma. You set still. Better for you if you had done a little asking before you sent them little devils out with this gun."
> "Was there . . . " We could hear her voice die away and then speak again, like she was behind it with a switch, making it talk. "Is he . . . it . . . the one who—"
> "Dead? Hell, yes! Broke his back and we had to shoot him!"
> "Had to—you had—shoot . . ."
> . . . "Yes, by God. Had to shoot him! The best damn horse in the whole army! The whole regiment betting on him for next Sunday——" (29)

(Afterwards Bayard will note, with a mixture of relief and disappointment, "We never killed him! We haven't killed anybody at all!") In "Raid" the names of two stolen mules, Old Hundred and Tinney, are transposed to the ear of one Colonel Dick, so that *one hundred and ten* mules are delivered, as settlement, to a baffled Granny; in "Skirmish at Sarto-ris," Drusilla is initially confused—and then outraged—when Martha Habersham expresses a clucking sympathy for her supposed "condition" (that is, unwed pregnancy).[2] And Ringo, "[trying] to understand about mountains," completely misreads John Sartoris's explanation: "At last he pointed out the cloudbank to tell us what mountains looked like. So ever since then Ringo believed that the cloudbank was Tennessee" (35).

Perhaps one of the reasons we so relish these moments of confusion and uncertainty in and between Faulkner's characters is that we, his readers, are usually the ones who are confused and uncertain. Faulkner's plots are famously difficult to unravel; his prose can hover on the edge of impenetrability.[3] Critics, too, have long wrestled with the idea of Faulknerian uncertainty—that is, with the question of what remains unknown, and what goes unsaid, in Faulkner's fiction. Richard Adams notes the reader's "cumulative, pervasive and fascinating sense . . . of temporal and epistemological disorientation"[4]; David Minter describes the novels as incessantly "strewing difficulties in our path, which is why readers often find themselves moving back and forth between fascination and frustration, engagement and resistance, insight and bafflement. Partial, filtered scenes, shadowy, elusive characters, and tentative, provisional stories are frequently all we have."[5] Indeed, no American writer can baffle quite like Faulkner. John Matthews has suggested that, in the dense landscape of Yoknapatawpha County, "the kernel of the story is precisely what vanishes into the words that describe it . . . the moment of the story's origin is lost in the novel"—that the texts are filled with holes that simultaneously demand and resist filling.[6] Or, as Robert Dale Parker puts it, "the main thing we know reading Faulkner's novels is that we *don't* know the main thing."[7]

But these are issues of *readerly* uncertainty: they speak to the mysteries that beset Faulkner's students and critics. As Faulkner's novels go, *The Unvanquished* does not seem particularly mysterious, or particularly difficult to unravel—especially when we compare it to, say, some of the knottier moments in *Absalom, Absalom!* or to Benjy's section in *The Sound and the Fury*. Its prose is clear; its plots are relatively straightforward; its structure is broken up into easily digestible, chronological units. But I find this clarity misleading: *The Unvanquished* is actually suffused with moments of mystery, with nuggets of uncertainty that are studded into the text so subtly and so organically that we discover them only when we seek them out: they are like the stock pen Bayard and Ringo bury "deep in the creek bottom, where you could not have found it unless you had known where to look, and you could not have seen it until you came to the new sap-sweating, axe-ended rails woven through and into the jungle growth itself" (11).

In our other encounters with the Faulknerian first-person (most notably the alternating narratives in *The Sound and the Fury* and *As I Lay Dying*) much of what is obscured to us—particularly in terms of plot—is still available to, and extant in, the consciousnesses of the characters. In other words, they—the characters—know things we—the readers—don't. *The Unvanquished* inverts this model. Consider this early exchange between the boys and Loosh:

> "Far don't matter. . . . Far don't matter. Case hit's on the way!"
> "On the way? On the way to what?"
> "Ask your paw. Ask Marse John."
> "He's at Tennessee, fighting. I can't ask him."
> "You think he at Tennessee? Aint no need for him at Tennessee now." Then Philadelphy grabbed him by the arm.
> "Hush your mouth, nigger!" she cried, in that tense desperate voice. "Come on here and get me some wood!"
> Then they were gone. Ringo and I didn't watch them go. We stood there above our ruined Vicksburg. . . . "What?" Ringo said. "What he mean?"
> "Nothing," I said. I stooped and set Vicksburg up again. "There it is."
> But Ringo didn't move. . . . "Loosh laughed. . . . What you reckon he know that we aint?" (6)

"What you reckon he know that we aint?" opens outward, so that the "he" is not only Loosh, but also the reader, who is privileged to "know" things—here and elsewhere—that the characters "aint." Even after the boys eavesdrop on Colonel Sartoris and Granny, their understanding remains incomplete and flawed: "Vicksburg *fell*?" Ringo asks Bayard incredulously. "Do he mean it fell off in the River?" (18). Meanwhile, though the conversation between Granny and the Colonel is obscured to us, the reader's understanding deepens.

Of course, history is on our side: to any Faulknerian reader, the outcome of Vicksburg is no mystery.[8] And the reader, like Loosh, has over Bayard and Ringo the advantage of maturity: the advantage of years, the advantage of experience. After all, through the largest part of *The Unvanquished*, the boys are just that—boys; even by its final story they are only twenty-four. Cleanth Brooks observes that the above exchange "beautifully suggests the troubling effect on the boy to whom Loosh is an adult, even though a slave"; and Loosh's retort—"Ask your paw"—indeed underscores the divide between his knowledge and Bayard's (Bayard thinks his father is "at Tennessee, fighting"; Loosh knows that, following the siege, "aint no need for him at Tennessee now").[9] It also highlights the fact that much, if not most, of Bayard and Ringo's understanding is mediated through and by the adults around them. How could Bayard realize the outcome of Vicksburg? Only, it seems, by "asking his paw"—or Loosh.[10]

The voice of the adult Bayard regularly interjects to reflect on (and to remind the reader of) the chasm between youth and adulthood, which is typically figured as an epistemological chasm: "I was just twelve then," he explains in "Ambuscade," so "I didn't know triumph; I didn't even know the word" (5). A few pages later, still reflecting on his mistaken childhood impressions, the adult Bayard insists that he "know[s] better now" (10). Arthur Kinney has suggested that "Faulkner's narrative poetics is first grounded . . . in human perception; he is in line with those modern thinkers who are as concerned with how we know as what we know"; and indeed, the idea of knowledge, of knowing, reverberates throughout the novel.[11] But we must also note the predominance of *not knowing*: Bayard incessantly notes the things he didn't—or doesn't— realize.[12] At the beginning of "Ambuscade," he confesses that he and Ringo "did not know where [Loosh] had come from; we had not seen him appear, emerge"; on the next page, he cannot interpret the "something curious" in Philadelphy's voice: "I didn't know which, urgency or fright" (4, 5). After the soldiers have left, when Granny moves to pray for forgiveness, the boys initially "didn't know what she was trying to do": only when she kneels do they understand (34).

The reader repeatedly witnesses, from outside the text, the moments of uncertainty that beset Bayard and Ringo within. Thus, I would suggest, the underlying ethos of *The Unvanquished* subtly mirrors one of the novel's most memorable scenes:

> Then [Granny] said, "Quick! Here!" and then Ringo and I were squatting with our chins under our knees, on either side of her against her legs, with the hard points of the chair rockers jammed into our back and her skirts spread over us like a tent, and the heavy feet coming in and (Louvinia told us afterward) the Yankee sergeant shaking the musket at Granny and saying,
> "Come on, grandma. Where are they? We saw them run in here."
> We couldn't see, we just squatted in a kind of faint gray light and that smell of Granny that her clothes and bed and room all had and Ringo's eyes looking like two plates of chocolate pudding. (28)

The boys' experience of this scene is—literally—veiled; their understanding of what has transpired must be delayed until Louivinia's ex post facto narration.[13] And throughout the novel, in some sense, Bayard and Ringo are burrowed under Granny's skirts, dimly aware of and yet distinctly separated from the actualities of the world around them. They understand—and as a result often misunderstand—their surroundings as if from beneath a "tent" of petticoats. The textual sensation of what I call *underskirtedness* becomes even stranger when such uncertainty applies not only to circumstances outside the boys' experiences, but also back onto those experiences, onto their own selves. Indeed, their personal histories can prove just as difficult to unravel as the mysterious

Colonel Sutpen's, even when considered retrospectively—so their lapses in understanding cannot be attributed to youth alone.

Abject uncertainty seems dissonant in a text of straightforward first-person narration; and yet Bayard regularly confesses to being baffled by the fabric of his own account. Of the Yankee officer who assaults Granny's wagon in "Raid," Bayard notes, "I dont know where he went anymore than I know where he came from"; and even after the chaos passes, he is at a loss to describe the scene: "Then maybe the band did cave, I dont know. I didn't even know we were in the river" (105, 107). The details of Granny's murder likewise remain ambiguous—"How many of them there were in the old compress, I dont know and when and why they took fright and left, I dont know" —as does the showdown with Grumby, after which Bayard admits, "I know what did happen, but even now I dont know how, in what order" (153, 182). There is some-thing strange—even a little unsettling—about this profusion of blind spots, of present-tense "I don't knows"; we may feel wary of a first-person narrator so frankly uncertain of the material he communicates, who confesses candidly to being "mixed up" in, and by, his own story (160). To borrow David Minter's terminology, perhaps we should conclude only that Bayard's account is "probably true enough."[14]

In *Faulkner the Storyteller* Blair Labatt observes that in Faulkner, "an occurrence can be believable and yet inexplicable. Faulkner appears to emphasize a general uncertainty about why things happen. In addi-tion to the multiplicity of named causes, there is the constant presence of superstition, the raising of the possibility of myriad causes that can never be traced or verified."[15] But there is an important difference between uncertainties of *why*, or *how*, and uncertainties of *whether*. When Bayard, silently watching the exodus of slaves, notes, "mostly they did not look at us. We might not have even been there," the obvious interpretation suggests the past subjunctive: *It was as if we were not even there*. But I would posit that it is equally worthwhile to consider Bayard's claim literally—to consider that they *actually* "might not have even been there." Such a reading is not unreasonable, given Bayard's uneasy—or, more accurately, uncertain—approach to knowledge: "We sat close together in the shadow again, listening to Father. Perhaps it was the dark or perhaps we were the two moths, the two feathers again or perhaps there is a point at which credulity firmly and calmly and irrevocably declines, because suddenly Louvinia was standing over us, shaking us awake. . . . Because there is that point at which credulity declines; somewhere between waking and sleeping I believed I saw or dreamed that I did see the lantern in the orchard, under the apple trees. But I don't know whether I saw it or not, because then it was morning and it was raining and Father was gone" (18–19). The passage suggests a multitude of compelling interpretive possibilities—earmarked by tell-tale serial "perhaps"es. Bayard is unaware whether he "saw" or merely "dreamed [he] saw," but the lasting effect—his impression of "the lantern under the apple trees"—is the same. Still, the fact of his uncertainty—of his underskirtedness—lingers. The moment is significant enough that Bayard exhumes it in the following chapter, in which he recalls, for no obvious narrative reason, "that night last summer while father was at home, while Louvinia stood in the door of the bedroom without even lighting the lamp while Ringo and I went to bed and later I either looked out or dreamed I looked out the window and saw (or dreamed I saw) the lantern" (40). But even upon revisitation, the facts of the scene—whether Bayard saw the lantern or merely dreamed he saw it—remain uncertain, inaccessible.

Just as Bayard doesn't know whether he saw it or not, Ringo doesn't know whether he *ate* it or not. In this case the *it*, the mysterious unknown, is "cokynut cake":

Ringo got the cook book from the kitchen and he and I lay on our stomachs on the floor while Granny opened the book. "What shall we read about today?" she said.

"Read about cake," I said.

"Very well. What kind of cake?" Only she didn't need to say that because Ringo was already answering that before she spoke:

"Cokynut cake, Granny." He said coconut cake every time because we had never had been able to decide whether Ringo had ever tasted coconut cake or not. We had had some that Christmas before it started and Ringo had tried to remember whether they had had any of it in the kitchen or not, but he couldn't remember. Now and then I used to try to help him decide, get him to tell me how it tasted and what it looked like and sometimes he would almost decide to risk it before he would change his mind. Because he said that he would rather just maybe have tasted coconut cake without remembering it than to know for certain he had not; that if he were to describe the wrong kind of cake, he would never taste coconut cake as long as he lived. (19)

It's an odd little moment, and one that might easily be passed over in favor of the more dramatic fare that is to come. But to overlook it would be a mistake: the anecdote of the "cokynut cake"—or, more to the point, the *hypothetical* "cokynut cake"—provides a lens through which to consider the way epistemology functions in the novel.[16] Ringo is so perplexed by, and so preoccupied with, this seemingly inconsequential hole in his own history that he continually returns to its subject: Bayard reports that "he said coconut cake every time" the question of cakes is raised. But unlike so many Faulknerian ambiguities, this mystery could easily be solved. Ringo could, as Bayard points out, simply describe the flavor or texture of the cake he remembers: if these adhere to actual properties of coconut cake, he has eaten; if they do not, he has not eaten. Either way—case closed.

What is so fascinating is that Ringo repeatedly defers, and then rejects, this option for certainty: the "risk" of "know[ing] for certain he had not" eaten coconut cake overtakes the potential benefit of knowing for certain that he had. (We also sense a hint of nihilism: "If he were to describe the wrong kind of cake, he would never taste coconut cake as long as he lived.") So uncertainty is preferable to an undesirable certainty (that is, the certainty of never having eaten coconut cake); but I want to suggest, further, that there is something desirable about uncertainty in its own right—even when it is not weighed against the possibility of an unpleasant discovery. And sometimes uncertainty is convenient, as well:

> "Where did you get that horse?" [Father] asked.
> After awhile I said, "We borrowed it."
> "Who from?" Father said.
> After awhile Ringo said, "We aint know. The man wasn't there." (62)

Interestingly, this scene is directly mirrored a few pages later, when Granny also appears with a pair of "strange horses" and responds to her son's queries about their origin in identical terms: "I borrowed them. . . . There was nobody there" (71).

Let's recall the way the passage opened. Granny puts away her sewing and offers to entertain the boys by reading to them out of an old cookbook. Ringo requests, as he apparently always does, that she take as her text the section on coconut cake: the item which most torments—and most tantalizes—his consciousness. I use the word "tantalize" deliberately: Ringo takes a kind of pleasure in returning time and again to the subject, and the substance, of his own uncertainty. The tension of possibility, of potentiality, of *not* knowing, becomes a strange force of titillation, and it makes the cookbook entry on coconut cake eternally exciting and eternally suggestive—no matter how many times it is read. Such is the real benefit in the risk-benefit dialectic I gestured towards earlier. That is, if risk is equivalent to "finding out you haven't had coconut cake," benefit is not "finding out you *have* had the cake"; it is, rather, the parallel existence, in Ringo's mind, of these dual possibilities—the continuing and continuous pleasure of ambiguity.[17]

We find a variation on the coconut cake theme in "Raid," with the introduction of a railroad, or, more precisely, an ex-railroad. This railroad is a site of an epistemological split between the boys: Bayard has seen a locomotive before; Ringo has not; therefore Bayard figures himself "ahead of" Ringo in knowledge (81). Ringo cannot stop thinking and talking about the object that separates the two when they arrive at Hawkhurst:

> "Hello," [Drusilla] said. "Hello, John Sartoris." She looked at Ringo. "Is this Ringo?" she said.
> "That's what they tells me," Ringo said. "What about that railroad?"
> "How are you?" Cousin Drusilla said.
> "I manages to stand hit," Ringo said. "What about that railroad?" (89)

(We sense that if Granny had a book on locomotives on the shelf with her cookbook, Ringo would also clamor to have it read aloud.) But when Ringo finally does see that elusive, mysterious railroad, he is disappointed: its tracks have been dismantled and burnt, and its rails are tied around tree trunks (prompting him to demand, "You mean hit have to come in here and run up and down around these here trees like a squirrel?") (88). We cannot know, of course, exactly how Ringo had imagined the railroad, but we can be sure that whatever vision he originally had in mind impacts what he actually sees; as Kinney notes, "Once we harbor certain thoughts . . . we precondition our future vision. Perception is not simply a matter of what we see, but of fulfilled anticipations of what we *expected* to see."[18]

Here we may posit that the coconut cake strategy—that of never seeing, or seeking, an undesired truth, and deliberately prolonging uncertainty—might have been preferable. But still, even after finding the railroad destroyed, Bayard reveals, "we sat there in that cabin and waited and watched that railroad which no longer existed . . . which for us ran still pristine and intact and straight and narrow as the path to glory itself": the boys return to a kind of epistemological innocence (96). For Bayard, this is simply an act of will: he replaces the destroyed railroad with his memory of the erstwhile, intact railroad. But for Ringo, who has no memory of the intact railroad, this is an act of will *and* imagination: he creates in his mind an ambiguity of dual-possibility—and returns to that uncertainty which is so unexpectedly satisfying.[19]

Walter Slatoff reads Faulknerian uncertainty less optimistically, writing in *Quest for Failure* that "many of Faulkner's leaps and shifts of ground are as much a way of escaping having to resolve his thoughts or feelings as they are a way of reaching for something further. It is as though he is determined to avoid clarifying or finishing his ideas, almost as though he feared to take hold of them, to give them full shape or realization."[20] But I find that the pervasive uncertainty of and in *The Unvanquished* is suggestive not of narrative indecision, but of profound narrative openness—it proposes, and embraces, an infinite set of narrative possibilities. This is similar to the apparent dual reality provided by Bayard's active (and incredibly realistic) dream life, which allows him to see multiple places simultaneously: "I was dreaming, it was like I was looking at our place and suddenly the house and stable and cabins and trees all were gone and I was looking at a place flat and empty as the sideboard and it was growing darker and darker and then all of a sudden I wasn't looking at it, I was there" (24). Bayard defers, or perhaps indefinitely suspends, any judgment of his own circumstance:

> We didn't know what time it was, we didn't care . . . we probably both crawled beneath the bridge already asleep, still sleeping, we doubtless continued to crawl. Because if we had not moved, they would not have found us. I waked, still believing I dreamed of thunder. It was light; even beneath the close weed-choked bridge Ringo and I could sense the sun though not at once; for the time we just sat there beneath the loud drumming while the loose planks of the bridge floor clattered and danced to the hooves; we sat there for a moment staring at one another in the pale jonquil-colored light almost before we were awake. Perhaps that was it, perhaps we were still asleep, were taken so suddenly in slumber that we had not time to think of Yankees or anything else. (60–61)

This scene of *underbridgedness* lines up nicely with the idea of *underskirtedness*: it refuses, with its "probably," its "if," and its "perhaps," any possibility for narrative certainty. The reader is just as unsure of what has actually transpired as is Bayard himself, who "didn't know" and "didn't care."

The ethos of uncertainty must originate somewhere—and I would suggest that it is *The Unvanquished*'s Civil War context that generates, and continually reinforces, its prevailing sense of underskirtedness. On the one hand this claim may seem counterintuitive: the war's enormity, and the reach of its impact, so suffuses the text that we may initially respond, *Mysterious? We can't get away from the thing!* If there is one thing of which these characters are certain, it would seem, it is the fact of the Civil War. But like so many supposed Faulknerian "facts," this one is squishy, full of holes, slippery to grasp. Brooks describes the world of the novel as "the exciting world of war," as "a world so topsy-turvy" (86). And indeed, despite the war's pervasiveness in the characters' consciousnesses, there is for them little ontological certainty, little understanding of what the Civil War actually *is*—or, for that matter, *whether* it is. By the opening of "Skirmish at Sartoris," Bayard confesses that "we didn't even know for sure if the War was still going on or not. All we knew was that for that three years the country had been full of Yankees, and then all of a sudden they were gone and there were no men at all there anymore" (188). That is, "all they know" for certain is only that to which they have immediate visual access: the changing face of Yoknapatawpha County. Of the marches and battles—and the bodies—that comprise the war itself, they have no confirmation, or, as Bayard puts it, "no proof" (94). "In fact," he continues, "we had even less than proof; we had thrust into our faces the very shabby and unavoidable obverse of proof" (95).

One of the manifestations of the "shabby and unavoidable obverse of proof," it seems, is plain old ignorance. It is not too strong a word: Bayard is so unaware of the politics underpinning the war that, after overhearing some slaves exclaiming over their emancipation, he rushes in to report to Granny that their family, too, will soon be emancipated: the Yankees "are coming here!" he announces excitedly. "They're coming to set us free!" (23) And of course the passage with which I began—"What you reckon he know that we aint?"—also hinges on ignorance: the boys are weirdly, and arguably blissfully, unaware of the Confederacy's true, flagging fates. But on further consideration this ignorance is understandable, and not only because of the boys' youth. Information from the front would have been scarce, transmission difficult, reports frequently garbled and/or inaccurate. Drew Gilpin Faust's recent study of the Civil War, *This Republic of Suffering*, argues that one effect of such limited information—and, just as often, *mis*information—is that those waiting at home found themselves "with abiding uncertainty and fantastical hopes, illusions that for them made the world endurable."[21] Faust cites a war wife named Sarah Palmer who fretted, "I do feel anxious to see the papers and get the list of casualties . . . and yet I dread to see it" (104).

The Unvanquished offers a host of Sarah Palmers, if briefly and anonymously: they are lumped together as "the women who would not know for months yet if they were widows or childless or not" (96). If we revisit the scene of the coconut cake, and Ringo's conviction "that he would just rather maybe have tasted coconut cake without remembering it than to know for certain he had not," surely the same principle holds for these women in the liminal ontological space between wifehood and widowhood, between motherhood and childlessness; surely it is preferable to be a maybe wife than a certain widow.

Still, it seems difficult in this case to argue for the pleasure of ambiguity, for an uncertainty so appealing it is superior not only to a negative outcome but also to a positive one. Put another way, surely the Sarah

Palmers of the world would rather know for certain that their husbands
were safe than to continue waiting on pins and needles for an unreliable
casualty list. But the introduction of Drusilla Hawk undercuts such an
assumption and suggests that, for some Southern women, the confusion and the uncertainty caused by the Civil War are ultimately forces
of empowerment, and as such ought to be embraced. Who can forget
Drusilla holding forth on the prototypical female trajectory?

> You lived in the same house your father was born in and your father's sons
> and daughters had the sons and daughters of the same negro slaves to nurse
> and coddle, and then you grew up and you fell in love with your acceptable
> young man and in time you would marry him, in your mother's wedding gown
> perhaps and with the same silver for presents she had received, and then you
> settled down forever more while your husband got children on your body for
> you to feed and bathe and dress until they grew up too; and then you and your
> husband died quietly and were buried together maybe on a summer afternoon
> just before suppertime. Stupid, you see. (100–101)

The stupidity Drusilla identifies is not just a function of the sequence's
banality (though that doesn't help matters); it is also, more searingly,
a function of its predictability—of its absolute, unwavering certainty.
The upheaval of war allows for a simultaneous upheaval of the carefully
ordered, entirely foreseeable female existence (which Noel Polk has
described as "the bourgeois life of endless, stultifying repetition of routine from generation to generation"); uncertainty emerges in the chaos,
and is embraced as a luxury.[22] Drusilla will take a completely unantici-
pated, even shocking, trajectory, and in so doing will become a narrative
mystery in her own right, "vanishing" somewhere between "Vendée" and
"Skirmish at Sartoris" to join John Sartoris's Confederate troop—and
again, for good, at the close of "Odor of Verbena."

In choosing this trajectory, Drusilla chooses her own Civil War—
or her own version of the Civil War. I use the possessive deliberately
here. There are in *The Unvanquished* many versions of the Civil War;
indeed, it has something of choose-your-own-adventure quality, in which
the thing itself is impossible to pin down. To Drusilla, the war is about
agency and adventure; to the Sartoris slaves, the war is about their freedom; to John Sartoris, the war is about honor; and to Aunt Louisa and
Mrs. Compson, the war is about—what else?—"purity and womanhood"
(193). In short, the hermeneutics of the Civil War are not so different
from the hermeneutics of Ringo's coconut cake: the multiplicity of possible versions, of potential realities, and the refusal to adhere with certainty to any of them, makes the war eternally mysterious. It is through

this mystery that the small space of Yoknapatawpha County is made, in Faust's terms, "endurable."

Let us return, then, to the very first pages of the text. When *The Unvanquished* opens, Bayard and Ringo are playing at war—*their* war (indeed, we recall Loosh saying: "There's your Vicksburg") (5). The pleasure of the game lies with its constant reimaginings and renegotiations (not in the least because the boys switch off between the roles of Grant and Pemberton), in the recreations and reconfigurations its unpredictable "living map" (3). And Bayard's description of their war is especially rich: "we ran, panting and interminable, with the leaking bucket between wellhouse and battlefield, the two of us needing first to join forces and spend ourselves against a common enemy, time, before we could engender between us and hold intact the pattern of recapitulant mimic furious victory like a cloth, a shield between ourselves and reality, between us and fact and doom" (4). The image of the cloth is what interests me most: the shield "between ourselves and reality, between us and fact and doom." From the very beginning of the novel, we see reality and fact—the ingredients of certainty—aligned with *doom*. The "shielded" boys may rest in a prolonged, and pleasurable, space of uncertainty, of partiality, of possibility; the "cloth" that shields them recalls the novel's ethos of underskirtedness. Perhaps, then, the only way to experience and process the devastation of the Civil War is from behind a veil of uncertainty—or from beneath the hem of Granny Millard's petticoats.

NOTES

1. William Faulkner, *The Unvanquished* (New York: Vintage International, 1991), 193. Henceforth this text will be cited parenthetically.

2. ". . . when Drusilla finally spoke, she sounded like Ringo and I would when Father would say something to us in Latin for a joke. 'Ma'am?'" (196).

3. Warren Beck memorably described Faulkner's style as, "though often brilliant and always interesting," "all too frequently downright bad": "baroque and involuted in the extreme, these sentences: trailing clauses, one after another, shadowily in apposition, or perhaps not even with so much connection as that; parenthesis after parenthesis, the parenthesis itself often containing one or more parentheses—they remind one of those brightly colored Chinese eggs of one's childhood, which when open disclosed egg after egg, each smaller and subtler than the last. It is as if Mr. Faulkner, in a sort of hurried despair, had decided to try to tell us everything, absolutely everything. . . . And it must be admitted that the practice is annoying and distracting." Robert Penn Warren, ed., *Faulkner: A Collection of Critical Essays* (Englewood Cliffs, N.J.: Prentice-Hall, 1966), 48.

4. Richard P. Adams, *Faulkner: Myth and Motion* (Princeton: Princeton University Press, 1968), 71.

5. David Minter, *Faulkner's Questioning Narratives: Fiction of His Major Phase* (Urbana: University of Illinois Press, 2001), 16.

6. John Matthews, *The Play of Faulkner's Language* (Ithaca: Cornell University Press, 1982), 21.

7. Robert Dale Parker, *Faulkner and the Novelistic Imagination* (Urbana: University of Illinois Press, 1985), 3.

8. Elsewhere, the reader reaps the benefits of a fuller narrative context: for instance, at the end of *The Unvanquished*, Bayard introduces Thomas Sutpen as an enigma in his own right: "a cold ruthless man who had come into the country about thirty years before the war, nobody knew from where" (222). But the Faulknerian reader *does* know from where (West Virginia, Haiti, Louisiana); the mystery of Sutpen's origins has been presolved for anyone who has had the patience to work through *Absalom's* knots.

9. Cleanth Brooks, *William Faulkner: The Yoknapatawpha County* (New Haven: Yale University Press, 1963), 85.

10. Ludwig Wittgenstein wrote that "the child learns by believing the adult. Doubt comes *after* belief"—"For how can a child immediately doubt what it is taught?" Ludwig Wittgenstein, *On Certainty* (Oxford: Basil Blackwell, 1969), 162, 288. Interestingly, Ringo appears preternaturally skeptical of secondhand information: he claims to trust Bayard's dream vision more completely than he would trust an adult source. "Then hit's so," he concludes. "If somebody tole you, hit could be a lie. But if you dremp hit, hit cant be a lie case aint nobody there to tole it to you" (21).

11. Arthur F. Kinney, *Faulkner's Narrative Poetics: Style as Vision* (Amherst: University of Massachusetts Press, 1978), 15.

12. Regarding claims of knowledge, Wittgenstein notes, "We just do not see how very specialized the use of 'I know' is. . . . For 'I know' seems to describe a state of affairs which guarantees what is known, guarantees it as a fact. One always forgets the expression 'I thought I knew'" (13).

13. On the other hand, the novel seems to suggest at this moment that visual evidence is not as meaningful or compelling as one might initially assume: the colonel ultimately dismisses the sergeant, despite his insisting, "But, Colonel, we *saw* them two kids run in here" (31, emphasis added).

14. Minter locates "in Faulkner's great novel . . . texts that withhold or defer meaning in order to bequeath it by giving us approximations or models of approximations, that are probably true enough" (18).

15. Blair Labatt, *Faulkner the Storyteller* (Tuscaloosa: University of Alabama Press, 2004), 21.

16. Charles Hannon reads the coconut cake scene as "an occasion to redraw the color lines that in fact determined experience in the plantation South," since it reminds us of its "basic inequalities": "Bayard and his family seated at their Christmas table and Ringo and his family of servants eating leftovers in the kitchen." It is also, Hannon suggests, a scene of subversion: "Ringo has learned the strategy of the subaltern—had learned (from his uncle?) endlessly to defer the moment of Bayard's self-ratification and thus to defer also the addition of one more category of experience that on grounds of race, would be denied him 'as long as he lived.'" Charles Hannon, *Faulkner and the Discourses of Culture* (Baton Rouge, Louisiana State University Press: 2005), 36, 37.

17. The empiricist David Hume insisted that, "though our thought seems to possess this unbounded liberty, we shall find, upon a nearer examination, that it is really confined within very narrow limits, and that all this creative power of the mind amounts to no more than the faculty of compounding, transposing, augmenting, or diminishing the materials afforded us by the senses and experience . . . all our ideas or more feeble perceptions are copies of our impressions of more lively ones." David Hume, *An Enquiry Concerning Human Understanding*, ed. Tom Beauchamp (Oxford: Oxford University Press, 1999), 97.

But Ringo is distinctly antiempiricist: his imagination soundly trumps would-be or actual experience.

18. Kinney, 22, emphasis original.

19. Ringo also suggests that Bayard's having seen the intact railroad ("Only I saw the track before they tore it up. I saw where it was going to happen") is actually meaningless, since Bayard did not or could not predict the railroad's ultimate fate: "But you didn't know hit was fixing to happen when you seed the track. So nemmine that" (99).

20. Walter Slatoff, *A Quest for Failure: A Study of William Faulkner* (Ithaca: Cornell University Press, 1960), 260.

21. Drew Gilpin Faust, *This Republic of Suffering* (New York: Vintage, 2008), 130.

22. Noel Polk, *Faulkner and Welty and the Southern Literary Tradition* (Jackson, University Press of Mississippi, 2008), 91.

Faulkner's Plots

MICHAEL GORRA

"A story has no beginning or end: arbitrarily one chooses that moment of experience from which to look back or from which to look ahead." These are the opening words of Graham Greene's 1951 *The End of the Affair*: one of the few books for which William Faulkner ever provided a blurb, calling it "one of the best, most true and moving novels of my time, in anybody's language."[1] Greene's first-person narrator is a novelist named Maurice Bendrix, a writer known above all for the skill of his narrative joinery, and the moment he chooses is an encounter with the husband of his former mistress on Clapham Common in 1946. He chooses, that is, to tell the story of his affair with Sarah Miles by beginning with a moment after what he has taken to be its end. It is a moment that asks us to consider the relations of endings and beginnings, of looking back and looking ahead; and the novel itself comes marked by a disjunction between the order of its events and the order of their narration. Moreover, *The End of the Affair* tells the story of Bendrix's attempt to solve a mystery. It "begins" when his conversation with Henry Miles leads him to think that Sarah has replaced him with a new lover. Why—and who is he? The pursuit of an answer leads Bendrix into a recapitulation of their affair's beginning and makes us realize that the end of their liaison was not, as it were, the end of the whole affair, not the goal toward which we move; there is a different teleology in play. But that answer, that solution to a mystery, also leads him to another mystery, a greater one. It introduces him to a mystery in the theological sense, one that cannot be understood but only accepted, a mystery whose solution lies behind a door that we cannot on this earth pass.

This essay considers Faulkner in terms of the questions that Greene's words raise, examining the relation in his work between narrative structure on the one hand, and mystery on the other, mystery in the several senses of the term. My argument falls into two roughly equal pieces. In the first I consider the concept of plot in itself, looking at the way some of Faulkner's contemporaries thought of it and then at a few of the narratological distinctions we can make about it. In the second I turn more directly to Faulkner himself, glancing briefly at those works of his that belong to the genre of fiction that we call "mystery," *Intruder in the Dust*

(1948) and the stories collected in *Knight's Gambit* (1949), and then moving on to the Compson novels before ending with *As I Lay Dying* (1930).

1

In his now-classic *Reading for the Plot* Peter Brooks associates Faulkner with a modernist suspicion that plot falsifies, that the "requirements of narrative design" too often force the novelist to sacrifice "more subtle kinds of interconnectedness." So the modernists "plot with irony and bad conscience," they work to lay bare the artifice of narrative structure.[2] Now certainly Faulkner's own sense of plot—of how to make them and why—differs from that of the nineteenth century. His work always demands that we notice the telling and the carpentry, and I draw upon Brooks in other ways later in this essay. But irony? I am not so sure. For Faulkner seems instead to have delighted in plot, in every sense of the term. He not only likes fitting his pieces of wood together, he likes having us watch him do it. You can see this in the pleasure with which he makes V. K. Ratliff squat down to tell us about a bit of Snopes skullduggery. You can see it too in the fact that he is the only major modernist who was willing to work, albeit with some ambivalence, in such popular forms as the mystery story. Or rather the only one who was willing to do it and—unlike Borges—to do it straight. We know he liked reading mysteries, and even that he once compared Simenon to Chekhov. The interviewer to whom he told that found it strange, and he stared her down; today that claim does not look so odd.[3] I might also mention *The Unvanquished* (1938) here, a series of well-made magazine tales that remind me of nothing so much as the school stories of Kipling's *Stalky and Co* (1899). I mean that as praise. *Stalky*'s pleasures are as simple and yet as real as ice cream, but I also admire the way Faulkner's book remains true to its sense of shenanigans while in the last story outgrowing it in the way that the Kipling finally does not.

Still, I cannot approach Faulkner's sense of these things directly. Writing about him inevitably requires a bit—a bit more—of digression and delay. So I need first to consider the range of things that can be meant by that crucial and complicated little word *plot*. A plot is a plan. Indeed the two words come together in surveying or real estate, where with a kind of builder's overspecification we can speak of a plot plan, a sketch of a building or a piece of ground. But the sketch itself may be called a plot, and in its verb form the term can also denote the act of making that sketch—plotting a plot. A navigator plots a course; that is, he plans one. A villain may plot out a crime. He might lay a plot, that is—we are back to nouns—a plot by which he will manage to sell a bunch of unbroken and unbreakable Texas ponies without any of the customers knowing to whom in fact they belong. It is a scheme, a purpose, a device; often secret, a conspiracy, something to be discovered, laid bare, foiled. Not all schemes are wicked, and sometimes the word merely denotes a design. So a plot is also the plan or the outline of a literary work, and often enough, as Brooks argues, those plots are about plots in that other large sense of the term: they are narrative structures designed to explore a world of secret and mysterious plans and purposes. For narrative is to him about desire—and our desire as readers lies in knowing or discovering what the characters themselves desire, in our experience of a plot about plots.

Which does not yet take us very far. I began with a British example and want to stay over there for a few minutes, in order to recall two central modernist statements, more or less contemporary with the start of Faulkner's own career, about the aesthetics of fiction. One of them can be found in E. M. Forster's 1927 *Aspects of the Novel* and the other in Virginia Woolf's essay "Modern Fiction," first published in 1919 and then revised for *The Common Reader* in 1925. Early on, Forster asks us to consider the most elementary and "fundamental aspect" of the novel—the fact that it tells a story. Or as he puts it himself, "Yes—oh, dear, yes—the novel tells a story. . . . That is the highest factor common to all novels, and I wish that it was not so, that it could be something different—melody, or perception of the truth, not this low atavistic form."[4] The more we think about stories, he suggests, the less we will find to admire about them. They are a kind of tapeworm, something paleolithic, primitive. Stories work when they satisfy what he calls the "primeval curiosity" of making us want to know what happens next.[5] But Forster finds that desire rather embarrassing and wishes that the novel were not so committed to sequence, to the representation of what he calls the "life in time."[6]

He is more interested in the "life by values," and the novel as a form is to him concerned above all with the relation of time to the question of value, to all the things that might pain or particularize our time, that might establish its worth.[7] Even in disparaging it, however, Forster recognizes that he can no more abolish the importance of time in fiction than could a young Harvard student who ripped the hands from his watch in 1910. (Or perhaps, depending on your point of view, in 1928.) And this is the moment to turn to the question of plot and to the famous though mistaken distinction that Forster made between story and plot. In common speech, of course, the two words are often used interchangeably. Few nineteenth-century critics made the distinction, nor do most book reviews today. Nevertheless Forster insists upon their difference. If a story is "a narrative of events arranged in their time sequence," then a "plot" is such a narrative with "the emphasis falling on causality." In his classic example, "The king died, and then the queen died of grief."[8] Not just events, but their causation, their motivation. Stories in Forster's schema make us want to know what happens next; plots make us need to know why.

Even here the concept of plot requires a sense of mystery, of something to be solved—a plot in the other sense of the term. Still, Forster's idea of what constitutes a fictional event seems to me terribly simplistic, and his definitions remain predicated upon a false distinction. For a motivation—the queen's grief—can be just as much of an event as a death or a punch in the nose. Thoughts, perceptions, desires—they are all events, and they have a sequentiality of their own. The inner life is an adventure in itself; so much we know from reading Henry James. Forster tries to bracket such things off from the crude pleasures of story, and he also chafes at the very idea of plot, even plot as he defines it. And he does so for reasons that fit Brooks's account of the modernists' suspicions. Plot imposes a shape. The interest in "cause and effect" gives the book an "air of predetermination,"[9] and Forster wishes he could simply say "To pot with the plot, break it up, boil it down. . . . All that is prearranged is false."[10]

Perhaps I have already said enough to suggest that the concept of plot and of story, and a dissatisfaction with sequentiality in itself, were on the table at the time Faulkner began to work. I will, however, add a bit from Virginia Woolf—her statement, even more famous than Forster's own, that most of the novelist's labor is thrown away in the service of "proving the solidity, the likeness to life, of the story." To her the writer seems enslaved by the need to "provide a plot, comedy, tragedy, love . . . probability." Woolf herself does not distinguish between plot and story—she lumps them together, interchangeably, as the enemy in the novelist's attempt to convey the "luminous halo, [the] semi-transparent envelope" of life itself.[11] And I suppose the endpoint of this modernist suspicion of narrative lies in the statement of the American novelist John Hawkes that he "began to write fiction on the assumption that the true enemies of the novel were plot, character, setting and theme," the obstacles on the way to some unspecified "totality of vision or structure."[12]

With this as background let me come to—or at least toward—Faulkner himself. For just as he is the one major modernist willing to draw upon popular forms, so he is also the one who was not in the least shy about the fact that the novel "tells a story." Indeed in narratological terms he is the most interesting modernist of all, interesting precisely because of his commitment to story. And stories, moreover, that can stand comparison with those of such predecessors as Dickens or Dostoevsky in tickling our hunger to know what happens next—or sometimes, and perhaps more characteristically, our hunger to know what has happened already. Having made that claim I must immediately qualify it. Hemingway has some of that quality too, at least in *A Farewell to Arms* (1929), and yet his linear narratives do without that other central aspect of Faulkner's work, the disruption of chronology that is the most modernist thing about him and on which much of that hunger depends. For once having aroused it, Faulkner usually refuses to satisfy it—not yet, not yet. A second qualification, once we note that disruption, would be the important precedent of Conrad. But of his other peers—Joyce, Woolf, Mann, Proust—no one else makes novels of such propulsive force.

To understand just how Faulkner works, though, we must first define—must refine—our terms. For there is a distinction to make between plot and story, even if it is not Forster's. So let me draw it. I have already noted that Greene's novel gains much of its power from the difference between the order of its events and the order of their narration: from the difference between what, in its characters' "life" that order would have been, and the order in which as a reader we experience them. His narration is not linear. Nor, of course, is Faulkner's. In *The Sound and the Fury* (1929), for example, we move from a Saturday in 1928 back to 1910 and then forward to the Friday before that Saturday; and end by skipping ahead to Sunday. And what happens between the book's individual sections happens within them as well, in those moments when the present drops away and a character's mind is filled with the past.

In their use of such a chronology the great narratives of the twentieth century's opening decades differ markedly from their Victorian predecessors. Flaubert, Dickens, Tolstoy—in their work we have what seems very nearly a coincidence between the order of events and the order of narration. Some opening exposition, to be sure, a bit of back story to fill in—but once we begin to move that motion is irrevocably forward. Just how these things became uncoupled is a complicated tale. But recognizing the disjunction between them remains a starting point in almost any consideration of narrative structure, and the different sides of that split have names. In French one speaks of the difference between *histoire* and *récit*, a story and its recitation, a distinction between a tale and the activity of its telling. The Russian formalists made a similar distinction between *fabula* and *sjinzet*, between "the action itself" and the way the reader learns of it, between events as they occur and events as they are told.[13] Some narrative theory translates these distinctions into terms of story and plot; with the word *plot* standing for the way, the structure, the discourse, through which we receive the story. These sets of terms are not precise equivalents, and it is easy enough to imagine cases where we might prefer one to the other, especially in considering the effects of voice or prose style. My own interest lies in one particular aspect of that distinction, and for the purposes of this essay I will indeed define the difference between the order of events and the order of their narration as that between *histoire* and *récit*, story and plot.

For Peter Brooks plot is above all concerned with a process of temporal unfolding. His argument depends on both linking the reader to the characters and on distinguishing us from them. For our experience of that unfolding—of turning the pages—is different from the characters' own experience of the novel's events. Only in the most linear of narratives does our experience match theirs, and in Faulkner especially our time is almost always different from theirs. We do not learn what is upstairs at Sutpen's Hundred until we're a few hundred pages into *Absalom, Absalom!* (1936) and sitting up on a winter's night in Cambridge. But Quentin Compson has known it—though not perhaps understood it—since the previous September and the night the book "began." We move forward to uncover the past, and so indeed do Faulkner's characters themselves, though not in anything like the same degree as his readers. Or to use the words of Kierkegaard so beloved of all narrative theorists, we live forward, but can only understand backwards.[14]

It is for this reason that Brooks defines plot as the "process of *sjuzet* working on *fabula*," the interplay of narration and event, the telling and the tale, the process of understanding and the thing understood.[15] Plot for him is finally the relation between these things, neither one nor the other but rather the tension between them. And it would be my claim—though not, I imagine, a very controversial one—that Faulkner's work finds its greatest power when that tension reaches its highest pitch, when the distinction between the sequence of events and that of their narration is most sharply drawn. From this standpoint the modernist suspicion of plot seems rather simplistic, or perhaps just misnamed. What it is really about is a distaste for linear narration. And it would also be my claim that it was in and through this radical disjunction that Faulkner both found and was able to represent his deepest sense of mystery, his sense of a world in which truth is always uncertain and knowledge forever incomplete.

2

If there's one place where we *do not* find that mystery-producing dis-junction, it is in those works that he actually called mysteries. Detective fiction does, admittedly, give us an easy purchase upon a number of narratological problems. It is the form in which we really do go forward in order to go back, in which the narration works to uncover the unrep-resented and often prior moment of the crime itself. Or as Tzvetzan Todorov has memorably argued, detective fiction tells a double story: the story of the crime, and the story of its investigation.[16] Sometimes this process of uncovering is accomplished through pure ratiocination, piecing clues together. More often the detective figure takes some action that serves to unlock the past. I think here of Chick Mallison digging up the grave in *Intruder in the Dust*: an action that produces another action on the part of the criminal, which in turn creates the conditions that will lead us to a solution.

Still, in Faulkner's detective fiction the past has only a minimal pres-ence. With *Intruder in the Dust* or "An Error in Chemistry" (1946) we typically get a few paragraphs of dialogue—Gavin Stevens talking with uncharacteristic brevity—that serve to tell us what happened before the narration began. It is a verbal description of what has already happened, as though one part of the tale's *récit* were a recitation of its *histoire*. But as for the order of *represented* events—of direct representation, as opposed to those indirectly presented through the dialogue—well, that order remains identical with the order of narration itself. In *Knight's Gambit* and *Intruder in the Dust* we respond to the same things that make a series mystery novel so attractive; the old shoe familiarity of the world they draw for us, however dark, as in the Los Angeles of Raymond Chandler or the Sicily of my current favorite, Andrea Camilleri. Only those worlds never get more complicated than they do in those particular novels, whereas even so slight a book as *Knight's Gambit* gestures toward every formal and historical complexity of Yoknapatawpha as a whole. Indeed with *Intruder in the Dust* the whole business of the murder in itself comes to seem inconsequential. It is a Hitchcockian MacGuffin, an armature upon which to place the rest of the novel's concerns, which include everything else we know about Lucas Beauchamp in particular.

Faulkner's mysteries are not nearly so complicated in structural terms as are many of his other books. They are not nearly so mysterious. I imagine, though, that he was drawn to the genre—that he chose this way to keep the pot boiling—by some of the same things that drew him to the spiraling form of *Absalom, Absalom!*, in which each new discovery seems only to make the problem more intractable, to postpone a solution yet again. And I would hazard that detective fiction as a form has a buried, almost hidden role in creating the possibility for the kind of disrupted chronology on which Faulkner's greatest fiction depends—Faulkner's, and Conrad's, and indeed modernism itself. You could even call it the secret plot of modernism's plots.

I am thinking here of the interpolated narratives of Wilkie Collins: the backing and filling of *The Woman in White* (1860) or *The Moonstone* (1868), themselves based on the form of court proceedings, in which one character offers his or her witness, only to be followed by another character who testifies to a different part of the story, in which one point of view serves to challenge another, and letters and documents and long-forgotten bits of the past are put into play. And often the last thing we are told, the last thing we learn, pertains to the very first events in the work's *histoire*. Even Conan Doyle does some of this. The second part of *A Study in Scarlet* (1887) contains a narrative of several chapters, and not in Watson's voice, that serve to explain the crime, the problem, with which the book has presented us at the start. Here the gap between the order of events and the order of narration becomes an object of genuine interest, and all the more so because it is at odds with the linear structure of most other Victorian fiction.

Such novels suggest that truth is not a given; it must be uncovered, or even made. Or as Frank Kermode puts it in *The Sense of an Ending*, the early twentieth century is marked by "an historical transition . . . from a literature which assumed that it was imitating an order to a literature which assumes that it has to create an order, unique and self-dependent."[17] The world does not disclose its meanings with the smooth linearity of a Victorian serial, an orderly unspooling of one event after another. Such a linearity suggests that some objective value or quality of meaning inheres in the world itself, and yet that is exactly what Faulkner's era was no longer able to believe. In fact, that lack of belief was in itself a reason for Forster's suspicion of story. I would not suggest that the invention of the mystery novel was enough on its own to produce that sense of things; there are many other reasons for the period's loss of faith in the grand narratives of a meaningful universe. But the mystery novel *does* stand as an early instance of the experiments that modernist fiction was to conduct with narrative sequence and point of view, and I think we must give it some explanatory power, if only because that explanation is one internal to the form and the history of the novel in itself.

The mystery novel insists that truth is hidden, that it must be discovered, and in Doyle or Agatha Christie it always is. Faulkner's greatest fiction, however, hangs upon the premise that such a truth can never be entirely known, no matter how many clues one accumulates. As though truth itself were a mystery, in the largest sense of the term. *Absalom, Absalom!* remains the obvious point of reference here, but I think we should approach its narrative procedures through those of *The Sound and the Fury*. We all remember the process by which the *histoire*, the *fabula*, the story of the Compson family emerges from its narration. It comes to us in fragments and shards, lightning blasts of illumination. We can spatialize it, as though it were a jigsaw puzzle, haphazardly assembled: a bit of the border, a spot in the center, something off in the corner, and most of the pieces forever absent. We can temporalize it, turning the novel into an archeological site, in which the digging seems to go on in several historical strata at once: Caddy's wedding, and Benjy following the ball, Jason's anger over his loss of the job he never had, and Quentin's despair not only at his sister's loss of virginity but also at his father's refusal to think that it matters. We read, we connect the spots of time, we ourselves become the detective.

What we learn as we do this, however, is that the past cannot, can never, be recovered. There may be a place in the mind of every one of Faulkner's Southern white boys "when it's still not yet two o'clock on that July afternoon" at Gettysburg, but it is not one they can ever get to, however willing they are to die trying.[18] His characters do not live on a Grecian urn, forever panting and forever young; that is, they do not know that they do. They live instead in a world that Mr. Compson describes as marked by the saddest of all words: "was."[19] And I take the mark of that impossibility to be the absence of Caddy's voice—the voice that is the biggest missing piece of the Compson's past. Its absence stands for all that we can never know, the questions we cannot answer. It is the gap in our memory, the family memory that we make by moving from the mind of one brother to another, the mystery we cannot solve. In Minrose Gwin's terms, Caddy is forever "*something more* than we can say," a voice that fades in and out of sound, forever on the edge of being lost.[20] We know it is there, just as we know the past is there, and yet it remains a presence that our ears, our arms, can never entirely hold.

In one sense *Absalom, Absalom!* is a simpler tale—simpler because there first Quentin and then Shreve do much of the work that we as readers had to do in *The Sound and the Fury*. They piece the evidence together for us, they make sense of its plot. Or rather the novel's plot consists of the process through which they try to make sense of Thomas Sutpen's design, of the old Colonel's own plots. They puzzle over that novel's equivalent of Caddy, the mysterious unspeaking presence of Charles Bon, with all that he represents of conjecture, of what they can never quite know. In other ways, of course, the later book presents us with a much more complicated structure. Benjy's and Quentin's interior monologues may offer certain technical difficulties, but those are puzzles we can solve. The later novel gives us no such assurance.

The story it tells is one that Quentin has always half known already. He knows Miss Rosa Coldfield's history, he has hunted quail over the grounds of what was once Sutpen's Hundred. And the book's narration depends upon a combination of prolepsis and reiteration—Faulkner is constantly dropping hints that he will then catch up to, and just as constantly reviewing where we have been. In *Heart of Darkness* the frame tale narrator describes Marlow's method of storytelling as one in which "the meaning of an episode was not inside like a kernel"—a bit of cracked nut—"but outside, enveloping the tale which brought it out only as a glow brings out a haze."[21] Faulkner, in contrast, gives us both the haze and the nugget of meaning. Each reiteration of Sutpen's story takes us at once further out and deeper in, as though its rippling band of knowledge were getting stronger and more powerful, more suggestive, the further away it travels from the tossed pebble of the initial chapter. Each repetition adds more detail, fills in a bit of the past, explains things once alluded to, and yet in doing so also introduces new mysteries. The story is told, and then told again, and again; and every chapter seems longer than its predecessors. Which is not, strictly speaking, true; though the claim is, like so much else about this novel, one that remains "true enough." [22]

So as we read we find ourselves circling around something already half-known, each new chapter another revolution, revelation. It is no surprise that Peter Brooks has given the novel a place in his *Reading for the Plot*. For the novel's plot is indeed built upon desire: Sutpen's ambitions and longings on the one hand, and on the other Quentin's and Shreve's desire to know, which is our desire as well. And it depends too upon secrets, upon knowing them and keeping them; the secrets the characters keep from each other, and the secrets that Quentin keeps from us, keeps until he is ready. As such, the character has been given all of Faulkner's own mastery of an impressionistic digression and delay. I think here in particular of the way the novel stalls its telling of Sutpen's early life. We are over halfway along before we learn of his early days in the Appalachian hills and the formation of his design in the shattering experience of a Tidewater plantation, of the West Indies and the slave revolt he worked to suppress. It is as though the order of narration were working to impede our understanding of the order of events, as though the book's *récit* were standing in the way of its *histoire*, blocking the doorway, keeping us out. But let us put it another way. In Faulkner a distorted chronology signifies above all an epistemological gap. It indicates, it defines, the uncertainty of our knowledge. In a world with answers, narration can have all the rationality of chronology. So it is in "Smoke" (1932) or *Intruder in the Dust* (1948), or for that matter *The Hound of the Baskervilles* (1902). But that simply won't do in the imagined world of *Absalom, Absalom!*. Its mysteries—its revelations, its sense of some mystic numinous presence—are not finally so explicable.

Let me here return to a point I made at the beginning of this essay. In Greene's *End of the Affair*, Bendrix's investigation of a secular mystery leads him to a theological one, to the discovery of a question, a problem, for which he has no answers. The past we come to know in both *The Sound and the Fury* and *Absalom, Absalom!* is never presented in objective terms. It is always a past as seen by, interpreted by, a particular point of view, one character's groping motion toward comprehension. And what such novels show us is that interpretation always reaches its limits. There is always a point at which it fails, beyond which it cannot go. "It just does not explain," Mr. Compson tells Quentin, in trying to understand the reason for Henry Sutpen's murder of his sister's fiancée. "We have a few old mouth-to-mouth tales; we exhume from old trunks and boxes and drawers letters . . . in which men and women who once lived and breathed are now merely initials or nicknames. . . . They are there, yet something is missing."[23] The past itself, which Faulkner's disruptions of chronology make so palpably and painfully present, is yet forever out of our reach and touch.

Or as Rosa Coldfield herself will say to Quentin, in speaking about the death of Charles Bon, "I heard an echo, but not the shot. I saw a closed door but did not enter it."[24] John Irwin has memorably described the role of the closed door in Faulkner's fiction, arguing that it serves to shut us off from something we know is there. Sometimes what's there is a murder; sometimes it is a sexual secret, a version of the primal scene.[25] Often, of course, the mystery concerns both, as it does in this novel and in *Light in August* (1932), where Faulkner cuts away from Joanna Burden's room just as Joe Christmas is about to enter with a knife in his hand. We see him at the door, we do not see what happens once he enters. The closed door may be the past, it may be another human heart, it is the Caddy we cannot quite hear, it is above all the mark of what we know we cannot know. It both defines and creates the point beyond which we cannot pass. It is the sign of mystery itself.

I will end by looking briefly at *As I Lay Dying*. The Bundren family's secrets are of course well known to us, if not to each other—Dewey Dell's pregnancy, Anse's desire to get them teeth, Addie's adultery. Their journey towards Jefferson is also for most of them a journey toward the fulfillment of private desires, even if some of those desires may be as unexceptionable as Cash's plan to purchase a graphophone. Donald M.

Kartiganer has argued that the novel is unusual in Faulkner's work in the degree to which it offers a linear narration.[26] *Histoire* and *récit*, the order of events and the order in which they're told, are here as close as they will ever get in his major work. But there are, of course, two important exceptions, exceptions that serve to define the limits of knowledge, the degree to which the book's characters can know the history that governs their lives.

The novel's central episode is the crossing of a river in flood—Addie's coffin braced on the wagon, Anse standing on the far bank, and Darl looking at him across a hundred yards of water in which it seems as though "the space between us were time: an irrevocable quality."[27] Just before we reach that river scene, Faulkner has allowed Darl to take us on an excursion into the family's past: the story of how Jewel got his horse, working nights to bust out a neighbor's fields. On the first night after the boy shows up with the animal, Darl sees their mother crying in the dark, and hiding it, and all the while hating herself for the tears and the deceit both. "And then I knew that I knew," Darl claims, knew it "as plain on that day as I knew about Dewey Dell."[28] We do not yet know what he knows—we will have to wait until after the river crossing, until after time's irrevocability has itself been revoked, and Addie Bundren can speak to us from behind the door of death. Which is a mystery in itself, though one that I think this novel's readers accept as readily as Christians accept the doctrine of the Trinity. We accept it as true though without knowing quite how, accept it because the creator has willed it.

We learn, once Addie speaks, of the laws that govern this family's past—of the early days of her marriage and then of her adultery, of Jewel's parentage and of her belief that words don't ever say what they are trying to get at. These two out-of-sequence chapters—the story of Jewel, and the story of Addie—serve to bracket the Bundren's most important moment of passage. So when Cash and Darl try to take their coffin-loaded wagon across the river and a "log appears suddenly between two hills" of waves, with a "long gout of foam" hanging to it "like the beard of an old man or a goat"—at that moment it is hard to escape the sense that what comes roaring down the stream of consciousness toward them is something like the past itself.[29] The past that will smash and destroy them, and all without their knowing why. For Faulkner's characters must live in a world of imperfect knowledge, never entirely aware of the forces that have shaped their lives. As readers we always know more about them than they do. We know the secrets with which Addie has been buried, the mysteries that Faulkner's plotting has revealed. Or rather we know, and Darl knows—and in consequence he has been sent to Jackson, gibbering with knowledge. "This world is not his world," Cash says, "this life his life."[30] He sees too much, he knows too much. It is as though, to quote George Eliot, he had died of the roar on the other side of silence, died to the world, anyway.[31]

"All plots tend to move deathward." So Don DeLillo suggests in *White Noise*, and I suppose he is right, that insofar as every plot supposes an ending they do indeed. "Political plots, terrorist plots, lovers plots, narrative plots. . . . We edge nearer death every time we plot."[32] Except that in Faulkner the death comes as often as not in the middle. It is a fixed point, and we move simultaneously toward it and away from it. But what we can never ever do is escape it.

NOTES

1. Graham Greene, *The End of the Affair* (1951; New York: Penguin Books, 2004), 1. Faulkner's own words appear on the back cover.

2. Peter Brooks, *Reading for the Plot: Design and Intention in Narrative* (New York: Knopf, 1984), 113.

3. See his 1955 interview with Cynthia Grenier in *Lion in the Garden: Interviews with William Faulkner, 1926–1962*, ed. James B. Meriwether and Michael Millgate (Lincoln: University of Nebraska Press, 1968), 217.

4. E. M. Forster, *Aspects of the Novel* (New York: Harcourt, Brace and Company, 1927), 45.

5. Ibid., 47.

6. Ibid., 49

7. Ibid.

8. Ibid., 130.

9. Ibid., 145.

10. Ibid., 152.

11. Virginia Woolf, "Modern Fiction," in *The Common Reader* (New York: Harcourt, Brace and World, 1925), 153–54.

12. John Hawkes, "An Interview," *Wisconsin Studies in Contemporary Literature*, 6:2 (Summer 1965): 159

13. Boris Tomashevsky, "Thematics," in *Russian Formalist Criticism: Four Essays*, trans. and ed. Lee T. Lemon and Marion J. Reis (1925; Lincoln: University of Nebraska Press, 1965), 67. See also Suzanne Keen, *Narrative Form* (Palgrave Macmillan, 2003), esp. chapter 5, for a lucid account of these distinctions.

14. Søren Kierkegaard, *The Essential Kierkegaard*, ed. Howard V. Hong and Edna H. Hong (Princeton: Princeton University Press, 2000). Kierkegaard put the thought in different ways in different works; the sharpest is perhaps in a journal entry quoted on p. 12 of Hong: "Philosophy is perfectly right in saying that life must be understood backward. But then one forgets the other clause—that it must be lived forward."

15. Brooks, 25.

16. Tzvetan Todorov, *The Poetics of Prose*, trans. Richard Howard (1971; Ithaca: Cornell University Press, 1977), 44.

17. Frank Kermode, *The Sense of an Ending* (Oxford: Oxford University Press, 1967), 167.

18. William Faulkner, *Intruder in the Dust*, in *Faulkner: Novels: 1942–1954* (New York: Library of America, 1994), 430–31.

19. William Faulkner, *The Sound and the Fury*, in *Faulkner: Novels 1926–1929* (New York: Library of America, 2006), 1014.

20. Minrose Gwin, "Hearing Caddy's Voice," in *The Sound and the Fury: A Norton Critical Edition*, ed. David Minter (New York: W. W. Norton, 1994), 406. Italics in original.

21. Joseph Conrad, *Heart of Darkness*, in Michael Gorra, *The Portable Conrad* (1902; New York: Penguin Books, 2007), 280.

22. William Faulkner, *Absalom, Absalom!*, in *Faulkner: Novels 1936–1940* (New York: Library of America, 1990), 276. My image of the water rippling around the stone of narrative is of course also borrowed from *Absalom, Absalom!*; see p. 216.

23. Ibid., 83.

24. Ibid., 124.

25. John T. Irwin, *Doubling and Incest/Repetition and Revenge: A Speculative Reading of Faulkner* (Baltimore: Johns Hopkins University Press, 1975), 171.

26. Donald M. Kartiganer, "By It I Would Stand or Fall: Life and Death in *As I Lay Dying*," in *As I Lay Dying: A Norton Critical Edition*, ed. Michael Gorra (New York: W. W. Norton, 2009), 367.

27. William Faulkner, *As I Lay Dying*, in *Faulkner: Novels 1930–1935* (New York: Library of America, 1985), 96.

28. Ibid., 89.

29. Ibid., 98.

30. Ibid., 178.

31. George Eliot, *Middlemarch* (1871–72), ch. 20.

32. Don DeLillo, *White Noise* (New York: Viking, 1985), 26.

"It Just Doesn't Explain":
"The Leg," "Mistral," Evelyn Nesbit, and
the Unreadable World

NOEL POLK

For Don Kartiganer and Ann Abadie, if only to give me leave to say that Don, Ann, and I have told each other stories for many years, always overpassing to love, which is also where the stories always begin.

Edgar Allan Poe begins "The Man of the Crowd" this way:

> It was well said of a certain German book that . . . it does not permit itself to be read. There are some secrets which do not permit themselves to be told. Men die nightly in their beds, wringing the hands of ghostly confessors, and looking them piteously in the eyes—die with despair of heart and convulsion of throat, on account of the hideousness of mysteries which will not *suffer themselves* to be revealed. Now and then, alas, the conscience of man takes up a burthen so heavy in horror that it can be thrown down only into the grave. And thus the essence of all crime is divulged.[1]

This man of the crowd is Poe's metaphor for all the unsolved and unsolvable enigmas that tantalize and threaten us because what we don't understand always seems to threaten us. We live with a constantly frustrated urgency to eliminate mystery, to thwart its control over us because it threatens the order, the dependable, knowable Truth that overlies so much of the surface realities of our lives. That Poe's narrator wants to see such unexplainable people as divulging "the essence of all crime" is important for my purposes here if only because at first it would seem a long step from "enigma" to the "essence of all crime." What's chilling, of course, is that any of us, isolated and viewed from a distance, is a "man of the crowd," so that in Poe's narrator's view we *all* harbor in ourselves the "essence of all crime." Perhaps that's the part in all of us that is fascinated with crime and detection—our ritualistic rehearsals of the violation and the restoration of order, our narrative stays against disorder—whether we prefer the subtleties and sophistications of P. D. James and Scott

Turow, say, or the shrieking outrage mongering of Nancy Grace and cable news in general.

Perhaps what Poe's narrator means is that the essence of crime is thus precisely the possibility of disorder that attaches itself to the inexplicable. But Poe, to be sure, not a simple man, didn't leave it at that: he countered this view of humanity with M. Dupin, who *can* read the seemingly unreadable, who faces the ostensibly incoherent circumstances of the murders in the rue Morgue and imposes on them a circumstance completely foreign to them, a chance reading of an item in the newspapers, which suddenly makes them readable—*The orangutan done it!*—and who finds the purloined letter by looking past the normal expectation that a thief would hide a stolen object in a remote, deeply secret place where no one could *ever* find it, and so with fiendish cunning locates it on the desk with all the other correspondence, in plain view of anybody who would have thought to look there. Like his later avatars Sherlock Holmes, Hercule Poirot, Miss Marple, Columbo, and Monk, Dupin thus brings order out of chaos, confounding and infuriating the rule- and logic-bound police because they can cut through the twin Gordian knots of felonious complications and procedural rules to reveal the single fact, insight, wherever it is, that everybody else has missed and that will reorganize the clues into a pattern that makes them readable and thereby solve the mystery. It is a good deal like what we literary critics do, of course, discovering a word or phrase in a text that others have overlooked, which allows us to reassemble the other parts, even heretofore very familiar parts, and, finally, to make sense even of Faulkner; or to bring to the text something from the outside—biography, Freud, Einstein, deconstruction, structuralism, what you will: orangutans all.

The stories I want to discuss here have long resisted the orangutan—not that we have tried all that hard to find one; we have mostly ignored them. But of course being Faulkner's stories, they are very much worth some attention. They are Poe-esque in their concern with those parts of our experience beyond the normal, our experience of a world where the inner and the outer, the here and the there, don't merely overlap but mix and mingle, meld and then separate again, morphing back and forth from one shape to another, so that they are often indistinguishable: I mean those parts of our experience that challenge what Davy, in "The Leg," calls the "certitude . . . which so arbitrarily distinguishes between verities and illusions, establishing with such assurance that line between truth and delirium which sages knit their brows over."[2] Both stories seem to take their characters and their readers to worlds beyond rational comprehension.

But I want to begin with a brief panegyric on a passage that has haunted me for years and that I now think I understand precisely in its reciprocities with these two stories. Probably the earliest articulation of Faulkner's seminal preoccupation with loss and discovery, the relationship between losing and having, between loss and desire, occurs latish in "Mistral" when the narrator sees a young woman as she walks through the little Italian village Don and the narrator are passing through to meet her lover, who has perhaps murdered for her, for whom she has perhaps murdered. The passage looks forward to *The Town* and the adulterous Eula Varner Snopes's unforgettable striding across the Jefferson square and the consternation it causes young Chick Mallison. This young woman comes

> up the street in her white dress, and I didn't feel like a Catholic any more. She was all in white, coatless, walking slender and supple. I didn't feel like anything any more, watching her white dress swift in the twilight, carrying her somewhere or she carrying it somewhere: anyway, it was going too, moving when she moved and because she moved, losing her when she would be lost because it moved when she moved and went with her to the instant of loss.

Seeing her walk thus across his vision, unattainable except in his eye, the narrator connects her to the public image of Evelyn Nesbit:

> I remember how, when I learned about Thaw and White and Evelyn Nesbitt [*sic*], how I cried. I cried because Evelyn, who was a word, was beautiful and lost or I would never have heard of her. Because she had to be lost for me to find her and I had to find her to lose her. And when I learned that she was old enough to have a grown daughter or son or something, I cried, because I had lost myself then and I could never again be hurt by loss. So I watched the white dress, thinking, She'll be as near me in a second as she'll ever be and then she'll go on away in her white dress forevermore, in the twilight forevermore. (*CS* 869)

The narrator's memory of Evelyn Nesbit,[3] whom he only knows as a public figure, thus destabilizes the moment he is describing, for reasons he does not explain and perhaps does not understand. Perhaps partly because it erupts so suddenly and dramatically and lyrically from another less immediate experience and wraps itself so sadly around his current moment as both a deflection from and a genuflection to the young woman in white, this is for me one of the most mysterious passages in Faulkner, perhaps the center of all the mystery in Faulkner—the gendered mystery, at any rate.

Such passages in Faulkner speak directly to our engagement with mystery in this life, all that is unknowable, all that is summed up in our problematic struggle with the word and the concept of "faith," what we hope for, what we dream about, how we structure our lives ideologically so as to impose a graspable, interpretable "meaning" on our experience—all the unsolved and unsolvable enigmas that resist our constant attempts to find order where there just might not be any. As rational creatures, of course, we understand the physiology, the facts, of loss and aging. But at another core level we remain mystified and pained by them, find ourselves crippled by regret for moments lost, half remembered, for opportunities missed, for the body and mind we had thirty or forty years ago, for desire forever unfulfilled; for our vulnerability to change, then: not just to *losing* something but to *being lost* in our insufficiency. We would be safer, happier, in an orderly world, where all things are explicable. So we are befuddled by the world's disorder, its rampant assault on the spiritual and ideological structures that we cling to for safety but that are no more permanent than the interstate bridge over the Mississippi in Minneapolis that suddenly collapsed a couple of summers ago. Crime, loss, is precisely a bridge that collapses.

What Faulkner begins to articulate here becomes a sort of leitmotif throughout his work. Evelyn Nesbit and her subsequent avatars *stand for* something so lost as to be not only unrecoverable but also ungraspable—an enigma within a mystery within a puzzle. The effect on us is like that of Original Sin: for all of us except Adam and Eve, the loss of paradise precedes the finding of it: we know it only through our loss of it, the finding is *in* the loss; it's already lost before we discover that we've lost it, so that we are born empty, incomplete and backward looking toward it, whatever and wherever it is. We are born with a lack, a gap between us and that Edenic security, which our culture, especially our religions, teaches us is somehow a deficiency in *us* that we can only overcome with Jesus, with love, with Barack Obama, or Rush Limbaugh. We thus live in a constant state of reconstruction and longing, of searching for the key, the one thing that will restore us to completeness.

The stories in the "Beyond" section of *Collected Stories* explore this gap through characters who move into the twilight between what we know and what we can never understand, and perhaps, as we shall see, do not want to know. What's *beyond* in these stories is precisely what's on the other side of that by no means liminal divide. Wilfred Midgleston, in "Black Music," claims that at a crucial point in his life he became something "outside the lot and plan for mortal human man to be" when he became a "farn"—a faun, one of "them little men" "the Bible says" "were myths"—in order to intervene morally in a modern couple's building in the Virginia woods a summer house for their pagan "frolics" because the gods "wouldn't like it about them married women running around nekkid" in the woods.⁴ "Carcassonne" continues Midgleston's adventures atop a buckskin pony *with eyes like blue electricity and a mane like tangled fire, galloping up the hill and right off into the high heaven of the world.*⁵ "Beyond" follows Judge Allison, in the liminal moments immediately following his death, into a sort of holding area between earth and an afterlife.

"The Leg" and "Mistral" follow "Divorce in Naples" to Europe. All three seem clearly to have their origins in Faulkner's walking tour of Italy and France in the mid-1920s that began in New Orleans on a ship with William Spratling; all three revolve around relationships between two men challenged or disrupted by a problematic female. Such triangles also form a kind of leitmotif throughout Faulkner; they are central to *The Sound and the Fury* with Quentin, Caddy, and Dalton Ames and in *Absalom, Absalom!* with Charles, Henry, and Judith. As usual, of course, the surround of the work is about so much more than that.⁶

To be sure, the stories allow us a way to avoid the inexplicable: just as Wilfred Midgleston's adventure as a farn might be an alcoholic fantasy, "The Leg" might be a Freudian dream, and "Mistral" might just be a bad story. But we miss their larger significance if we take them that way. "The Leg" and "Mistral" confront the limits of rationality perhaps as a function of their youth and of the war that is in their immediate backgrounds. In the war-torn world of the very young, the rational may be a distant memory.

✳ ✳ ✳

Much of "The Leg" takes place in dreams that at least invite the provocative psychoanalytic insights that James Gray Watson has given it.⁷ It begins in June 1914 when two "Oxford young gentleman" (826)—as Simon, Everbe Corinthia's father, calls them in disdain of their boorish undergraduate behavior—continue a flirtation with Everbe Corinthia begun at least three years before. George and Davy, sculling on the Thames just below Abdingdon, near Oxford, must or at least do pass through a lock that Simon oversees, apparently so that they can flirt with Everbe Corinthia. George makes a dangerous game of the flirtation by holding to a pole to keep their scull from passing through while he recites to her Comus's second speech, a formal attempt to convince a maiden to give up her chastity and celebrate the pleasures of the flesh with him.⁸ Davy keeps hollering at him to let go of the pole so that Everbe Corinthia can open the lock and they can pass; George perhaps deliberately relents just as she opens the lock; the scull "sho[ots] away"

(825) and George clings momentarily to the pile before dropping into the filthy Thames. A flurry of activity ensues: Jotham, Everbe Corinthia's brother, home from London, rescues George with a boat hook. For some reason, she sits "on the ground, weeping hopelessly and quietly. 'You damned fool. Oh, you damned fool'" (826), she says, though we do not know the cause of her tears and her hopelessness. Is she merely relieved that nobody was hurt? Does she weep because George and Davy will soon be in France, in the war? Does she have a relationship with either George or Davy? We do not know, and cannot know from what the story provides, but her tears, and perhaps her hopelessness too, play an indecipherable role in what follows.

The story moves ahead to August 1915. George is dead[9] and Davy is having his leg amputated, obviously from battle wounds. Davy begs George to "wait" (829), to delay his departure to the other world, to find Davy's leg and make sure it's dead, so that it will "lie quiet" (830). There is some talk of the war and whether either of them, in their condition, will have to "go back to the front." Then, curiously, they discuss Everbe Corinthia's tears of over a year ago.

The story's final sequence takes place three years after those tears. Her brother has been arrested and faces execution for desertion; for three and a half months he has been AWOL, mostly in Abingdon seeking the cause of his sister's death. He has been caught after a failed attempt to kill Davy: failed because he tripped over Davy's detached wooden leg and Davy, awakened, was able to defend himself. The padre who counsels Jotham as he faces execution comes to see Davy twice. Davy denies knowing any reason why Jotham would want to kill him, since he knows him only from the attack and from that episode three years before, at the lock. The padre tells him that both Simon and Everbe Corinthia are dead, Simon having died a week after Everbe Corinthia—apparently, though we do not really know, because of Everbe Corinthia's death.

The priest leaves, to go back to Jotham's execution, and Davy continues, apparently but not certainly repeating what the priest has told him of Jotham's narrative; perhaps of course Davy was there, though the story he tells seems based on things about Jotham and Everbe Corinthia that he could not possibly have known—what Jotham thought, for example. He begins with Everbe Corinthia's very curious behavior, which Jotham and the priest understand as that of a woman in heat. She leaves the house every evening for an hour; her manner causes Jotham "to question her," upon which she becomes "evasive, blaz[ing] suddenly out at him in anger which was completely unlike her at all, then bec[omes] passive and docile." Jotham interprets her behavior as "secretiveness," her docility as "dissimulation." One evening, surprising her as she leaves, he drives her back into the house; she goes to her room and locks the door; he then *thinks* he catches "a glimpse of the man disappearing beyond a field," but he can't find him. Later that night he awakens and from his window sees "something white flitting along the towpath." He pursues, noting an empty punt by the towpath, and overtakes his sister: "it could not have been very pretty," Davy reports, as though he were *not* there and has gotten the story from somebody else. "Then she collapsed as suddenly and from the tangled darkness of the coppice behind them a man's laugh came, a jeering sound that echoed once across the moonlit river and ceased." Jotham rushes into the coppice and finds nothing, but hears the laugh again and notes that the boat is gone. He locks Everbe Corinthia in her room, but in the morning she is gone, the door still locked. Jotham and Simon find her and bring her back, unconscious; when she revives, she starts "screaming," Davy says. "She screamed all that day until sunset. She lay on her back screaming, her eyes wide open and perfectly empty, until her voice left her and her screaming was only a ghost of screaming, making no sound. At sunset she died" (839–40).

Nothing explains any of this—how or why she dies, what she is running from or to, why she is so exercised. Since Jotham's behavior is not unlike that of other brothers in Faulkner, who want to control and/or otherwise take an inordinate interest in their sisters' sexual lives, we may easily understand Everbe Corinthia's behavior as consonant with other of Faulkner's repressed women who suffer the consequences of repressive strictures at home. The episode makes it at least as likely that repression at home causes Everbe Corinthia's curious behavior as that Davy has done something to her. You may recognize here my own pet orangutan, which allows me to presume to understand this by reference to similar moments in other Faulkner texts. But Faulkner here presents what happens as simply what happens, not as part of a tissue of patterns that we can impose on them; and to be sure when he bases his themes in such family dynamics in individual works, Faulkner does not reference them as part of any pattern, but simply as what happened.

The priest returns after Jotham's execution, hands Davy what he calls Jotham's "incontrovertible" evidence against him, and leaves him with a cruel accusatory prayer: "May God have mercy on your soul." Davy tells us the "evidence" is a "photograph, a cheap thing such as itinerant photographers turn out at fairs. It was dated at Abingdon in June of the summer just past"—at which time, Davy claims, he was "lying in the hospital talking to George." He sits still, "looking at the photograph," because "it was my own face that looked back at me. It had a quality that was not mine: a quality vicious and outrageous and unappalled, and beneath it was written in a bold sprawling hand like that of a child: 'To Everbe

Corinthia' followed by an unprintable phrase, yet it was my own face" (841–42). Davy seems here to admit the proof, and thus his guilt, in spite of his claim that he couldn't have been at Abingdon at the time. Why does he do so? James Watson argues that the "heavily psychological" nature of the plot allows Davy's dreams to "represent a world of apparent illusion in which the unconscious, animal self is freed to perform real acts. Released in sleep from his conscious inhibitions—represented by his earlier disapproval of George—he becomes his own manic alter ego, the mangle dark self who evades the good spirit (George) and corrupts female chastity. In the final scene, faced with a demonic photograph of himself inscribed to Everbe Corinthia and dated during the month of his dreaming, the conscious self is brought face to face with its own dark shadow, "vicious and outrageous and unappalled" (81).

Perhaps. But the photograph, as Davy presents it, is by no means "incontrovertible" evidence of anything; it proves nothing. It could have been taken at any time or any place and the "yet" in the sentence describing the "bold sprawling hand like that of a child" may suggest that it's not even his handwriting even if it is somehow his face in the photograph and even if the face has a "quality that was not" his. Further, the padre tells Davy that Jotham gave him the picture "to destroy." Why doesn't he do so? What's the priest's interest in prosecuting Davy spiritually, wishing him to hell? If this is the incontrovertible proof that Jotham used to justify his attack on Davy, why does Jotham now want it destroyed?—an act of repentance before he dies? Did the outraged brother or the priest manufacture the evidence from a picture found in his sister's bureau? Is that Jotham's childlike handwriting? The priest's? Everbe Corinthia's? Simon's? The photograph is as insubstantial a proof that Davy murdered her as the laugh that Jotham tells the priest he remembers hearing at Abdingon during Everbe Corinthia's tribulations.

Simply, *nothing* in the story connects Davy to Everbe Corinthia's death or to her corruption, if corruption there was, even if Davy is lying to us about his whereabouts the previous June; certainly nothing "incontrovertible" connects the opening episode at the lock to her death, except perhaps Jotham's jealous rage at her presumably sexual behavior. Unless what Davy tells us about the circumstances of her death comes from some source other than what the priest claims Jotham told him, the story leaves wide open the possibility that Jotham or old Simon themselves harassed, abused, and otherwise drove her to distraction—or killed her themselves. The story provides no indication that Davy did anything at all to her or that he even wanted to, though of course his delirium might have brought to the surface a repressed desire. Indeed, there is a repressed desire, I suspect, but it has little to do with Everbe Corinthia.

The story ends upon a sort of incantation: "I told him to find it and kill it. . . . I told him to. I told him" (842). Why does he want the leg killed? Why does he think it still lives? Perhaps the amputated leg symbolizes the whole rotten chaotic world that he has no control over, that indeed nearly killed him? Perhaps its death would give him control over *something* in a war-torn world, even if only the disposition of the castrated member. The story explains nothing, but subsumes all such considerations in the *Absalom*-like ending, leaving us, like Davy, only with what he calls the "dread and disgust," the "horror and the dread" (834).

❀ ❀ ❀

Like "The Leg," "Mistral"[10] comes to us through so many filters—evasions, interruptions, miscommunications, gossip, innuendo, assumptions, scenes, visions, needs that take place in the dark—that we cannot know exactly what happens, much less explain it. All of what we do get insists upon but absolutely resists interpretation. Don and our narrator, on a walking tour of northern Italy, encounter in the countryside an old couple, who trade them wine for cigarettes and introduce the story's major players and the mystery that Don and the narrator will find themselves observing. But Don's and the narrator's Italian is minimal, the old couple has no English, and the old man is deaf, though he can speak. The woman communicates with him in sign language, but has to put her signing fingers very close to his face because he is probably nearly blind as well: his "blue eyes" have "dissolving irises, as if they had been soaked in water for a long time" (844–45), so that he probably cannot see her signs. Thus "Mistral" comes to us through language multiply occluded, through gestures that may or may not signify, mysterious body language and looks, statements begun, interrupted, and never completed, things that seem to happen in shadows and on the other side of doors and fences and shrubs. It's a narrative of signifiers that never quite connect up with a signified—and vice-versa.

The young Americans are, as usual, drinking heavily and arguing, we can never tell whether in the good sardonic humor of the very young or whether with a spiteful edge to their dialogue that springs from irritations they never explain: if they hadn't spent so much on Milanese brandy they might be able to afford a second heavy coat, so that they would not have to alternate days wearing it against the cold nights and the freezing mistral. The narrator is a reasonably serious soul who tries throughout to be rational, to describe and absorb and understand what they are experiencing; Don is a wisecracking Shreve, who keeps their growing angst at bay with his running mordant commentary. A young soldier passes them pushing a bicycle up the hill, gives them a "surly good day" (843), and moves on.

The old couple tells them that the church bells in the distance announce the funeral of a wealthy man who was to have wed the priest's ward, a young woman of illegitimate birth he had rescued from a poor mother, had raised as his ward, and arranged her marriage when she got old enough. But, the woman insists, the girl, a wild, unruly child, has scandalized the village by her behavior and will have none of the arranged marriage. She prefers the company of Giulio Farinzale—the young man with the bicycle—who, when the priest discovered their relationship three years ago, suddenly got drafted into the army. To the extent that Don and the narrator can understand them, the old couple claims that there is much gossip in the town about the priest's struggles with the girl; they "have heard" how she defies him, how they quarrel, and they wonder why the wealthy man would want a girl who is, as they say, "no good, when there are daughters of good houses who had learned modesty and seemliness." Don asks the woman whether she has unmarried daughters who might qualify and she admits that she does; we therefore might not want to trust her testimony completely. The village also speculates about the priest and the girl: the "holy are susceptible to evil, even as you and I, signori," the old woman says, and her husband tut tuts her: "It was nothing. The priest looked at her, too," he says. "For a man is a man, even under a cassock. Eh, signori?" (849–50).

The girl's intransigence makes the priest and the fiancé delay the banns for three years, but finally the priest reads them, for the third and final time, on the Sunday just prior to the boys' arrival. "And now the fiancé is dead," the old man says. "Was he very sick?" Don asks. The old man answers: "It was very sudden. . . . One day he was well, the second day he was quite sick. The third day he was dead" (851). Then Don, a complete stranger begins, like Shreve, to "play, too," to assemble these fragments into a coherent story that makes a case for murder: "And he died suddenly. And he got engaged suddenly. And at the same time, Giulio got drafted suddenly. It would have surprised you. Everything was sudden except somebody's eagerness for the wedding to be. There didn't seem to be any hurry about that, did there? . . . In fact, they seemed to stop being sudden altogether until about time for Giulio to come home again. Then it began to be sudden again. And so I think I'll ask if priests serve on the draft boards in Italy."[11] When they wonder why Giulio has returned just now, Don quips: "for the funeral" (854); maybe, he scoffs, the priest wrote him a letter and told him about the service (854). Perhaps he's to be "one of the pallbearers" (859), and he came home for his own wedding, now possible no matter how the fiancé died. And since the fiancé may have died from poisoning, Don proposes to give Giulio a stomach pump for a wedding present (856), thus solving the murder that, so far as we can tell, he has created: the girl has killed the fiancé.

The old couple tells them that they may find food and shelter for the night at the priest's home; on their way there, they stop at a tavern run by Giulio's aunt, who seems suspicious of them. When Don proposes to her another, an eminently reasonable, explanation for Giulio's sudden return home—that he's home because he has finished his tour of duty (855)—she agrees perhaps because she believes that to be true, because she wants to cut off the conversation, or because she may fear that they are police, here to investigate the sudden death. Then they go to the church, noticing Giulio's bicycle just outside; they attend the funeral and the burial, after which they notice Giulio emerging out of the mourning throng. Don says, "He was one of the pallbearers" (859), though we have no idea how or whether he emphasizes the word *was* and so no way to tell whether he is still being ironic or stating a fact. Clearly, they cannot figure out why he would attend the funeral of a man he or the girl has poisoned. Just as clearly, perhaps Giulio did not murder him; perhaps the fiancé even died of natural causes; perhaps Giulio and the dead man had been good friends, even if rivals for the girl's affections. Perhaps, indeed, he was a pallbearer if only to act an innocence he does not possess.

At the priest's house, the housekeeper offers them food but refuses them a room for the night. The possibility that Giulio is waiting in the garden of the priest's house, in the cold, fills the boys with dread: they admit that they don't even want to know what they don't know (862). Faulkner never makes clear what they fear: do they worry that Giulio might kill the priest too? that he might assume that they, Don and the narrator, are also here as suitors for the girl's hand, and that they too might become his victims? What follows suggests that he is just waiting for her to come out to play, a fact which should not concern them.

As they eat, the priest enters, more than a little agitated and distracted; we of course do not know why. He greets them, "excusing his tardiness in one breath, in a low rapid voice," and says "a Latin grace." While he prays his hands "writhe" "slowly on either side of his plate." The woman enters silently and they enact a bizarre relationship, one suggesting a pathology that the story leaves completely unexplained. She interrupts him with "a sharp word." He then looks up at his guests out of "weak, rushing eyes. They were brown and irisless, like those of an old dog. Looking at us, it was as though he had driven them up with whips and held them so, in cringing and rushing desperation. 'I forget,'" he says: "There come times—," he continues, but the woman interrupts by "snapping" at him, standing so that the "shadow of her arm [falls] across his face and remain[s] there," sharply and deliberately cutting off his communication. She stands thus "for a time, the priest's face in the shadow of her arm; she seemed to be holding us all so until the moment—whatever it was—had passed." She leaves and the men begin to relax just a bit, until she returns and places her shoulder again between them and the priest. "There come times—" he begins again, only to have her interrupt him again in "that shrill, rapid patois." He pushes back and the boys again note his "driven eyes." He tries a third time: "There come times—" though this time he continues talking even though she "drowns" what he says and puts herself "completely between" them and the priest (863-64). This odd relationship is as mysterious as any in the story: the priest seems like a henpecked husband, she like a dominatrix trying to keep the lid on a Gothic family secret. What does she know of the priest and his ward? Is she more than a housekeeper? Is she his mother? His lover? Both? The story supplies no answers. But things get even stranger.

The priest and the woman leave the room; when she returns, alone, they hear the priest's voice in another room, as "a sustained rush of indistinguishable words. He was not talking to anyone there; you could tell that. In whatever place he was, he was alone: you could tell that. Or maybe it was the wind. Maybe in any natural exaggerated situation— wind, rain, drought—man is always alone. . . . The voice was muffled and sustained, like a machine might have been making it" (864-65). For some reason, the boys need to establish, to believe, that the priest is alone; but if he is, to whom is he talking so intensely? Perhaps their repeated assertion that he is alone means only that they don't want to believe that he is shouting at his ward, perhaps instructing her about what he assumes to be her part in the death of her fiancé or that he is accusing her of using the occasion of the funeral or of the meal to leave the house, apparently to meet Giulio and perhaps go off with him. They—and we—just cannot tell.

The boys finally leave the mysterious house in the freezing blow of the mistral but, curiously, not before interrupting the priest's frantic pacing up and down beside the wall by kneeling and asking him to bless them. They then head downtown to a friendlier tavern, where the talk is of the funeral; the tavern keeper also worries that Giulio is a policeman. A woman and a child come into the bar, then leave. Don proposes that they follow the woman and the child to see if they can sleep at her house. The narrator recalls the previous summer when Don worked for three days to seduce a barmaid, so he knows that his companion is not now interested in sleep, and they agree to part company for the night. Then occurs the scene that vouchsafes the narrator the vision of the troublesome girl herself, heretofore unseen, for whom, perhaps, a man has killed, who perhaps has killed, who perhaps is as innocent as the virginal white she wears, the village's opinion notwithstanding. As she passes, meets Giulio, and walks off with him, he reflects on Evelyn Nesbit.

Then Don, obviously having struck out with the young mother, rejoins him and they follow her and Giulio "into the full sweep of the wind," apparently losing them until they hear a "smothered whimpering sound that seemed to come out of the air overhead." They think it's a child, a baby, an animal of some sort. Ahead they discover that the sound comes from a copse just "this side of darkness, before a wall."

> But the sound was nearer than that, and after a moment we saw the priest. He was lying on his face just inside the wall, his robes over his head, the black blur of his gown moving faintly and steadily, either because of the wind or because he was moving under them. And whatever the sound meant that he was making, it was not meant to be listened to, for his voice ceased when we made a noise. But he didn't look up, and the faint shuddering of his gown didn't stop. Shuddering, writhing, twisting from side to side—something.

The boys are terrified and begin bickering, wondering what the hell is going on: is the priest watching Giulio and the girl? If so, what can he see in the dark? Maybe he's imagining things? Is he masturbating? Weeping for grief over his vows of chastity? Grieving the death that his attempts to control the girl have caused?[12] Does he merely regret the mistake the girl is making? The copse, which when they first saw it "blobbed shapeless on the gloom," now, "against the gloom," "seemed to pulse and fade, as though it breathed, lived." Perhaps it does: perhaps what they thought was a copse is the joined bodies of the two lovers, and the voyeuristic priest is bereft, having lost his love too. Perhaps the boys only imagine that it is Giulio and the girl the priest is watching: indeed, they seem to have lost them in the dark, and we might expect to see at least a glow, even a faint illumination, from the girl's white dress even in the dark, but Faulkner does not give us that marker. We all, readers and characters, might well be simply imagining what's going on in that copse. Thus we all might well agree with the narrator that "night, darkness, is terrible to young people. . . . Young people should be so constituted that with sunset they would enter a coma state, by slumber shut safe from the darkness, the secret nostalgic sense of frustration and of objectless and unappeasable desire" (874–76)—objectless because they cannot openly direct their unappeasable desire toward the one object because it's forbidden or toward the other because they cannot generate it.

Hastily departing the scene, the boys suddenly, inexplicably, begin to curse each other, somehow responding to an "unappeasable desire" that they do not understand. Don appears to the narrator "ludicrous;

he looked like a clown; he was terrible and ugly and sad all at once. . . .
And so was I: ugly and terrible and sad." They fight over who has the
cigarettes and depart not side by side but with Don just behind, the
narrator looking at him over his shoulder as if he's being followed—or
rejected—by some one or some thing he's trying, but does not really
want, to lose (876). Their descent into this kind of bickering is extremely
curious, since there's nothing in the story, except perhaps the bickering,
the cursing, and the narrator's sudden discovery of their both being "terrible and ugly and sad," that would suggest what's at stake for them in
these circumstances, nothing to suggest whether or how they feel physically or even psychologically threatened, though clearly they do.

❊ ❊ ❊

Certain connections between "The Leg" and "Mistral" may help us
understand what's going on in both stories. In "The Leg" George and
Davy, in Davy's dream, also descend into that kind of bickering and
name-calling. In both stories, trouble occurs when the narrator's male
companion abandons him for a heterosexual liaison; the same occurs in
"Divorce in Naples," though with more harmonious results, as Theresa
Towner has pointed out (6). "The Leg" is explicit about the implications: in one of his dreams, Davy smells "a rank, animal odor. It was an
odor which I had never smelled before, but I knew it at once, blown
suddenly down the corridor from the old fetid caves where experience
began. I felt dread and disgust and determination, as when you sense
suddenly a snake beside a garden path." The odor leaves and George
is there, looking at him, asking "What is it?" Davy responds: "It's nothing. . . . It isn't anything. I won't again. I swear I shan't any more." But
George continues to accuse: "You said you had to come back to town.
And then I saw you on the river. You saw me and hid, Davy. Pulled up
under the bank, in the shadow. There was a girl with you." Davy swears,
"I won't again!" The dream is so powerful that he fears sleeping. When
George returns, Davy feels a "sulphur reek . . . all about" him, as though
George has just returned from hell. He feels "horror and dread and
something unspeakable: delight. I believe I felt what women in labor
feel." But George is only there to say goodbye, though Davy begs him
not to go, screaming, again, "I shan't again. I shan't any more, George"
(834), as though George is leaving, has been killed, *because* Davy has
betrayed him for having or wanting to have a woman. Where George has
been sounds so much like the setting of the scene when Jotham catches
Everbe Corinthia sneaking out—the moon, the punt under the bank,
the hiding, the spying, the laughter—that we might well conclude that
George accuses Davy of having somehow sneaked back to Abingdon to

Everbe Corinthia and causing her death somehow. Indeed, while Everbe Corinthia weeps in the opening scene, George accuses Davy of "envying me" (826). Does he mean Davy envies him for Everbe Corinthia's tears, for having a heterosexual lover? Perhaps: but since this is *Davy's* dream, in which George scolds *him*, Davy, for sneaking off to a liaison with a female, why should Davy be the one desperately promising that he won't go to females any more?

A Freudian reading of his dream would surely allow us to understand it as invoking Davy's pain in a homosexual attraction to George that George doesn't completely return—not, at any rate, to the point of giving up heterosexuality. I suggest that the "rank animal odor" and the "feeling of dread and disgust" in his dream as George appears are functions of the homoerotic. The "old fetid caves where experience began" can only be a womb, the "rank animal odor" a symbol of the "dread and disgust" that many of Faulkner's men feel in reaction to female biology. The phallic snake completes the problematic image of heterosexual union. If so, we may understand Davy's agitation at the end of the story, his seeming admission of guilt. That the "something unspeakable" he feels simultaneously with the "horror and "dread" is "delight" may indeed suggest something of his confusion in the combination of pleasure in their homoerotic attachment, however deeply it goes, and the shame and self-loathing that that delight causes. That he believes he felt "what women in labor [feel]" feminizes him, makes him at least feel himself as the passive, perhaps helpless partner in this relationship and in the betrayal, though why he feels "determination" is not at all clear. It could also be his dream's, and so his own, last desperate grasping toward reproductive heterosexuality. Almost certainly, then, George, in Davy's dream, is right: Davy *does* envy George's hold on heterosexuality.

In "Mistral" the narrator's sudden sadness at seeing the young woman at the center of the storm and his reflections on Evelyn Nesbit and loss, then, constitute a meditation on his loss of heterosexuality. At the crux of the homosexual experience, in Faulkner, is the loss of a presumptive sexual normality that spirals out into other presumptive abnormalities that in turn alienate homosexuals and make them vulnerable not just to social ostracism but to shame and self-loathing and, too often, to violence. The apparently heterosexual longing for the girl and for Evelyn Nesbit, I propose, is not heterosexual desire but rather a longing for that desire, which he's never had; heterosexuality itself is what he's lost, what he wants. Nesbit thus represents not so much the desirable women that he cannot have but rather the desire itself that he cannot have, which he knows he should want but simply cannot generate. Not that he can't have a given woman, because perhaps he can. Or perhaps Evelyn Nesbit and

Eula Varner and the white-dressed girl of "Mistral" are farther away than even that. Perhaps he wants *her*—Nesbit, Eula, the girl—the iconic, the fabulous, the perilous, instead of a girl he actually might have, precisely because he knows he can't have *her*; she thus becomes symbol not even of all women but of heterosexual desire itself, not so much through her unavailability as through something in him that simply shuts down at the very thought. Quentin may want Caddy for the same reason, not really for reasons of incest but for her simple availability and her presumed sympathy. It ought to be easy to get laid in the right and proper heterosexual way, Quentin thinks, "with so many of them walking along in the shadows and whispering with their soft girlvoices lingering in the shadowy places and the words coming out and perfume and eyes you could feel not see, but if it was that simple to do it wouldn't be anything and if it wasn't anything what was I. . . ."[13] What he *is* is terrified of his homoerotic impulses, and I suspect that's a more likely cause of his suicide than his family's curious history.[14]

But the loss of heterosexual desire does not explain everything in "Mistral" or "The Leg" by a long shot, and I do not pretend that it does. Questions abound. Maybe Davy's castrated leg is the heterosexuality that he wants George to kill so that it will "lie quiet" (830), sacrificing it to George as a love offering, to convince George that he, Davy, has given up heterosexual desire; perhaps Everbe Corinthia's inexplicable screaming and painful death is precisely the death of Davy's heterosexual longings—or at least the death that he wants to bring about. But our believing so does not explain how or why she dies, who is lying and who is telling the truth, or whether we can assemble anything resembling "truth," complete truth, from the materials of these stories at all, wherein the narrated manifest "plots," which present themselves as murder mysteries, occur simultaneously with but do not seem otherwise related to the other, buried, latent stories that they are telling—the real subject of the narratives.

"The Leg" and "Mistral" spiral away from their own clues. Both leave us with mysterious deaths that may or may not be murders, with dozens of unanswered questions locked behind doors and shadowy copses, with the companions' sudden bickering, and, in "Mistral," with the freezing wind of the mistral itself, an ill wind indeed that blows no good and against which the boys have only the protection of a single coat that they use on alternate days, a shared shield that leaves them individually vulnerable to the mistral's invisible but impacted constant sourceless assault—the inescapable inexplicable terrifying truth, in a nightmare of confusions, deflections, and anxieties. Like Judge Allison in "Beyond," they do not know what's beyond and cannot commit themselves to finding out without committing themselves also to the consequences of discovery. No matter how we rearrange the clues, no matter how many criminals we convict and put away, we never quite put *it* away sufficiently to feel safe from it. On this side of beyond we live according to the "certitudes" that "arbitrarily distinguish between verities and illusions" (833); the other side, we fear, removes those illusions and the ways we construct ourselves so as to negotiate between those verities and illusions. It's all there, waiting, that mysterious damned *unknown* separated from us not even by a wall or gate or door or darkness but barely by our own intractable denial.

At the core of "The Leg" and "Mistral," then, is not so much a crime as something criminal, something that breaks laws not by being enacted but just by being thought, that move us toward the moment, as Phil Weinstein reminds us in speaking of Freud's uncanny in this collection, when "the normal traffic between ourselves and the world comes to a halt." What works on the narrators, I think, is not at all that they don't know what's beyond, it's precisely that they do know. It's not a matter of who done it but of what they might do, what chaos they might stumble into that's always barely a micromillisecond or two the other side of the door, the gate, the wall: the denial. It's the mocking laughter coming from the dark copse, summoning them to discover and confront a truth that will not make them free but will commit them to the horror and the dread, the self-loathing and the self-destructive bickering that supplies the specific energy of both stories. It's not that it just does not explain, not that we aren't supposed to know, but rather that we refuse to know. We are constantly undone, unmoored, by the mockery of the unsourced laughing voice we suppress and deflect. We are thus all perhaps Poe's man of the crowd, self-indicted as "the essence of all crime," and in these two stories it is indeed the Truth that lurks in the beyond that's in our hearts, the orangutan waiting not to solve the crime but to commit it, not to restore order but to destroy it.

NOTES

1. Edgar Allan Poe, "The Man of the Crowd," in *Edgar Allan Poe: Poetry and Tales* (1840; New York: Library of America, 1984), 388–96, 388.

2. William Faulkner, "The Leg," in *Collected Stories* (1931; New York: Random House, 1950), 823–42, 833.

3. At the turn of the century, Nesbit was a fabulously popular chorus girl and model, one of the Gibson Girls, one of the *IT* girls, in hundreds of advertisements and illustrations in magazines and newspapers all across the country. At a very early age she became the mistress and plaything of the famous architect Stanford White and, soon after, the

wife of a wealthy Philadelphia playboy, Harry K. Thaw, who, learning particulars of Evelyn's relationship with White, murdered the architect, very publicly, in the rooftop restaurant of the Madison Square Garden. The newspaper coverage of the subsequent sensational trials made all three household words. Nesbit published memoirs, *The Story of My Life* (1914) and *Prodigal Days* (1934). In 1926 she gave an interview to the *New York Times* that rehashed the whole sordid story. Given his virtual obsession with the nubile, it is also easy to imagine that Faulkner's early and continuing encounters with Nesbit in the tabloids and even in the respectable press in his adolescence and young manhood forced her upon him, as upon America, as the very ideal of unattainable feminine sexuality: girl next door though she be. Her connection to a murder scandal is part of her enduring charm and perhaps not without some connection, in the narrator's mind, to the events he is describing. See Paula Uruburu, *American Eve: Evelyn Nesbit, Stanford White: The Birth of the "It" Girl and the Crime of the Century* (New York: Riverhead Books, 2008). See also Lisa Paddock, "'Trifles with a tragic profundity': The Importance of 'Mistral,'" *Mississippi Quarterly* 32 (1979): 413–32.

4. "Black Music," in *Collected Stories*, 799–821, 805.

5. "Carcassonne," in *Collected Stories*, 895–900, 895.

6. "Divorce in Naples" and "The Leg" are considerably less enigmatic to me now after Theresa Towner's fine explication at the 2008 Faulkner and Yoknapatawpa Conference, though my discussion of "The Leg" moves in a different direction from hers. Towner, "The Weird Stuff: Textual and Sexual Anomalies in Faulkner's Fiction," in *Faulkner and Formalism: Returns of the Text* (Jackson: University Press of Mississippi, 2012), 178–92.

7. James Gray Watson, "Short Story Fantasies and the Limits of Modernism," *Faulkner Studies* 1 (University of Miami, 1980), 80–85.

8. See Watson (81) on the resonances of "Comus" in "The Leg."

9. James B. Carothers suggests George dies as a result of the episode at the lock: "Faulkner's Short Stories: 'And Now What's to Do,'" in *New Directions in Faulkner Studies: Faulkner and Yoknapatawpha, 1983,* 221.

10. "Mistral," in *Collected Stories*, 843–76.

11. Ibid., 851–52.

12. A. Nicholas Fargnoli and Michael Golay, *William Faulkner A to Z: The Essential Reference to His Life and Work* (New York: Checkmark Books, 2002). 161.

13. *The Sound and the Fury* (1929), in *William Faulkner: Novels 1926–1929* (New York: Library of America, 2006), 990.

14. Noel Polk, "How Shreve Gets in to Quentin's Pants," in *Faulkner and Welty and the Southern Literary Tradition* (Jackson: University Press of Mississippi, 2008), 22–30.

Contributors

Hosam Aboul-Ela is associate professor of English at the University of Houston. He is the author of *Other South: Faulkner, Coloniality, and the Mariátegui Tradition*; a translation from the Arabic of the novel *Distant Train*, by Ibrahim Abdel Meguid; and critical articles appearing in *American Literature, Mississippi Quarterly*, and other journals.

Susan V. Donaldson is the National Endowment for the Humanities Professor of English at William and Mary. She is the author of *Competing Voices: The American Novel, 1865–1914*, coeditor of *Haunted Bodies: Gender and Southern Texts*, and the author of over fifty articles and book chapters, largely on writers of the South.

Richard Godden teaches in the Department of English at the University of California, Irvine. He is the author of *Fictions of Labor: William Faulkner and the South's Long Revolution* and *William Faulkner: An Economy of Complex Words*.

Michael Gorra is Mary Augusta Jordan Professor of English at Smith College. He is the author of *The English Novel at Mid-Century*; *After Empire: Scott, Naipaul, Rushdie*; and *Portrait of a Novel: Henry James and the Making of an American Masterpiece*. He edited *The Portable Conrad* and critical editions of *As I Lay Dying* and *The Sound and the Fury*.

Lisa Hinrichsen is assistant professor of English at the University of Arkansas, Fayetteville. She has published articles on Bobbie Ann Mason, Elizabeth Madox Roberts, Robert Frost, and Faulkner and is currently working on a book-length study, "The Fantasy of Mastery: Southern Literature 1930 to the Present."

Donald M. Kartiganer is Howry Professor of Faulkner Studies Emeritus at the University of Mississippi. He was director of Faulkner and Yoknapatawpha from 1994 to 2009 and coedited seven of the conference volumes as well as two special Faulkner issues of the Mississippi

Quarterly. He is the author of *The Fragile Thread: The Meaning of Form in Faulkner's Novels* and numerous essays on Faulkner and other writers.

Sean McCann is professor of English and director of the Center for Faculty Career Development at Wesleyan University. He is the author of *A Pinnacle of Feeling: American Literature and Presidential Government* and *Gumshoe America: Hard-Boiled Crime Fiction and the Rise and Fall of New Deal Liberalism*.

Sarah Mahurin has been a visiting assistant professor of English and African American Studies at Wesleyan University since completing her PhD in English at Yale University in 2011. "The Southern Expatriate in American Literature" is the working title of her book based on her doctoral dissertation.

Noel Polk was professor emeritus of English at Mississippi State University and editor of the *Mississippi Quarterly*. He was the author or editor of over a dozen volumes, including *Outside the Southern Myth*, *Children of the Dark House, Eudora Welty: A Bibliography of the Work*, and *Faulkner and Welty and the Southern Literary Tradition*, and he was the coauthor of *Reading Faulkner: "The Sound and the Fury."*

Esther Sánchez-Pardo is associate professor of English at Universidad Complutense de Madrid. She is the author, editor, and translator of a dozen books, including *Cultures of the Death Drive: Melanie Klein and Modernist Melancholia* and a forthcoming translation and critical edition of the poet Mina Loy, *Antologia Poetica*.

Annette Trefzer is associate professor of English at the University of Mississippi. She is the author of *Disturbing Indians: The Archaeology of Southern Fiction* and coeditor with Ann J. Abadie of several volumes of critical essays on William Faulkner, including *Global Faulkner*, *Faulkner's Sexualities*, and *Faulkner and Formalism: Returns of the Text*. She is also coeditor, with Kathryn McKee, of "Global Contexts, Local Literatures: The New Southern Studies," a special issue of *American Literature*.

Rachel Watson received a PhD in English at the University of Chicago where she wrote a dissertation titled "Capturing the Individual: Race and the Forensics in American Literature, 1894–1959." She is the author of an article on the film *To Kill a Mockingbird* and has presented conference papers on Rudolph Fisher, Richard Wright, and Mark Twain.

Philip Weinstein is Alexander Griswold Cummins Professor of English at Swarthmore College. His publications include *The Semantics of Desire: Changing Models of Identity from Dickens to Joyce*; *Faulkner's Subject: A Cosmos No One Owns*; *What Else But Love? The Ordeal of Race in Faulkner and Morrison*; *Unknowing: The Work of Modernist Fiction*, and, most recently, *Becoming Faulkner*.

Index

www.ingramcontent.com/pod-product-compliance
Lightning Source LLC
Chambersburg PA
CBHW020054030726
47498CB00006B/1784